The Private Pilot's Guide to
Renting and Flying Airplanes Worldwide

The Private Pilot's Guide to
Renting and Flying Airplanes Worldwide

Geza Szurovy

TAB BOOKS
Blue Ridge Summit, PA

FIRST EDITION
FIRST PRINTING

© 1991 by **Geza Szurovy.**
TAB Books is a division of McGraw-Hill, Inc.

Library of Congress Cataloging-in-Publication Data

Szurovy, Geza.
    The private pilot's guide to renting and flying airplanes
worldwide / by Geza Szurovy.
        p.   cm.
    Includes index.
    ISBN 0-8306-7633-3
    1. Private flying.   I. Title.
TL721.4.S98   1991
629.132′5217—dc20   91-10363
                                                 CIP

TAB Books offers software for sale. For information and a catalog, please contact TAB Software Department, Blue Ridge Summit, PA 17294-0850.

Acquisitions Editor: Jeff Worsinger
Book Editor: Norval G. Kennedy
Production: Katherine G. Brown
Book Design: Jaclyn J. Boone   AV1
Photography by the author unless stated otherwise.

Contents

To Endre Szigeti

Acknowledgments

PERHAPS THE MOST PLEASANT EXPERIENCE about flying for fun in foreign countries is the realization that flying is a great leveler of cultural barriers. Climb into a cockpit with a foreign pilot in a strange land and you will instantly feel as if you were back home, flying with the guy whose airplane is tied down next to yours. Invariably you will find generous hospitality and intense curiosity about flying in your country. And so it was with writing this book. Many of the people who made it possible had no reason to provide so much help, other than their shared love of flying.

A special thanks to Ron Campbell of AOPA-UK and IAOPA in London; Jud Milgram, Günther Marsch, and Andrew Szurovy in Munich; John and Claudette Khoury in Paris; Ricardo Schillaci in Buenos Aires; Barry Sadler in Sydney; Martine Berenstein in Boston; Bernard Grand, Joe Verronau, Rod Bater, Ron Saunders, Lutz Paap, and Segun Agbetuyi in Africa; and Ray Dorman, who unhesitatingly flew with me in any winged bucket of bolts.

Much credit is due to the Aircraft Owners and Pilots Associations and national aeroclubs worldwide, who responded so promptly to my many requests.

Thanks also to Dennis Shattuck and Mary Silitch at *Private Pilot*, where several of these stories first appeared, and Jeff Ethell at *Warbirds* for their support and advice, and Anne, fellow pilot, fellow traveler.

Introduction

YOU ARE ABOUT TO BOARD AN AIRLINER for that special trip to some far off land. Your seat has been assigned, your carefully planned itinerary is in your pocket, and you are ready to browse through the guidebooks again as soon as your flight is off the ground. For the next few weeks, with family, friends, or on your own, you will have a great time discovering new places and getting to know a little more of the world. And, if you are like most recreational pilots, you will also feel a tinge of regret about having temporarily grounded yourself to spend time wandering around foreign ruins, museums, and the countryside. But if you have really done your homework, your itinerary will also include a stop at an airfield where pilots like you fly just for fun. And the flying adventure that awaits you there will be a highlight of your trip.

In many countries, it is a lot easier than you might think for the visiting private pilot to fly. In recent years, licensing requirements for private pilots have been converging toward a standard. The 40-hour private pilot's license has generally become the worldwide norm. There are only minor differences in standards among most countries, having to do with local regulations, night flying qualifications and restrictions, the airspace structure, visual flight rules (VFR) minimums, and the like. A good briefing and a little cramming and note taking is usually sufficient to see the visitor through.

There are also similarities in the airplanes and equipment. A veritable recreational air force of Pipers, Cessnas, Beechcraft, and Mooneys still dominates the world. Such foreign contenders as the light aircraft of Aerospatiale are not much different to fly. Almost everyone sits behind a Lycoming or a Continental, and is brought to a stop on rollout by a set of Cleveland brakes. The worldwide fleet of popular touring airplanes is complemented by a wonderfully diverse collection of "exotics," many of them available to the visitor: surplus military trainers like the Chipmunk, antique biplanes like the Buecker and the Tiger Moth, motorgliders, Piper Cubs, and an assortment of indigenous light aircraft, popular in their own neighborhood but little known elsewhere.

Thanks in large measure to developments in commercial aviation, radio

The Swiss Trainer is under development as a low-cost two-seater of modular construction.

navaids are standard throughout the world; the VOR on the Ngong Hills outside Nairobi is the same as the one at Albany, New York. NDBs are still popular in some areas, and DME transmitters are not always as widespread as they are in the United States. More importantly, many recreational airplanes available for rent are not loaded with expensive navigation equipment. The art of pilotage is still highly respected and widely practiced throughout the world. The visitor intending to go cross-country had better be up on pilotage.

A common, but needless deterrent to many would-be recreational fliers traveling abroad is the fear of not being understood among foreigners who speak with many tongues. For English speakers this is not a problem because English is the official language of aviation, and in most countries anyone with whom you need to talk on the radio will speak it to some degree. Accents sometimes conspire with scratchy radios to create a situation requiring a lot of patience, but if you stick to standard, professional radio phraseology, usually all will be well. If you suffer from general radiophobia and are willing to stay within certain airspace restrictions, there are still ways, just like at home, to avoid radio communications all together, or limit it to a brief exchange of grunts with a tower controller.

In many countries the authorities have recognized the similarities in the training and skills of private pilots and have made it remarkably simple for a visiting private pilot to rent an airplane for day VFR flying. Often, a local checkride and proof of your qualifications is all you need if your stay is fewer than 90 days. In some countries, to fly as pilot in command, you will need to have your license

Airplanes that are familiar in the United States turn up in the strangest places: Tomahawk on the ramp in Douala, Cameroon.

validated, or a temporary local certificate issued based on your license, but in most instances this is easily accomplished.

For longer stays, and to use your instrument rating, a combination of license validation, testing on local regulations, and a checkride is required in most places. The time and effort this takes varies, but persistence will usually pay off even in the more bureaucratic countries.

There are many ways to enjoy recreational flying on a trip abroad. What you should know before leaving is what you want to accomplish during your stay and how to find out what is possible.

WHAT KIND OF FLYING?

The kind of flying you are likely to do can be broken down into two general categories: aerial sightseeing and touring where the airplane is a tool to get you over the scenery, or specialty flying where the airplane itself or a flying technique practiced in it is your primary interest. How much flying you want to do will depend on how much time you can spare from museum hopping and haute cuisine, and how much you want to spend. This will help you decide whether to check out or not check out.

On a tight schedule, when you are only looking for a taste of local recreational flying, an excellent option is some well planned dual where your host, an experienced local pilot or instructor, lets you do the flying and conducts the guided tour. A full checkout to operate as pilot in command in the foreign environment might be more satisfying but will take more of your time and resources. Let's consider the options in greater detail.

Aerial sightseeing and touring

This kind of flying interests most recreational pilots on trips abroad. The view of a strange new land from above is always revealing and often spectacular. The airplane is a means to an end, an armchair aloft.

In its simplest form, an hour or two of dual, it is the most efficient way to sample how the locals fly. To get the most out of such a flight it is important to choose an airplane in which you are experienced, and to be specific in explaining to your hosts what you want to accomplish. Let them know that you want to do the flying, you want to see certain specific sights, and you want a brief explanation of local customs and regulations. You will rarely need more than half a day including getting to and from the airport, and the experience is likely to be more rewarding than you had initially imagined. In a two-hour rental block you can view London from under 2,000 feet; you can go chateau hopping over the French countryside; you can tour the length of the Panama Canal; or you can loiter over Rio de Janeiro. All you have to know is how to make the arrangements.

If you have a full day to go flying, the dual option might be the way to go. You will learn more about flying locally and can do more scenic flying on a day-long dual cross-country than if you spend the morning getting checked out and the afternoon rushing through a solo cross-country in an unfamiliar environment.

A good preflight is important everywhere.

If flying is an integral part of your vacation plans and you have set aside several days for it, the obvious choice is to get checked out and to make plans to go touring. Again, you will want to pick an airplane in which you are experienced, to keep your flying simple, which allows you to concentrate fully on navigation and the scenery. The checkout will usually be thorough, much like a private flight test, and you will have to spend some time learning local customs and regulations. A half a day to a day should usually be enough to get checked out, and then you are ready for the ultimate adventure, touring on your own. You can plan a series of day trips, a good strategy where the weather is notorious for rapid changes, or you can set out on a trip taking several days, an appealing choice where there is lots of sunshine. Whatever your decision, don't overstep your capabilities and scrupulously observe your personal safety limits. It is just as insane to press on through a closing Alpine pass as it is to press on through a developing thunderstorm back home.

Specialty flying

Another form of flying in a foreign country that can be a rewarding experience is a checkout in an exotic airplane not available at home, or instruction in a particular form of flying with which you have little or no previous experience, such as soaring or aerobatics.

The experimental aircraft movement is alive and well in Europe.

You can sample these opportunities informally on an introductory flight if you are short on time, but because they require learning a new skill, you will get little out of the experience if you don't opt for the checkout or a good dose of formal instruction. This usually means a time commitment of a few days, and you could turn it into a whole vacation.

Throughout the world you have a chance of encountering rental airplanes that you couldn't easily find back home. Today's antique open-cockpit biplanes were yesterday's run-of-the-mill trainers, and they have endured. The odd Tiger Moth, Buecker Jungmann, or Stampe is occasionally available in Europe, and sometimes farther afield. Arranging a Chipmunk checkout is not too difficult in Britain, and at last count was even available in Zimbabwe. And it is always fun to get checked out in light airplanes fairly common regionally, but not well known back home, such as the French Jodel, the Swiss Bravo, the Brazilian Uirapuru, the British Slingsby T-67, and the Japanese Fuji.

You should also always be on the lookout for the opportunity to begin learning a special skill. In some countries aerobatics are much more on the mind of the average pilot than might be the case where you fly, and the chance to learn is readily available. When that chance is in a Chipmunk or a Stampe it is difficult to pass up.

Another popular form of flying in many countries is soaring. It is especially spectacular among the jagged peaks of the Alps. Checkouts and high performance composite rental sailplanes are available for the licensed glider pilot and courses of various duration can be arranged. Several British gliding operations offer all-inclusive week-long soaring vacations for the novice, which takes participants through their first solo.

COMMERCIAL SCHOOLS AND AEROCLUBS

The choice of operators who provide recreational flying varies from country to country, but can be generally broken down into commercial flight schools and aeroclubs. In most countries both are available and each has its advantages and disadvantages. In selected countries recreational flying is available only through a nationwide chain of aeroclubs, but the visitor is usually welcome.

Commercial flying schools will be familiar to American pilots because they are the equivalent of the fixed-base operator in the United States. They will usually be equipped with a fleet of trainers like Cessna 150s and Piper Tomahawks or Cherokees, and a number of touring aircraft. They are used to serving walk-in customers and will get you airborne with a minimum of fuss. Their big drawback is price because they are trying to earn a living; therefore their rates tend to be well above those available at the aeroclubs.

Aeroclubs in most countries play a much bigger role in recreational flying than they do in the United States. The higher cost of flying and the prohibitive cost of airplane ownership for most flyers has made the aeroclub a popular haven for the private pilot worldwide. Fleets usually consist of a mix of trainers and touring airplanes, and your chances of finding something exotic, either owned by the club or owned by one of the more affluent members who might be willing to rent or give dual, are also good. A few aeroclubs specialize in such activities as flying antiques or aerobatic airplanes.

The usual aeroclub is much more than a place to rent for less. It is also a social organization, often complete with restaurant, bar, and in some cases even a swimming pool and a tennis court.

If you are under time constraints, but want to find out a lot about recreational flying and are content to fly dual, head for the local aeroclub. You will always be welcome as a fellow pilot from abroad. Although they might not be able to rent to you directly on short notice because you are not a member, they can send you up with one of their members or instructors, renting in their name. And in most cases the costs will be well below what you would pay at a commercial operator. Most aeroclubs have a small professional staff, so you can reach someone throughout the week. Your best bet is to give them a call and ask for the chief pilot, with a clear idea of what you would like to accomplish.

Aeroclub rules that give visitors direct flying privileges vary. Some offer temporary memberships, usually for the annual dues prorated for the visitor's length of stay. Temporary membership approval might take a few days and if your time is short it might not be worth the fuss. However, if you will be in the area for a week or two, or for an extended stay, a temporary membership might be the best way to go.

USING THE COUNTRY CHAPTERS

The country chapters serve three basic purposes:

- Provide specific information on the licensing regulations visitors wishing to fly must meet.

- Provide basic summary information on the flying opportunities available to visiting private pilots, describe the likely costs, and discuss how reasonable it is to opt for checking out as pilot in command, given local regulations and opportunities and considering the visitor's available time.

- Tell the reader how to arrange his or her own flying opportunities and present additional sources of information.

Each chapter is organized into sections with applicable information.

Country Rating. The first entry rates by category the ease of recreational flying by the visitor, based upon all the information collected on the country. Below are the ratings and definitions:

- Easy. Regulations are unrestrictive, opportunities abound, solo flying is easy to arrange.

- Moderate. Regulations are a bit cumbersome, solo flying might be time consuming to arrange, the availability of rental aircraft for solo flight by foreign visitors might be limited, flying with a safety pilot is readily available.

- Difficult. Great effort and patience needed to meet regulatory requirements, limited opportunities for flying with a safety pilot, but worth a try.

ONC Chart Number. Specification of the 1:1,000,000 scale ONC aviation chart covering the country. The maps are available from the National Ocean Service and through AOPA's chart department. They show good topographic detail and cover the world. They are useful for getting an idea of destinations and distances.

Rental Cost Range. Lists in United States dollars the range of hourly rental rates for various aircraft. The low number is usually the solo rate at a noncommercial operator. The high number is the dual rate at a commercial operator. These ranges are indicative only, and are subject to significant fluctuation with changes in the exchange rates and the ever changing costs of flying.

Qualifications and license validation

Describes the local regulations in effect at the time of writing, concerning the extent to which a foreign private pilot's license and supporting qualifications, such as ratings, medical certificate, and radio operator's license are recognized, and the steps to be taken before visitors can fly solo. This section also lists the length of time for which validation is in effect and what can be done to extend it.

Documents you should take

A list of licenses, medical certificates, logbooks, and other supporting documents you should have with you to meet the host country's requirements. Pay careful attention to this section. Bureaucratic officialdom can be insistent on all

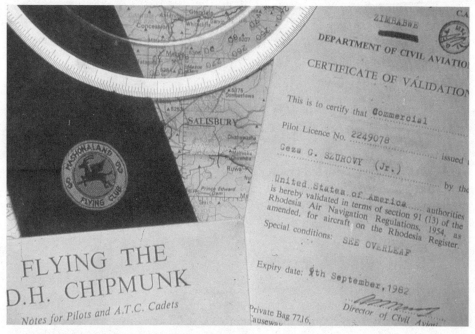

A validated license is the ticket to foreign checkouts.

sorts of seals and pieces of paper that you have never imagined to be relevant to flying for fun. In many countries your own signature verifying your flights entered in your logbook is not enough. Local regulations might demand traces of official-dom, such as a big rubber stamp on every page—complete with illegible authorized signature. A notarized copy of a visitor's logbook will usually do the trick. Your pilot certificate, with appropriate ratings and limitations, and medical certificate should be original, although some countries do accept notarized copies.

Useful flying organizations

Every country has at least one national organization representing the interests of recreational flying. In most cases this is the national aeroclub, and depending upon the country it might be a lobby similar to AOPA, or it might be a governmental or quasi-governmental institution. Often it has an important role in administering recreational flying, and it might be a useful source of information. There might also be national organizations catering to special interests, such as aerobatics or homebuilding. This section lists and briefly describes the purpose of these organizations. Where appropriate, the local AOPA is listed, including the address and phone number. For most countries this section also lists the national civil aviation authority responsible for aircrew licensing.

Where to fly, what to fly

An overview of local recreational flying that discusses operations that provide recreational flying, describes the major centers of general aviation, highlights local airplanes to watch for, and lists a selection of popular recreational airfields. Because FBOs and aeroclubs come and go, rather than provide an exhaustive list, the section describes a few that have endured, and guides the reader to the airport managers (including phone numbers where possible), who will be happy to give up-to-date information.

Touring

Selected countries have a broad scope of touring possibilities; therefore it is addressed in a separate section that suggests a selection of popular flights of various length and complexity. It describes in broad terms the areas of a country best suited for touring.

VFR question & answer

Commonly asked questions about VFR flying that are intended only to give a flavor of local VFR regulations as they were at the time of writing. It is not to be used as a guide to VFR regulations. All pilots should consult applicable primary sources for regulations and guidelines prior to any flying in a particular country.

Bush flying is widely available in the right places.

Additional sources of information

This section describes where and how to find out more. It lists the country's more important aviation sources: books, pamphlets (often free), and magazines. It also comments on the local yellow pages, a surprisingly useful source of information.

INSURANCE

The statistical odds of something going wrong while flying have been diminishing steadily over the years. Remaining risks can be minimized by carefully selecting the best aircraft you can afford and flying responsibly. Training and mental preparation for emergencies will stand you in good stead if something does go wrong. But what about the aftermath, the potential financial burden of an accident or incident? You can be prepared for that, too, by having sufficient insurance.

Consider two insurance questions before renting an airplane:

Are you covered for any damage you might cause and personal liability you might incur?

Does your regular health insurance provide coverage in case of personal injury in a rental airplane?

Most pilots probably think that the operators who rent you airplanes worth tens of thousands of dollars surely have adequate coverage. The operator probably does, to get off the hook and stay in business in case of a mishap. But that doesn't stop their insurance company, or third parties, from attempting to recover their losses from you, the renter.

You can cover yourself against such claims by obtaining renter's *hull* and *liability* insurance where it is available. In the United States, especially, some excellent and reasonably priced renter insurance programs exist that are suitable.

Health insurance coverage in case of a mishap in a rental airplane depends on the health insurance you have. Some policies will cover you, some will not. You owe it to yourself to ask, and get additional coverage if you feel unprotected.

And what about insurance when you rent airplanes in foreign countries? The simple answer is that there are no hard and fast rules. Let's consider health insurance first. It would be especially foolish to fly around in a strange land without health insurance coverage. Regular health insurance might not cover you for rental flying abroad, so it is imperative to check with your health insurance provider. They can either provide additional insurance for the trip, or advise you where to get such coverage.

Renter's hull and liability insurance is a trickier affair. Most operators in most countries have hull insurance, and some form of liability insurance, usually a specified amount per seat, applicable to the occupant of the seat. Claims that can be made against you by all parties to an accident or incident is much less clear and might vary greatly from country to country. It is your responsibility to ask, and your decision whether or not the insurance arrangements are acceptable to you. At a minimum, ask the following questions from the operator renting you the airplane:

- What hull and liability insurance does the operator have covering the airplane?
- What does a renter pay for damage to the airplane if (a) the damage is your fault, (b) the operator's fault, and (c) a third party's fault?
- What liability claims are you likely to be open to in case of an incident or accident?
- Is renter's insurance available, and is it available for the short term you need it?

In comparison to the United States, the rest of the world tends to be a lot more reasonable about liability litigation, but you can end up facing a big bill anywhere if you bend an airplane or cause any damage or personal injury with it. Let the buyer beware.

Lastly, though not directly an insurance issue, be aware of liability waivers that you might be asked to sign by some operators, usually nonprofit flying clubs. In these statements, you waive your rights to make any claims against the operator in case of any mishaps, a way for them to control their own liability insurance cost. The enforceability of such waivers varies from country to country, depending on the legal system.

A WORD OF CAUTION

The world of private flying is forever changing. Flying schools, aeroclubs, and airports are at the whim of the economy, the regulators, and a host of interests competing with the private, recreational flyer. While every reasonable effort has been made to ensure that the information in this book is accurate, you might discover that some flying opportunities have been curtailed and there are great

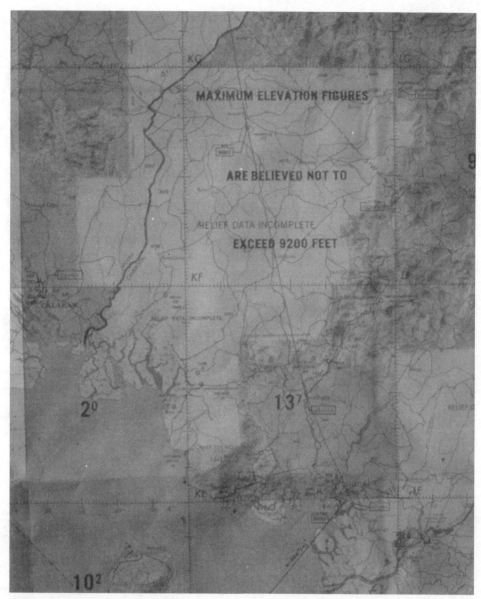

Watch out for the gaps in some maps.

opportunities where none are listed. Flexibility, good humor, and patience is the key to making the most of the changing recreational flying environment around you.

And remember, this guide is as much a book on how to find out what is possible, as it is a source of information on what is out there now.

Any reference in this book to aviation regulations, routes, and procedures is merely a descriptive interpretation at a moment in time, and is under no circumstances to be used as a source of information for an actual flight. It is the responsibility of every pilot in command to consult all official sources of information relevant to every aspect of a proposed flight and personally assure compliance with all laws, regulations and procedures.

ICAO VFR MINIMUMS

ICAO, the International Civil Aviation Organization, headquartered in Montreal, Canada, has the task of standardizing the structure and technical aspects of civil aviation worldwide. ICAO recommendations are not binding on the 156 member nations, but are generally accepted out of self-interest, especially the recommendations affecting international commercial air transportation.

The organization has also established recommended Visual Flight Rules (VFR), in *Rules of the Air*, Annex 2, Chapter 4. An important component of the rules is the recommended VFR minimums listed below. Many member nations have accepted these minimums entirely, or with minor modifications. The country chapters that follow frequently refer to these ICAO minimums.

ICAO VFR Minimums

	In Controlled Airspace		Outside Controlled Airspace	
	Above*	At or Below	Above*	At or Below
Visibility	8 kilometers (5 miles)	8 kilometers (5 miles) 5 kilometers (3 miles)**	8 kilometers (5 miles)	1,500 meters (0.9 miles)
Distance from cloud				
(a) horizontal	1,500 meters	1,500 meters	1,500 meters	Clear of clouds,
(b) vertical	300 meters (1,000 feet)	300 meters	300 meters	surface in sight

*900 meters (3,000 feet) MSL or 300 meters (1,000 feet) agl, whichever is higher

**When so prescribed by the appropriate ATS authority.

(Not to be used for flight planning; consult official sources.)

Europe

1

Fun flying with an Old World flair

NEXT TO THE UNITED STATES, private VFR flying is most easily and widely available in Europe, particularly in the countries covered in this section. But while Europe's population is greater than that of the United States, it is home to many separate countries, each with its own laws and regulations, and this can sometimes be a bit of a constraint on recreational flying by foreign visitors. The situation is changing rapidly for the better as the drive for European unity increases, especially among the 12 countries of the European Economic Community.

The IFR system has been standardized not only in Europe, but also worldwide for a long time to meet the needs of international commercial air transportation. Private license requirements are converging, and European borders are becoming simpler to cross. National VFR regulations in Europe are increasingly in conformity with the standards recommended by the International Civil Aviation Organization (ICAO). In these changing times you might wish to consider a few issues and practices common to the continent.

LICENSE VALIDATION—REGULATIONS

In the summer of 1990, the European Parliament (the European Economic Community's supranational governing body) passed a law for the automatic recognition without validation, by all 12 EEC member countries, of private pilot certificates issued by each member country. The 12 EEC members are the United Kingdom, France, Germany, the Netherlands, Belgium, Luxembourg, Italy, Portugal, Spain, Greece, Ireland, and Denmark. The EEC countries are treaty bound to accept this legislation, and it will come into effect as each country's national government ratifies it. This step forward coincides with the economic unity of the EEC countries to be in effect by 1992. Pilots holding EEC certificates should note that as soon as their countries ratify the new legislation, the validation section of the country chapters on the EEC countries will no longer apply to them.

Old and new: Wichita iron discreetly surrounds this slick new German-built Grob G-115 at an English field.

Foreign visitors to EEC countries from outside the EEC will have to continue to comply with the national requirements outlined in the country chapters, but there is hope for simplification. There are signs that in the near future it will be enough for visitors from outside the EEC to obtain validation in one EEC country, which will be automatically valid for all other EEC countries. Stay tuned.

LICENSE VALIDATION—LOCAL OPERATORS

Some local flying schools and aeroclubs are woefully ignorant of their country's license validation requirements, and will usually err on the conservative side, telling you that you will first have to take at least written tests given by the civil aviation authorities, when that is not the case. On a recent trip to Switzerland one operator insisted that I had to take a written exam, and half an hour later another operator offered me his entire flight line fleet after a glance at my United States certificate. (They were both wrong; I had to get a validation issued upon the inspection of my certificate by the civil aviation authority, but I didn't have to take any tests.) How do you tell people in their own country that they don't know their laws? As tactfully as possible. Hear them out, and, if they are wrong, tell them politely how you understand the requirements, and offer to call the civil aviation authorities to confirm your information. In most cases you will have no problems at all, but be prepared.

GAFOR

GAFOR stands for *general aviation visual flight forecast*, and is a coded VFR weather forecast summary in widespread use throughout Europe. Four letter codes for the summary usually explain the type of weather (check the national AIPs for variations on ceiling and visibility values):

- Oscar (open), ceiling 2,000 feet or better, visibility 5 nautical miles or more.
- Delta (difficult), ceiling 1,000-2,000 feet, visibility 2 nautical miles or more.

- Mike (marginal), ceiling 500-1,000 feet, visibility 1 nautical mile or more.
- X-ray (closed), ceiling less than 500 feet, visibility as low as zero.

These codes are applied to divided and numbered sections of the country laid out on a map, or to numbered routes depicted on the map. These form maps are usually available in pads at all the airports. GAFOR is available over the phone, or at airports in teletype form. GAFOR information is especially useful on cross-country flights as an update when you have already received a thorough weather briefing earlier in the day, or on local flights.

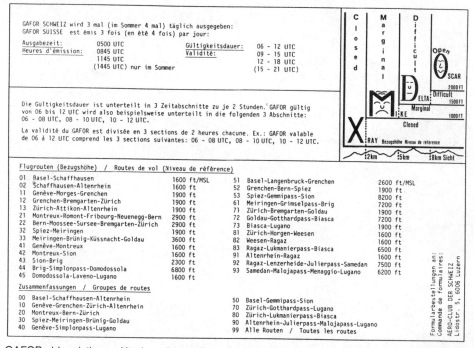

GAFOR abbreviations, altitudes, plus additional information are found on this side of a Swiss flight planning document.

BORDER CROSSINGS

Border crossings used to be a real hassle in Europe because there are so many borders. You invariably had to leave from airports of exit and land at airports of entry, and the paperwork would choke a goat. This, too, is getting easier. By the time this book is in print, aerial border crossing formalities will no longer be required among EEC countries (verify this information on arrival). The bureaucracy will still reign in other countries but might become simpler on cue from the EEC. Get advice on the border crossing paperwork requirements when you rent the airplane.

In selected countries, border crossings in locally registered rental aircraft might be prohibited for holders of validated certificates, or recognized foreign certificates. Always check with the operator renting you the airplane, before you blast off for the country next door.

PRIOR PERMISSION REQUIRED

Throughout Europe you will encounter *prior permission required* (PPR) airports, especially when landing at a privately run field. PPR means calling on the phone before departure, not hollering on the radio on downwind. Always check before takeoff to see if the destination is PPR.

JEPPESEN-BOTTLANG AIRFIELD MANUAL

If you intend to do any serious VFR flying throughout Europe, an excellent (though expensive) airfield guide is the *Jeppesen-Bottlang Airfield Manual*, which provides good airport diagrams and detailed frequency and facility information. Many of the bigger European airports have unique VFR arrival and departure procedures over a series of specific checkpoints, which are also depicted in great detail. The manual is also available in individual sections, country by country. It is bi- or trilingual, depending upon the country covered, and one language is always English.

2

United Kingdom

Country rating: **Easy**

ONC Chart: **E-1**

Rental cost range:

  2 seat trainer **$65-110**

  4 seat fixed gear **$100-175**

  4 seat retractable **$150-220**

QUALIFICATIONS AND LICENSE VALIDATION

Pilots holding licenses issued by ICAO members require no license validation in the United Kingdom to fly UK-registered aircraft solo on private VFR flights. The United Kingdom automatically recognizes private pilot licenses from all ICAO member states, for any length of stay. Recognition is also extended to instrument ratings.

To rent an airplane for noncommercial, recreational flying, you have only to go to an FBO or club of your choice with the documents listed below, and pass a checkride. Expect a comprehensive check, similar to a private pilot flight test.

UK airspace regulations differ slightly from United States and ICAO standards. It is, therefore, important to get a thorough briefing on regulations from a local instructor, as well as a briefing for each specific route you plan to fly until you get used to the local airspace system.

DOCUMENTS YOU SHOULD TAKE

Pilot license

Current medical

Logbook

Radio operator license (if separate from pilot license)

The Slingsby T-67 is a delightful British airplane available for rental.

Bring your original license and medical. For a short-term stay, a notarized photocopy of the logbook is sufficient. Notarize the last page containing summary flight experience, and pages containing checkflights and endorsements. For a long-term stay, bring the original.

USEFUL FLYING ORGANIZATIONS

Royal Aero Club
Kimberley House
Vaughan Way
Leicester
Telephone   (0533) 531051

This is the national organization coordinating recreational and sport aviation in the UK. It can provide information on local aeroclubs.

AOPA UK
50a Cambridge St.
London SW1V 4QQ
Telephone   (01) 834 5631 or 834 4307

AOPA UK is a particularly active and effective general aviation lobby. Its senior officers also play an important role in coordinating AOPA activities throughout Europe. AOPA UK is a good source of information for visiting private pilots, especially AOPA members.

Civil Aviation Authority
Aviation House
129 Kingsway
London WC2B 6NN
Telephone   (01) 405 6922

This government agency is responsible for general aviation pilot licensing and publishes *Conduct of VFR Flights Within the U.K.*

FAA Regional Office
c/o American Embassy
Grosvenor Square
London W1AE
Telephone   (01) 499 9000, extension 2497

The FAA's regional representative is helpful to visiting American pilots with questions about flying in the UK.

WHERE TO FLY, WHAT TO FLY

The United Kingdom has been a driving force behind the development of aviation since the earliest days. This island nation with a tradition of far-flung overseas interests, has always eagerly embraced any mode of transportation that hastened mobility. Even before World War II, Imperial Airways had established regular and frequent service on the routes leading to the Far East, Australia, and the remotest corners of Africa. British airplanes have also shouldered their share of the burden in two world wars. Who hasn't heard of the Sopwith Camel, the Hurricane, and the Spitfire?

Private flying, too, prospered under these conditions. Many a ragwing biplane carried its adventurous amateur pilot to destinations thousands of miles away. Sir Francis Chicester flew to Australia in a tiny de Havilland Moth long before he sailed solo around the world. Britain's aviation heritage is cherished in its excellent aviation museums, and the spirit of amateur flight lives on in the recreational airfields that still dot the land. There are great opportunities for cross-country flying over the beautiful countryside in the average four-seat touring aircraft or two-seat trainer. There are also good possibilities to get checked out in a variety of unusual aircraft. And if you want to try something really different, you can take one of the week-long glider courses available at the country's many soaring fields.

Aircraft to watch for

Britain still makes a number of interesting light aircraft, although not nearly on the scale as during the 1930s. Today's production lines are small, and the airplanes that roll off are aimed at a niche market. The Slingsby T-67 series is a sleek side-by-side two seater, intended primarily for low-cost basic military training and civilian aerobatic training. Slingsby, the builder, is best known for its sailplanes, and the influence is clearly visible in the clean lines and high aspect ratio of the T-67. The airplane comes with a range of engines. It was first built out of wood, and is now made of fiberglass. The switch in building materials has not changed its appearance.

The ARV Super 2 is a cute wasp-like side-by-side two-seat, all-metal, high-wing airplane aimed at the low-cost trainer replacement market, and built on the Isle of Wight. Its novel feature is a high tech, super-efficient, in-line liquid-cooled two-stroke engine (the airplane is not an ultralight).

With their particularly keen sense for history, the British are great preservers of the past. There is a lively vintage aircraft movement, and a respectable number of vintage and classic airplanes are available for rent. Be especially on the lookout for Tiger Moths, Chipmunks, and Austers.

The classic Chipmunk is also available for rent at several British airfields.

Airports

Airfields are near almost every large town, many of them dating back to World War II, when Britain was one large unsinkable aircraft carrier. What follows is a nationwide sample of airfields, large and small, selected for location, and the availability of rental touring aircraft or special flying opportunities. Because clubs and schools might come and go, the telephone numbers of airport management are listed. It is best to give them a call to get the most recent rundown of who is doing what at a particular airfield.

The London area

Britain's majestic capital is a major destination for most visitors to the United Kingdom, and its environs offer many recreational flying opportunities. Four good places to start are Ellstree to the north, Biggin Hill to the south, and Wycombe-Booker and Blackbushe to the west. All four airfields have a number of flying schools with large fleets available seven days a week.

Ellstree, (01) 953 3502, is north of London off the M1 Motorway, convenient if your itinerary continues up toward the Lake District and Scotland. Available aircraft include a wide selection of Grummans and Pipers. There is a good pilot shop.

Biggin Hill, (0959) 71111, is south of London near the M25 ring road and is an excellent flying location if you intend to spend time in the delightful Kent, Surrey, and Sussex countryside. It is also a good jumping off point for flights along the southern coast and across to the continent. Local fleets include a wide range of Cessnas, Pipers, Grummans, and a full line of Aerospatiale light aircraft. One operator also offers two fully aerobatic Slingsby T-67s. Biggin Hill was one of the most famous Spitfire and Hurricane bases during the Battle of Britain, remembered today by an RAF chapel memorial near the main gate.

Wycombe Air Park-Booker, (0494) 29261, is northwest of London and has a good selection of Cessnas and Pipers and a Chipmunk. One club offers aerobatic training in a CAP 10, a feisty little low-wing French airplane made famous in the United States by *The French Connection*.

Blackbushe, (0252) 873338, is west of London and very close to Farnborough, which is the site of the famous biannual air show and home of the Royal Aircraft Establishment. There is a large Cessna fleet, and a chance to fly an ARV Super 2. Blackbushe is a good staging spot for flights over Oxford, the Cotswolds, and into Wales.

The rest of the United Kingdom

White Waltham, (062882) 3272/3/4/5, is near Maidenhead in Buckinghamshire. It is the home of the West London Aero Club. In addition to a large Piper fleet, the club also offers instruction in two Chipmunks, a Super Cub, and a Slingsby T-67.

Cambridge Airport, (0223) 61133, is just outside the famous university town. Spectacular aerial views of the university and the idyllic countryside are made better by the possibility of viewing them from a Tiger Moth. The Cambridge Flying Group operates several of these old biplanes. Cessnas are also available.

Goodwood, (0243) 789660, in Sussex is the home of the Condor Flying Club, which specializes in aerobatics and taildragger training, and flies a Slingsby T-67, a vintage Condor, and a J-3 Cub. Flying schools with conventional training fleets are also based here.

Headcorn, (0622) 890226, in Kent, is the new home of the Tiger Club, dedicated to aerobatics and the preservation of Tiger Moths and similar aircraft. The club operates the world's oldest Tiger Moth, as well as several other Tigers and Stampes. Two member recommendations and 100 hours of taildragger time are requirements for joining. Take the first step and introduce yourself. To start, expect dual on a member's account. If they like you and you have the experience, you are in.

Old Sarum Airfield, (0722) 23385, in Wiltshire, is close to Stonehenge. The local aeroclub offers a Chipmunk among its varied fleet.

Staverton, (0452) 712005, near Cheltenham and Gloucester, is an ideal base for aerial day trips around the Cotswolds wool country. You will find a good selection of Cessnas and sporty French Robins here.

Sutton Bank, (Thirsk 597237), is a glider field in Yorkshire near the village of Thirsk, home of James Herriott, the literary vet. To pilots, it is known for the huge white horse carved into the embankment at one end of the field. Aerial views of the Yorkshire countryside and villages are soothing. The field is operated by the Yorkshire Gliding Club, which offers week-long (and longer) residential gliding courses. Flights in a Bergfalke motorglider are also available.

Inverness, (0463) 232471, is smack in the middle of some of the most scenic parts of Scotland. There are good aerial sightseeing opportunities in the mixed Cessna and Piper fleet based here. Other airports in Scotland where good rental touring fleets are available are Edinburgh (031) 3331000, Glasgow (041) 8878918, and Prestwick (0292) 79800.

TOURING

Whether you decide to fly dual or get checked out to fly solo, you might want to consider touring. The good news is that distances are short. The whole country is easily covered in a day or two. The bad news is that the United Kingdom has some of the world's worst and most changeable weather. If you are on a tight schedule, you might do best with day trips. Lovely scenery is around each of the locations listed above. Check for details with the locals, but bear in mind the following suggestions.

Southern England is especially suited for day trips. From the Biggin Hill area you can pick any combination of airports for a round robin that would take you out to the Cliffs of Dover, over the beaches of Brighton, and on toward perhaps the Isle of Wight for lunch before heading back. Westbound, an attractive area to head for is the Cotswolds sheep country, with a bit of loitering over Oxford before landing there for a break, followed by a return to home base.

A particularly pleasant excursion is a flight to the airport at the lovely village of Compton Abbas, west of London, near Stonehenge. The village is within walking distance, and you can also fly around Stonehenge before you return home.

If you have an interest in aviation history, a delightful experience is to fly into Duxford, north of London near Cambridge. The airport is home for the Imperial War Museum's aviation collection, a vast complex of hangars filled to the gills with historic warplanes. Many of these airplanes fly on the air show circuit. A short hop from Duxford is Old Warden (call ahead to determine if landing permission is required), housing the Shuttleworth Collection, flying antiques, mostly from the days of Bleriot. Give yourself plenty of time to see the aircraft.

Flights over the Lake District and Scotland are also rewarding, but be especially wary of the weather.

VFR QUESTIONS & ANSWERS

What are good sources of VFR regulations? Consult the *UK Air Pilot and Conduct of VFR Flights*. The pilot shops and flying schools usually carry a good selection of publications that cover the VFR regulations. The most recent edition of *Pooley's Flight Guide, United Kingdom and Ireland* is highly recommended.

How can I get a weather briefing? You call for one at the meteorology office of a major airport. Get the phone numbers at the local airport. You can also get a recorded GAFOR.

What are VFR ceiling and visibility minimums? In controlled airspace and uncontrolled airspace above 3,000 ft. MSL, minimum visibility is 5 nautical miles, and the minimum ceiling is 1,000 feet. In uncontrolled airspace at or below 3,000 feet, the minimum visibility is 3 nautical miles, and the aircraft is to remain clear of cloud.

Is night VFR permitted? Yes, outside controlled airspace, if you have a night VFR endorsement.

Must I file a VFR flight plan? You must file only for international flights.

May I fly the airways VFR? No. All VFR traffic must be off airways.

May I cross an airway VFR? Only if you are IMC/IFR rated and obtain the permission of the controlling authority. Otherwise, you should descend below the airway (they don't extend to the ground) to avoid the airspace.

What are VFR cruising altitudes? Instead of dividing airspace from 0 to 179 and 180 to 359 degrees, according to the ICAO standard, the British divide airspace into 90-degree quadrants and have different cruising altitudes for each quadrant. Consult the *UK Air Pilot*.

Is there radar advisory service in the UK? Yes. It is called LARS, and except for parts of Scotland, coverage is quite extensive.

Must I maintain en route radio contact with ATC on VFR flights? No, except to enter control zones and control areas.

Is VFR on top permitted? You may fly VFR on top only if you have at least an *IMC rating*, which is a curious British "preinstrument" rating that primarily requires a demonstration of basic aircraft control on the gauges.

ADDITIONAL INFORMATION SOURCES

If you plan to do any serious solo touring in the UK, an indispensable publication, full of regulations, procedures, and airport diagrams, is the current edition of *Pooley's Flight Guide, United Kingdom and Ireland*.

Airplanes are included in the British preservation movement: Tiger Moth and Auster.

Britain also has some excellent aviation magazines, full of current information on recreational flying opportunities and matters of interest to the aviation history buff. All these magazines can be picked up at any UK newsstand and most newsstands in Europe. American pilots will find them at selected speciality magazine shops in the United States.

Pilot magazine is the local recreational flyers' primary magazine. The back is full of ads for aviation schools and clubs throughout the United Kingdom (including current rental rates). The annual March or April issue contains a comprehensive "Where to Fly" listing of commercial operators and flying clubs, including rates and equipment.

Aeroplane and *FlyPast* are both popular aviation history magazines of a quality rarely found elsewhere. Both contain good current information on upcoming aviation history events and aviation museums.

Flight International is a prestigious commercial aviation magazine. Topics include good general aviation coverage.

Last but not least, the local yellow pages contain substantial information on local flying schools and airplane rentals, especially commercial operations.

You should also obtain the latest edition of the Civil Aviation Authority's pamphlet entitled *Conduct of VFR Flights Within the U.K.* Call the CAA's Aeronautical Information Service at 0242 35151 or get it from a pilot shop.

3

Tale of a Tiger

THE FIELDS AND WOODS OF THE ENGLISH COUNTRYSIDE slide beneath the wings of your silver and burgundy Tiger Moth. Built by de Havilland in 1933, it is the oldest operating Tiger in the world. For more than 11,000 hours, its wings have watched the hedgerows below create a mosaic pattern in infinite shades of green, broken only occasionally by the rusty browns of a village or the cool grays of a castle dating back to the time of the mythical King Arthur. Somewhere in the haze, beyond the oil-speckled windshield and the clattering Gypsy Major, lies London, beckoning you for a look at the Thames and Tower Bridge. This is the 1990s and your Tiger Moth is rented. Is this a dream? A mad illusion? Not if you fly with the Tiger Club of England from Headcorn in Kent, southeast of London.

Founded in nearby Redhill in l956, the Tiger Club did not set out to preserve antique biplanes for the use of its membership. Its goals were much more modest; among the goals, according to first point in the "Rules," the club aims "to provide a means of meeting for those who take an active interest in light airplane racing, displays, aerobatics and other forms of flying," and "to provide its members with good sport flying at the lowest possible cost." The fledgling aeroclub bought two Tigers because they were cheap, the last of them having been mustered out of the Royal Air Force training squadrons only three years before. Then, as the years passed and everyone else rushed out to buy what the British refer to as modern "spam cans," the Tiger Club suddenly found that yesterday's surplus trainers had become envied antiques, and the club, their highly respectable keeper.

Three Tiger Moths and two Stampes form the biplane fleet today, and the rest of the flightline also is an unusual collection, dating back mostly to the 1950s. There are several Jodels and a Condor for touring, a Fournier RF-4 motorglider for aerobatics and soaring, and four tiny Turbulents and a Super Cub for fun. When it gets warm in the summer, the Super Cub is put on floats, standing in for the club's famous red Sea Tiger that sadly was turned into a reconstruction project by a hard landing.

Typically British, the charter of the Tiger Club asks a member only to "always go out of his or her way to assist other members in aeronautical matters, always

G-ACDC, the world's oldest Tiger Moth, flies with the Tiger club.

to fly with courtesy and with special attention to the safety and comfort of others, and [I like this one the best] never to use an airplane for any disreputable or unworthy purpose." If you can live with that, and have a private license and 100 hours of in-command time, all you have to do is persuade two club members to say they like you and you, too, can join. The initiation fee is about $200 at the current exchange rate, and the dues are surprisingly modest, about $150 for overseas members and not much more for residents. Airplane rentals also are very reasonable. The Tigers and Stampes go for rates comparable to those for a standard four-seater at an American FBO, a bargain for the world's oldest flying Tiger, and what an alternative to the "You wanna' fly it? Buy it!" routine that is typically encountered when one wants to fly something exotic.

There is a loyal band of members, many of them scattered overseas, scheming forever for another trip to London. "I hope you won't sell the house and quit your job back home just to move near the Tiger Club. People have, you know," said the club secretary when I joined a few years ago. American airline pilots have retired nearby, and British members have been known to turn down promotions so they would not have to move from the area.

New members first learn to fly the Tiger Moths, and getting checked out in *Delta Charlie*, the oldest of the lot, is a very special feeling indeed. Its wings are silver, its fuselage burgundy, the traditional colors of de Havilland. It looks like it did 53 years ago when it left the factory, the fifth Tiger off the production line. A plaque on its side announces a designation of "historical aircraft" by the Royal Aeronautical Society. You have to swing its propeller to start it and it has no brakes, so you must be especially careful with the wheel chocks. It has a tailskid instead of a wheel, you talk to your instructor through a World War II oxygen-mask intercom and set your course by a huge gray horizontal compass from the 1930s. Its only discreet concession to our modern times is a radio.

The Royal Aeronautical Society has declared G-ACDC an official historic aircraft. The registration plate dates back to Red Hill days. The Moth can be rented by any qualified club member.

The instructors are demanding, the flying standards high. They make you spin from straight and level, they make you spin from turns, they open the throttle only when your emergency field is really made, they make you slip left and they make you slip right and they make you land, land, land, and land again.

First come the normal full-stall landings, throttle closed as you pass the threshold on downwind, a 180-degree descending turn to final. (Everyone at the Tiger Club knows that airplanes are meant to fly around in circles, not squares.) The next step is to perform wheelies for better traction on rainy days. In a perfect wheelie, you touch down on the mains and progressively push the stick forward to keep the tail from settling as long as possible, and finally, just as the tailskid gently touches the grass, the stick should hit the forward stop.

Then come the emergency landings with the power on, the nose way up, dragging her in a fraction above the stall, and when you chop the throttle as the three points touch, you roll to a stop in about 100 feet without any brakes. Finally, you do all of this from a pattern that never gets above 300 feet. England's weather is capricious and can surprise anyone in the slow defenseless Tigers, thus it pays to be well practiced in the routine precautionary landing techniques of the 1930s, all the more so because the countryside is dotted with inviting fields.

Learning by doing is the order of the day. I asked Chris Jesson, my checkpilot who flies Boeing 737s for a living, to explain just how a Tiger will flick into a spin from an overdone slip, a thought that often crossed my mind. Jesson said, "Climb in, old chap, and we will see." Up we went to 3,000 feet and we certainly saw, from every possible attitude, again and again. The loss of altitude and the view as the nose took off on its own accord made a stronger point than any discussion ever could have. Later that day, Jesson went up in a Stampe for a session with another club member who had questions about inverted spinning. They also practiced in-flight restarts, stopping the engine over the airport several times and restarting by diving toward the ground, windmilling the prop, because none of the biplanes have starter motors. The dive has to be literally vertical to work. The timid restart attempts typical of pilots who have never practiced the maneuver are unlikely to succeed should a cranky Gypsy Major give up the ghost because of, perhaps, a momentary mixture problem.

Once you are signed off for general flying in the Tiger Moths, you are free to checkout in any of the other aircraft. Most people immediately move into the Stampes to benefit from the Tiger Club's well-deserved reputation as one of England's foremost aerobatic schools. Two national aerobatic champions have emerged from the club over the years, and members compete in all classes, some in their own high-performance competition machines.

The Stampe is the creation of a Belgian designer who set out to improve upon the Tiger Moth. In fact, it looks like a beefed up Tiger, with a stronger wing, stronger tail surfaces, and upper and lower ailerons. Originally powered by a 140-hp in-line Renault engine, it has served long and well as a trainer in the air forces of France and Belgium and was a frequent participant in aerobatic competitions during the '50s. The somewhat fragile Renaults proved to be quite a drain on civilian purses, so many Stampes have been converted to the more rugged Gypsy Majors. Though long obsolete for top-level competition, the Stampe is still one of the best training airplanes and introduces many a novice to sportsman class aerobatics.

Minutes into your first flight in a Stampe, you quickly realize what a sloppy machine the Tiger really is, and how pure nostalgia must have had a lot more to do with its attraction than you first suspected. The Stampe responds lightly, precisely and instantly—a sheer pleasure to fly. And in experienced hands, there is little that it will not do. Both Stampes at the Tiger Club have inverted systems and smoke.

After a sufficient amount of aerobatic instruction, requiring you to fly sequences as in competition, you go for a checkride, and if you pass, you are signed off for solo aerobatics. Beyond that, it is up to you. You are encouraged constantly to test and expand your personal limits, using your own good judgment and the membership's bottomless pool of expertise. Formation flying, air show routines, competition aerobatics, formation aerobatics—the sky's the limit!

If you don't feel like air-show work and competitions, you can just take one of the old biplanes and do a little cross-country flying the old-fashioned way. A run up to Old Warden, where the Shuttleworth collection lives, is a favorite. To get a close look at London on the way, you set course for Croydon, from where big multiengined biplanes with names like Hannibal and Heracles once set majestically forth in the colors of Imperial Airways to the remotest parts of the British Empire. The immense grass field is there still, though airplanes have not used it for years. Then you head north and Greenwich is soon on the right and Tower Bridge, spanning the Thames, is down below. London sprawls to the left. You can pick out St. Paul's Cathedral, Parliament, and even Buckingham Palace on a clear day. But stay below 2,000 feet, or else you'll intrude on Heathrow's TCA. As you approach the city's north side, carefully pick the correct road, and Old Warden will be straight ahead. The trick is to sneak up early one weekend, during the season when the collection puts on a flying display. There is no telling what you will see taking to the air; a Bleriot monoplane, a Mosquito from World War II, or anything in between.

You also may take the club's planes for extended touring in Britain or abroad. The Tiger Club logo is a welcome sight on the continent, just a short hop across the English Channel. The club also organizes en masse aerial tours, a popular European pastime, when the entire fleet descends upon some pleasant spot for a day or perhaps the whole weekend.

But despite its other attractions, for many, the appeal of the Tiger Club is the nostalgia of the Tiger Moths. As you cruise homeward in *Delta Charlie* late in the afternoon over Kent's rolling countryside, you can't help but feel that it is 1935. And when you land, there will be white wicker chairs, cucumber sandwiches, and tea. That is quite a sensation for someone who wasn't even born when the last of the Tiger Moths were being unceremoniously drummed out of the Royal Air Force.

4

France

Country rating: **Easy**

ONC Charts: **E-1, E-2, F-1, F-2**

Rental cost range:

  2 seat trainer   **$65-110**

  4 seat fixed gear   **$100-175**

  4 seat retractable   **$150-220**

QUALIFICATIONS AND LICENSE VALIDATION

France has had a longstanding policy of recognizing for private VFR flight, without validation, licenses issued by EEC member states. Pilots from other countries need to have their licenses validated. This is an administrative procedure, easily accomplished at any one of the 21 District et Délégations Régionales de l'Aviation Civile (DRAC), provided that your license is issued to ICAO standards. Check for the DRAC nearest you with the local aeroclub or flying school. No theoretical or flight test is required by the authorities. Expect a thorough checkride from the organization renting you an airplane.

If you are not a citizen of an EEC nation, the United States, Canada, or Japan, you will also need a security background check arranged by the DRAC and performed by the French police concurrently with license validation. Depending on how risky the French consider your country, the security check might take some time. Check the length of time with them up front.

Your validation will be in effect for one year and is renewable for another year.

To validate your IFR rating you have to take a checkride with a government appointed checkpilot. Dual instruction might be necessary to learn local practices in preparation for the checkride.

Below is a list of DRACs and their telephone numbers, serving France's aeronautical districts.

Aeroclub lineup of Robins at St. Cyr.

Northern region

Alsace; Aéroport de Strasbourg-Entzheim   (88) 78 26 01
Bourgogne-Franche-Comté; Longvic   (80) 66 37 06
Centre; Aéroport de Tours-Saint-Symphorien   (47) 54 26 05
Lorraine; Aéroport de Nancy-Essey   (28) 29 03 81
Pays de la Loire; Aéroport de Nantes   (40) 75 80 00
Ile de France, Haute Normandie; Aérogare Orly   (1) 687 35 63
Basse-Normandie; Aéroport de Deauville-Saint-Gatien   (31) 88 31 27
Bretagne; Aéroport de Rennes-St. Jacques   (99) 50 72 54
Champagne; Aéroport de Reims   (26) 07 01 34
Nord; Aéroport de Lille-Lesquin   (20) 95 92 00
Picardie; Aéroport de Beauvais-Tille   445 12 30

Southeastern region

Auvergne; Aéroport de Clermont-Ferrand-Aulnat   (73) 91 11 98
Côte-d'Azur; Aéroport de Nice   (93) 83 11 31
Provence; Aéroport Principal de Marseille-Marignane   (42) 89 90 10
Corse; Ajaccio   (95) 21 01 94
Languedoc-Roussillon; Montpellier   (67) 58 69 85
Rhône-Alpes; Aéroport de Lyon-Bron   (7) 841 00 35

Southwestern region

Aquitaine; Aéroport de Bordeaux-Mérignac   (56) 34 84 49

Limousin; Aéroport de Limóges   (55) 50 40 20

Midi-Pyrénées; Aéroport de Toulouse   (61) 71 01 80

Poitou-Charentes; Aéroport de Poitiers   (49) 58 24 91

DOCUMENTS YOU SHOULD TAKE

Pilot license
Current medical
Logbook
Radio operator license (if different from pilot license)

You will also have to show evidence of permission to be in France, such as a visa. For validation, notarized photocopies of your documents are sufficient, but it is best to bring the originals, just in case. Apply in person on arrival.

USEFUL FLYING ORGANIZATIONS

Service de la Formation Aéronautique et du Control Technique (SFACT)
246 Rue Lecourbe
75732 Paris, CEDEX 15

SFACT is the supervisory organization for the DRACs. Contact them to clarify issues if you run into a problem at the regional level.

APPA (AOPA France)
Bâtiment Paul Bert, Bureau 25
93350 Aéroport Le Bourget
Telephone   (1) 48 35 92 94

Helpful to visiting general aviation pilots, especially AOPA members. Offers a useful pamphlet (available in English) on flying VFR in France.

Aéro Club de France
6 Rue Galilee
75782 Paris, CEDEX 16

Coordinating organization for French sport flying (standards, records, etc.). APPA is a better initial contact for the visitor.

RAID International Association
288 Ave Victor Hugo
94120 Fontenay Sous Bois
Telephone   (1) 48 75 13 54
Facsimile   (1) 48 75 50 17

RAID is a private venture dedicated to organizing international air rallies, a sport the French are particularly fond of. Morocco, Greece, Egypt, Norway, and the Soviet Union were destinations for one-week trips on a recent annual calendar.

RAID arranges all the groundwork, fuel, permits, and accommodations. Participants must bring their own airplanes. RAID can tell you who might be looking for partners to fly in a particular rally.

WHERE TO FLY, WHAT TO FLY

French pilots and airplane makers have figured prominently in the annals of aviation history since the earliest days. Today, the French aviation industry is among the most dynamic in the world. It is no surprise then, that France is one of the least restrictive European countries for private, recreational flying (although here, too, VFR pilots justly complain about constant government pressure to expand airspace restrictions). Flying opportunities abound from lazy, afternoon chateau hopping to cruising over Mediterranean beaches and flying the Alps. You are never far from an airfield anywhere, and can usually expect to find an assortment of French light aircraft and the usual Cessna or Piper fleet.

Aircraft to watch for

For private pilots an especially welcome feature of the French aviation industry is that it is one of the few left that still produces light aircraft in reasonably large numbers. For visitors the locally built fleet might offer the chance to fly some types not widely available back home. The two biggest builders of light aircraft are Aerospatiale and Avions Pierre Robin.

Aerospatiale's line of four-seat light aircraft has received a fair amount of worldwide attention in recent years and mirrors in function and configuration Piper's Cherokee line. The various models share as many structural elements as possible, and have a common cockpit layout. The fixed gear, fixed-pitch propeller

While others talked, the French acted, producing Robin's recreational airplane, the Avions Tres Leger.

Tampico is the low-end, no frills, trainer of the line. The more powerful fixed-gear Tobago is available with various engines and a fixed-pitch or constant-speed propeller. The top of the line is the retractable gear, constant-speed-propeller Trinidad. All are good, solid airplanes and they all have style with a capital S. Their designer cockpits are more reminiscent of a fancy European sports car than a run-of-the-mill light airplane.

An out of production but still well liked predecessor of the current Aerospatiale line is the four-seat Rallye with a bubble canopy; you fly it with a stick!

Less known in the United States but very popular in Europe are the airplanes of Avions Pierre Robin. Robin is the sport pilot's airplane maker. Its aircraft are famed for crisp handling, and outstanding visibility—the low line of the big bubble canopy is at your waist as you sit in the cockpit. Most models are built out of wood, the old-fashioned way, though from the sleek lines you would never know. A sporty aerobatic trainer is the Robin 2000 series, available with engines of various horsepower. Another Robin product worth sampling is the dainty, two-seat, V-tail, butterfly-like ATL. The name stands for Avions Tres Leger, and the design was the winner of the Aeroclub de France's affordable basic recreational aircraft competition. Available only in France because it was built to special local certification standards developed for it, the ATL should be an inspiration to recreational pilots and designers everywhere.

If aerobatics is your game, flying Avions Murdy's CAP-10—the side-by-side, two-seat, taildragger made famous in the United States by *The French Connection*—is a must.

Airports
Paris area

Several good general aviation airports ring Paris, from small grass strips to acres of concrete with all the bells and whistles. Although both Charles de Gaulle and Orly, which are the two main commercial airports, are also close to town, the airports' airspace does not overwhelm the smaller airports.

Toussus Le Noble, (39 56 34 75), is to the south of Versailles, and is considered by many to be the primary general aviation airport of Paris. It is big, with several aeroclubs, commercial flight schools, and a good pilot shop at the base of the tower. The Aerospatiale representative on the field offers for rent, on short notice, brand new examples of the company's light aircraft line at reasonable cost by local standards.

St. Cyr L'Ecole, (30 45 01 86), also to the south, is a delightful grass strip a stone's throw from the Versailles Palace. On takeoff toward Paris, you will be over the royal moats instantly, and will have to turn left or right as soon as practical, to avoid overflying the palace itself, which is prohibited airspace. There are a number of clubs and commercial operators at St. Cyr, offering a wide selection of French and American airplanes.

Lognes, (60 05 37 57), is to the west approximately 10 miles from the city center. On takeoff toward Paris in good visibility you will get a fine view of the skyline.

Coulommiers, (64 03 04 67), is another popular field to the west, a bit farther out than Lognes.

Pontoise, (30 31 23 08), is a suburban airfield northwest of Paris for the recreational pilot.

La Ferte Alais, (64 57 52 89), is a grass strip 20 miles to the south of Paris that is France's premiere aerobatic center. EAA conventions and warbird shows are also held here regularly.

The rest of France

Rouen-Boos, (35 80 10 53), is a nice general aviation field in the city of the Cathedral made famous by Monet's paintings.

St. Malo, (99 81 34 17), is a pleasant grass strip near the abbey of Mont-Saint-Michel in Normandy.

Rennes, (99 31 92 44), is a good staging point for flights over Bretagne.

Annecy, (50 22 02 41), near a beautiful lake ringed by mountains is an ideal airport for Alpine flights.

Grenoble-Le Versoud, (76 77 25 73), airport is also well situated for exploring the Alps. It is home to several clubs and schools offering rental aircraft.

Megeve, (50 21 41 33), elevation 4,823 feet, **Meribel,** (79 08 61 33), elevation 5,636 feet, and **L'Alpe-d'Huez,** (76 80 41 60), elevation 6,102 feet, are high-altitude mountain strips in the French Alps. All are suitable destinations from Grenoble or the Annecy-Geneve area. They are open to pilots not holding a mountain rating, but rental operators might require a thorough mountain checkout before letting you fly into the Alps solo. Local flying is also available at these fields (call ahead). Watch the weather and beware density altitude.

Lyon-Bron, (78 26 77 77), is the general aviation airfield for the town of Lyon, which has some of the best restaurants in France. The scenic Burgundy wine region is just to the north.

Bordeaux-Merignac, (56 55 80 00), is a launching port to explore another great French wine region.

Cannes-Mandelieu, (93 90 40 75), is the French Riviera's premiere general aviation airport, well run and popular with recreational pilots from all over Europe.

Well known glider sites are **Buno-Bonneveaux** (1 64 99 49 41) about 30 miles south of Paris and a short hop from the aerobatic field of La Ferte Alais, **Bailleau** (37 31 43 74) just northeast of Chartres, and **Fayence** (94 76 00 68) and **Vinon** (92 78 80 43) east and northeast of Marseille.

TOURING

Unlimited opportunities abound for scenic flying over France's varied and historic terrain. A satisfying flight over uniquely French settings can be had in as little as an hour. There are excellent day trip destinations, and touring for several days is also an attractive option, especially toward the south of France, where the weather tends to be better.

Chateau hopping is a highly recommended and easily arranged aerial pastime. The aristocrats of the Ancien regime littered the countryside with extravagant chateaux—only one of their many excesses for which a number of them literally lost their head. Fortunately for visitors to Paris, these men of means liked to be within a coach ride from the seat of power, so the capital is surrounded by dozens of lovely chateaux. On one recent flight out of St. Cyr, we were clicking off one chateau every 10 minutes.

Chateau hopping is best done from an altitude of approximately 1,000 to 1,500 feet, and is most efficient in the company of a good local pilot/guide who knows how to find them from the air. Pinpoint on a map in advance the chateaux you want to see and perhaps read up on them before departure. Be mindful of any overflight or low flying restrictions that might be in effect in any particular area.

Some of the largest and most beautiful chateaux dot the wine country of the Loire River Valley, within easy reach of Paris by light aircraft. A 3.5- to 4-hour round trip by Cessna 172 will get you there and back with ample time for sightseeing. Alternatively, take your time over the chateaux and stop for lunch at Amboise.

You will find the most impressive chateaux not only along the Loire itself, but also along its tributaries. A good plan is to intercept the Loire at Orleans (there is a divided highway you can follow all the way from Paris) and turn southwest to follow the river. Within a few miles the chateaux will be upon you fast and furiously: Chambord, Blois, Chaumont, Amboise, Villandry, Langerais, and Usse. Be careful about the airspace restrictions around Tours, just west of Amboise. Get a good briefing and check the NOTAMs before you go. Shortly after passing Usse, turn southeast along the River Vienne where it joins the Loire and follow it a short distance until you reach Chinon. Then head due northeast to intercept the River Indre at one of the smaller but most beautiful chateaux, the Azay le Rideau. Reintercept the Loire to the north and follow it back toward Orleans until you reach the River Cher flowing in from a southeasterly direction. Follow the Cher upstream and you will find Amboise airport on its banks. Fly beyond the airport to view Chenonceau, the most fairytale castle of them all, built, in part, right over the river. Land at Amboise for a break, or retrace your route toward Orleans or wherever home base is. It is highly recommended that before the flight you read about these chateaux in a good guidebook.

On the shores of Normandy you will find one of the most often photographed sights of France, the abbey of Mont St. Michel. It straddles a 264-foot rock sitting on sand flats a few hundred yards off shore. The tide varies up to 45 feet here, and Mont St. Michel is at its best during high tide when the water cuts it off completely from the mainland. As you circle it, remember that the monks started building it a 1,000 years ago and it took generations of them 500 years to finish. You can fly to Mont St. Michel in a comfortable daytrip, or you can arrange local flights from nearby airports. A nice grass strip recommended by the locals is Saint Malo about 20 miles west of the abbey. There are few VORs and no four-lane highways between Paris and Saint Malo, so prepare to fly by pilotage.

For those who feel a sense of emotion at the word D-Day, a rewarding experience is a low flight along the Normandy beaches where the landings took place, east of Cherbourg toward Deauville (there are good airports at both cities). The French are faulted from time to time for being critical of America. Let their aeronautical charts speak for them: there, in plain English, you will find Omaha Beach and Utah Beach.

Favorite destinations for pilots from around the continent are France's many wine regions, and a top choice among them is Bordeaux. The main airport in the region is Bordeaux-Merignac serving the provincial capital on the banks of the Gironde. Vineyards are everywhere, many of them overlooked by splendid chateaux. Pomerol, St Emilion, Graves, Sauternes, Medoc; look at a bottle of Bordeaux back home after you have flown over the vineyard from which it came and you will see so much more. Be especially careful to watch the bottle to throttle rules.

Alpine flying in France is as rewarding and its traditions as strong as in any of the other countries lucky enough to claim a piece of these magical mountains. Good jumping off points for alpine flying are the airports of modern Grenoble to the south and the much more quaint Annecy on the shore of a crystal clear lake embraced by snowy peaks. The high altitude mountain strips are accessible from either airport. An especially rewarding flight is into the Chamonix Valley, France's oldest alpine resort area nestled at the base of Europe's highest peak, 15,771-foot high Mt. Blanc. The high altitude strip of Megeve nearby is worth a landing, or you might be able to organize a local flight from there (call first if you want to fly locally from Megeve).

When you have tired of chateaux, cathedrals, and alpine air, there is always the French Riviera and serene cruising above the blue Mediterranean. One of the best general aviation airports is in Cannes, an ideal staging point for coastal flights and even farther afield to the islands of Sardinia and Corsica. There are several aeroclubs and commercial schools at Cannes, and it is also a favorite training ground for a number of British flying schools that bring students here for concentrated training in the good weather.

VFR QUESTIONS & ANSWERS

What are good sources for VFR regulations? Consult the French AIP. APPA (AOPA France) has put out a pamphlet called *Flying VFR in France*, which is available in English.

How can I get a weather briefing? In person or by telephone from the met offices at the major airports. You should manage in English if your French is rusty, but it might pay off to have contingency arrangements for a French speaker to be standing by on your end. Get the phone numbers from the local club or flying school. A comprehensive prerecorded GAFOR system is also available.

What are VFR visibility and ceiling minimums? France has adopted the ICAO VFR minimums.

Is night VFR permitted? Yes, but with some limitations. You must file a flight plan, and only certain routes are available. Check the AIP.

Must I file a flight plan? No, except for flights crossing FIR boundaries, flights across the Mediterranean to and from Corsica and Sardinia, and night flight.

May I fly the airways VFR? Yes. Maintain altitude according to the standard ICAO hemispherical heading standards.

Must I maintain en route radio contact with ATC on or off the airways? No.

Is VFR on top permitted? Yes, if you have a two-way radio, and a VFR descent and landing is assured at your destination.

ADDITIONAL INFORMATION SOURCES

For the serious flyer in France, the latest edition of the *Guide Delage* is a must. It has diagrams and information on practically every airport in France, and it also covers VFR regulations.

There are a number of good French aviation magazines available at most newsstands.

Aviasport is an outstanding magazine for the private pilot. It provides extensive coverage of light aircraft and the flying they do, and avoids commercial and military topics.

Aviation & Pilote is another magazine intended primarily for the private pilot. It also carries selected articles of general interest beyond the world of light aircraft.

Air & Cosmos is a high quality magazine for aviation enthusiasts, providing general coverage of all aspects of aviation and space flight.

Info-Pilote is APPA's (AOPA France) periodic publication. It is in newspaper format and contains a wealth of information for recreational flyers, but is available by subscription only. It might be worth your while to get some back issues at an aeroclub or flying school.

5

Chateau hopping around Paris

I OPENED THE THROTTLE OF THE CESSNA CUTLASS and we started to accelerate down the grass strip. Rotate, positive climb, gear up, and we had to turn left to avoid something most Cutlass pilots never find in the way: the Versailles Palace. It was Sunday morning, the grass strip we had departed from was St. Cyr-L'Ecole, barely 10 miles southwest of the Eiffel Tower, and we were going chateau hopping. Three others joined me on the flight: a friend of mine who had just moved to Paris and joined one of the local aeroclubs; Jean Jacques who knew where the chateaux were and would fly while I took pictures; and another aeroclub member.

I had wanted to fly to Chartres to see the famous cathedral from the air, and hoped to see a chateau or two on the way. But when we asked Jean Jacques, he whipped out a map and pointed to a dozen spots on the way, all chateaux. Among them were royal palaces, but many were aristocratic family seats where the founders' descendants still lived. There were better known chateaux, but it would be interesting to glimpse from above the layout of the "ordinary" aristocrats' domain.

From the standpoint of meeting regulatory requirements for our low level flight, the situation could not have been simpler. We could just get in and go. No flight plan and no communications as long as we stayed out of control zones, except the tower at St. Cyr to clear the area. The French have some weird minimum VFR altitude requirements, with which we had to comply. Among the altitudes we had to maintain were 1,000 feet over factories, hospitals, and motorways, 1,500 feet over open air gatherings and herds of cattle, and 4,500 feet over gatherings of 100,000 persons. So, keeping our eyes peeled for herds of cattle and gatherings of 100,000 persons, we were off at 1,000 feet.

The scenery was unexpectedly rural the minute we turned away from Versailles, and Jean Jacques said the first chateau would be upon us in two minutes. It was Dampierre, finished in its present state in the 1670s for the Duc de Luynes

Well-heeled mystery chateau on the way to Chartres is absent from the guidebooks.

as the family seat, by François Mansart, the famous architect of the time. The grounds were laid out by Le Nôtre, Mansart's equally famous contemporary. The Duc's descendants still live here today. The chateau is open to visitors, and much of the interior has been preserved in its seventeenth century condition. But from our vantage point the interesting vision was how clearly the chateau formed an integral part of the surrounding village community, and what a symbol of power it must have been for the villagers in its day. Such a structure is logical, especially for the older chateaux, given all the logistical problems an isolated estate would have faced in those immobile days. This pattern would be encountered repeatedly during the flight.

The next chateau was Breteuil, a few miles to the south, and also still a family seat since the early seventeenth century. We came in low over the surrounding fields. Shrubbery blocked all signs of modern times, and we were looking at a scene essentially unchanged in 350 years. A tidy estate of gray brick and steep slate roof, surrounded by woods, it had refreshingly clear lines and an informal and inviting look from above. Its upkeep is not cheap and the family has opened it to visitors, hoping to attract them with wax figures of the famous personalities who have stayed there over the years. The dummies were mercifully invisible from 1,000 feet.

Not five minutes down the road, as the Cutlass flies, was Rambouillet, the only chateau on our route with prohibited airspace directly above it. It is still used by the French president as a residence and to entertain visiting heads of state. From the air the eye is drawn by the pleasingly asymmetric cluster of turrets that form the chateau and date back as far as the fourteenth century. Dwarfing the chateau are the acres and acres of elaborate formal gardens and lakes, which are at their best in high summer.

Next was a mystery chateau, near the town of Epernon. It was in no guidebook, and no one knew of it, though it was the biggest and most beautifully landscaped chateau we were to see that day. It didn't look as old as the others. Judging from its formal, square dimensions, light finish, and somewhat frilly appearance, it was most likely middle to late nineteenth century. It must have been owned by a family keen to preserve its privacy and able to afford it without resorting to tourist gimmickry.

There was nothing private about the Chateau de Maintenon down the road, once the residence of Madame de Maintenon, the very public mistress of Louis XIV. Though occupied by madame at a later date, the buildings that remain today date back to the twelfth and fourteenth centuries. Its substantial grounds are a golf course now, and running across the greens, best appreciated from the air, are the remains of a giant aqueduct, one of the Sun King's many outrageous schemes. It was to supply Versailles with water from the Eure River, and was to extend for 30 miles. More than 30,000 workers toiled on it between 1684 and 1688 before the project was abandoned. But what a backdrop it is, along with the chateau, for a round of golf.

The cathedral at Chartres was next, an appropriate foil to visions of the era conjured up by madame's chateau. The cathedral is impressive in size from aloft, and is pleasing to the eye in spite of the hodgepodge style in which it was built piecemeal between the twelfth and sixteenth centuries. As we looked closely we noticed that one of the spires was shorter than the other. An earlier church on the site burned down in 1194, but an alleged relic of the virgin housed in it survived the fire and the cathedral has been an important shrine ever since. What caught our eye was how the cathedral towered above the town clustered around its base, much as it must have for the last 1,000 years. Its immensity compared to its surroundings and the power it represented was perhaps even more noticeable from above than it would have been from the ground.

Breteuil has been the family seat since the 17th century.

From Chartres we headed north. Suddenly Jean Jacques remembered another chateau and told me to bank right. Soon we were over a simple, gray, pentagon of a manor house, somewhat run down, another mystery chateau, most likely a private residence. Unlike the others, it was isolated, a dense forest to one side, fields on the other, and a dried up moat around it. I would move in as soon as they refilled the moat . . . .

We pushed on farther north to the Chateau de Thoiry (22 nautical miles west of Paris), built in 1564 in magnificent formal gardens set out by Le Nôtre. It is one of the best restored chateaux and the present owner, the Vicomte de la Panouse, and his American wife pay the bills by maintaining a delightful museum of gastronomy in the chateau and a safari park complete with lions, elephants, and hippos out back.

We were nearing the end of our block time so we set course back to St. Cyr, passing another endearingly shabby mystery chateau on the way that appeared to earn its keep from the surrounding farmland. By now I was certain that I preferred the mystery chateaux, and could spend hours loafing over them in the early morning summer air in a Piper Cub with the door open.

They had changed the runway at St. Cyr, so we had to turn final over the grounds of Versailles and got a good low level look at the Sun King's immense extravagance, surpassed perhaps only by the size of his ego. It had been quite an hour and a half. And we had barely scratched the surface. "There are over a hundred more chateaux just around Paris," said Jean Jacques. And the most magnificent ones are in the Loire Valley, less than two hours south by Cutlass. The sights to be seen could fill up years of flying before I would start getting bored. And our hop down to Chartres had it hands down over the usual Sunday morning flights next door for the $50 doughnut.

6

Germany

Country rating: **Easy**

ONC Charts: **E-2 and F-2**

Rental cost range:

  2 seat trainer **$90-130**

  4 seat fixed gear **$120-160**

  4 seat retractable **$150-200**

QUALIFICATIONS AND LICENSE VALIDATION

In recent years, Germany has considerably simplified the temporary validation of foreign licenses for private VFR flight. If you are current (three takeoffs and landings within the past 90 days) and have held your license for at least two years, validation is an administrative procedure provided that your own country is reciprocally cooperative in validating licenses issued by Germany. Your license will be given a "general validation" by the regional Luftfahrtbehörden (aeronautical authority) or its authorized local office (Luftaufsichtstelle) responsible for the area where you are. You need only to present your license, information on your temporary stay in Germany, and proof that your license is valid (a valid medical in the case of United States licenses). No government imposed theoretical or flight test is required.

A problem common in Europe and acute in Germany is that flying school and club operators usually have very little knowledge of the legal requirements for the validation of foreign licenses. Based upon the bureaucratic traditions of their country, they will often insist that validation is far more complicated than it actually is. They might be confusing temporary private validation with permanent commercial validation, or they might simply remember laws that are no longer in force. It is important to be diplomatically insistent if you encounter difficulties. Politely and firmly refer your host to the *German AIP, Volume III, Gen 2-1.1: "General Recognition of Foreign Airmen's Licenses."*

A general validation will be in effect for six months.

If your license is less than two years old you have to apply for "individual

An aristocratic Bavarian country estate.

validation" at the Luftfahrt-Bundesamt, Flughafen, 3300 Braunschweig, Telephone (0531) 3902-1. This is the federal civil aviation authority. Based upon your flight experience, the authority will determine on a case by case basis if you need any additional dual or theoretical instruction before validating your license. To use your instrument rating, you must also apply at this authority for "individual validation" of the rating. Expect a written examination and some dual IFR requirements prior to validation.

Below is a list and telephone numbers for the regional Luftfahrtbehörden (Aeronautical Authorities):

Baden-Würtenberg; Innenministerium Baden-Würtenberg, Stuttgart (0711) 2072-1.

Bayern; Bayerisches Staatministerium für Wirtschaft und Verkehr, Munchen (089) 2162-01.

Berlin; Der Senator für Verkehr und Betriebe, Berlin (030) 2122 - 2414.

Freie Hansenstadt Bremen; Der Senator für Hafen, Schiffahrt, und Verkehr, Bremen (0421) 361-1.

Freie und Hansenstadt Hamburg; Behörde für Wirtschaft, Hamburg (040) 34912-1.

Hessen; Der Hessische Minister für Wirtschaft und Technik, Wiesbaden (06121) 815-1.

Niedersachsen; Der Niedersächsische Minister für Wirtschaft, Technologie, und Werkehr, Hannover (0511) 120-1.

Nordhein-Westfalen; Der Minister für Wirtschaft, Düsseldorf (0211) 837-02.

Rheinland-Pfalz; Ministerium für Wirtschaft und Verkehr, Mainz (06131) 16-1.

Saarland; Der Minister für Wirtschaft, Saarbrücken (0681) 501-1.

Schleswig-Holstein; Der Minister für Wirtschaft, Technik, und Verkehr, Kiel (0431) 596-1.

The N-number option

The opportunity exists for holders of United States licenses to fly N-registered aircraft VFR or IFR without validation requirements; N-registered aircraft are available at Tannheim, west of Munich, and Egelsbach, outside of Frankfurt (see the list of airports in this chapter). Flights must remain within Germany and must not be for commercial purposes.

DOCUMENTS YOU SHOULD TAKE

Pilot license
Current medical
Logbook
Radio operator license (if separate from pilot license)

Take the original documents. You will have to present evidence to the aeronautical authorities that your license is valid. Such evidence varies among issuing countries. American licenses are made valid by a current medical certificate, UK licenses by a Certificate of Validity, and Canadian licenses by a License Renewal Certificate.

USEFUL FLYING ORGANIZATIONS

Luftfahrt-Bundesamt
Flughafen
3300 Braunschweig
Telephone   (0531) 3902-1

Germany's federal civil aviation authority. Need only be contacted if the regional aeronautical authorities have a problem validating your license.

AOPA Germany
Haus 1, Flugplatz
D-6073 Egelsbach
Telephone   (06103) 42081

Helpful to all visitors, especially AOPA members. Conveniently located at a popular general aviation airfield just south of Frankfurt. Refer to its file of Europewide trip reports filed by the membership (in German).

Deutscher Aeroclub
Lyoner Strasse 16
6000 Frankfurt/M 71
Telephone   (069) 66 30 090

Coordinating body for all sport aviation in Germany that can provide helpful advice to visiting recreational pilots.

WHERE TO FLY, WHAT TO FLY

Some of Europe's most picturesque aerial sights are found over Germany. Sections of the Rhine Valley are a fairytale land of castles perched atop narrow gorges towering above the winding river. Southern Germany is a land of soothing fields and forests, and "gemütlich" villages. You can wing your way over the Black Forest, the Blue Danube, and such medieval market towns as Ulm, Lindau, and Meersburg. You can fly over the historic Bodensee where Graf Zeppelin's airships and Dornier's flying boats were once built and took to the air. And then there are the Alps. Not only can you indulge in some of the best mountain flying, but you can also arrange some thoroughly German instruction.

Airplanes to watch for

Germany is the land of gliders and motorgliders. Who hasn't heard of Otto Lilienthal's gliding experiments in the late 1800s, or the restrictions placed on German power flying by the Versailles Treaty at the end of World War I that made gliding practically a national sport during the 1920s and 1930s. It was also in Germany during the 1960s that the sleek, high-performance fiberglass sailplane was developed and came into its own. Soaring is widely available and you are encouraged to try it, especially at the more scenic locations.

For the power pilot, perhaps the most interesting and efficient form of local flying worth sampling is the motorglider. These graceful aircraft, that, with their engine on, easily match the performance of a Cessna 152 on less gas, and with their engine off, turn into sailplanes of respectable performance, have become particularly popular in Germany as the ultimate sport flying and touring machine.

Motorgliders to watch for are the modern fiberglass Grob G-109, the Schempp Hirth Taifun, and the Austrian Hoffman H-36 Dimona. Older, but popular models of mixed construction are the Bergfalke and the SF-27. All are side-by-side two seaters.

Germany also produces powered light aircraft in limited numbers. An intriguing powered airplane is the Gyroflug Speedcanard. It is similar to the VariEze and Long EZ, but being a production aircraft, it is constructed in a mold. The workmanship is excellent and the airplane is great fun.

A fiberglass-powered light aircraft of more conventional layout is the side-by-side two-seat Grob G-115. Its production has been on-again-off-again for reasons unrelated to the airplane's abilities. It is aimed at the trainer market, but its sleek airframe and delightful handling characteristics also make it a speedy and economical touring machine.

Airports

Germany is blanketed with a vast network of general aviation airports and airfields where you will find the friendly local "Flugschule" and its fleet of American and/or European (mostly French) light aircraft. You will generally also find someone on the instructor staff who speaks aviation English well. Below is a sample of airports and airfields chosen for their proximity to popular destinations and the speciality flying some of them provide.

Egelsbach, (06103) 4181, is Frankfurt's main general aviation airfield. It is south of town and the international airport. A short hop farther south under the 1,500-foot floor of the formidable Frankfurt control zone in this area will bring you to less restrictive skies. Egelsbach is home to numerous flying schools, and is also the headquarters of AOPA Germany, whose offices are well worth a visit. Some N-registered Cessnas and Pipers are available for rent.

Aschaffenburg, (06026) 4933, is a private airfield east-southeast of Frankfurt, under the control zone with 3,500 feet to spare. In addition to the usual fleet of modern training and touring aircraft, Aschaffenburg is also homebase to several vintage airplanes and their restorers. Ragwing biplanes you might see are the Buecker Jungmeister and the rare Focke Wulf FW 44 Stieglitz.

Bad Nauheim/Reichelsheim, (06035) 3106, is a short drive northwest on the autobahn from the northern suburbs of Frankfurt. Here you will find several flying schools, a helicopter school, and an ultralight school.

Tannheim, (08395) 1244, is a pleasant grass strip about halfway between Munich and Stuttgart with a lot going on. It is one of Germany's handful of private airstrips. From here the Dolderer family offers a fleet of American and French airplanes, including an N-registered Cessna 182. The field is also home to rental motorgliders, a sailplane club, ultralights, and private sport aircraft, including some nice antiques. Away from control zones, it is a popular fly-in destination for private pilots. The Dolderers and their staff are active in sport aviation events. Several of their instructors are ex-Luftwaffe and speak English well. The Dolderers also run a flying school for German students in Naples, Florida, affording an easy rapport with visiting American pilots.

Augsburg/Mülhausen, (0821) 76115, is directly off the Munich-Stuttgart autobahn serving the more than 2,000-year-old town of Augsburg. It is a large airfield and thoroughly general aviation oriented. Here you will find Europe's largest Beech Aircraft dealer, a good selection of flying schools, and even a gliding club. The airport is also home to a fine antique collection including a famous World War II German liaison airplane, the Fiesler Storch.

Landshut, (08765) 463, is a short distance northeast of Munich and has become a popular refuge of private pilots because Munich's main international airport introduced a slot system due to ever increasing traffic.

Kempten/Durach, (0831) 65969, is Germany's premiere Alpine airfield. It is ideally located in a wide valley a short distance from the serious mountains, so that when conditions among the peaks turn tricky, the airfield is often still tranquil. Kempten has been in continuous operation since 1932, and is home to the Deutscher Alpenflugschule, an excellent mountain flying school. You can take several courses from a basic one-day 2.5 hours of flying, to courses lasting several days and exploring such topics as the intricacies of glacier flying and Alpine soaring.

Leutkirch, (07561) 3156, is approximately 20 nautical miles northwest of Kempten and is another good staging point for alpine flying, as well as general touring in southern Germany.

Juist, (04935) 399, is a long and narrow island on the East Frisian coast and is a popular sport aviation field and a big soaring center. An inviting sandy beach is at the airport's doorstep, and scenic flights over the Frisian Islands are the thing to do.

Oerlinghausen, (05202) 72421, approximately halfway between Düsseldorf and Hannover, is one of Germany's biggest soaring schools. Another is Burg Feierstein (09194) 8098, north of Nüremberg.

Wasserkuppe, (06654) 364, straddles the Fulda Gap northeast of Frankfurt and is Germany's, and the world's, most famous historic soaring site. Soaring continues to be taught here in a big way, and there is also a quaint but rich soaring museum.

TOURING

Germany offers excellent opportunities for touring, from scenic hops of approximately an hour and a half, to days of cruising throughout the land. A good feature of the country is its varied terrain within a relatively small area. By light aircraft, no part of Germany is more than a few hours away. The most attractive areas are sections of the Rhine, the Black Forest and southern Bavaria, the Alps, and the Frisian Islands up north.

The Rhine Valley's most scenic portion is between Wiesbaden and Bonn. The whole area is an easy daytrip from the airports near Frankfurt. Heading upriver from Maintz you overfly the Rhine Gorge, where the river is at its narrowest for about 40 miles, and vineyards cover every inch of soil. The village of Kaub and its castles dating back to the thirteenth century, one on a tiny island, the other on the hillside, are the first noteworthy vistas from the air. Then comes Burg Katz and Burg Maus, products of ancient power politics, followed by ruins of less enduring castles. Then it is over Koblenz and on to the bridge at Remagen of World War II fame and the ruins of Drachenfels castle dating back to the twelfth century. At this point you will be sufficiently close to the Köln-Bonn CVFR area to be encouraged to head back.

A favorite VFR haunt of German recreational pilots is the Black Forest, once the wildest corner of superstitious, ancient Europe, now a friendly land of dark, rolling forests and broad, green valleys. It is within close proximity to virtually all airports on or south of the Heidelberg-Munich line. The region roughly falls in the area defined by the spa town of Baden Baden to the north, the twelfth century market town of Freiburg to the southwest, and the Bodensee's western tip to the southeast. Freiburg is particularly attractive from the air. There are good airports both at Freiburg and Baden Baden.

Another popular area in the south is the Bodensee (Lake Constance) and points east, including the Alps. Excellent airports for flights into this region are Tannheim, Augsburg, Kempten, and Leutkirch. Have great respect for the Alps and at first venture in only in the company of an experienced local mountain flyer, but do venture in because you will experience some of the most exhilarating flying you will ever do. To get the full effect, cross over into Austria and perhaps even Switzerland. Do not miss the aerial view of Germany's most photographed fairytale castle, Schloss Neuschwanstein built for the mad King Ludwig in the 1870s, nestled in the Alpine foothills overlooking the Forgensee about 15 nautical miles southeast of Kempten. To give you an idea of distances, a flight in a Cessna 172 from Tannheim southwest to Lindau on the Bodensee, east to Ludwig's Castle, and back to Tannheim takes about 1.5 hours. Two old towns especially worth viewing from the air in this region are Mengen and Nordlingen.

In the extreme north of Germany do not miss a chance to fly over the wild and windswept East Frisian Islands on the North Sea. A good staging point for such flights is Juist airport on the 11-mile-long island by the same name. Several inviting airports are on the other islands too.

An intriguing option, available for some time even before the collapse of the Berlin wall, is flying into what was formerly East Germany. As more information becomes available and such flights become routine, greater detail will be included in future editions. For the moment check with your local German flight school or club if you want to visit this hitherto taboo land to see what all the fuss was about.

VFR QUESTIONS & ANSWERS

What are good sources for VFR regulations? The German AIP and *Flying Under VFR Within the Federal Republic of Germany* (in English and German), an excellent pamphlet published by the Bundesanstalt für Flugsicherung, Hansallee 2, D-6000 Frankfurt (Main) 1, Telephone (069) 2108 761 (free).

How may I get a weather briefing? The major airports throughout Germany have excellent met offices. Briefings are available in German and English. German VFR pilots usually rely on a comprehensive prerecorded GAFOR system that meets the legal requirement for a preflight VFR weather briefing. Get met office and GAFOR phone numbers at the local airport.

What are VFR visibility and ceiling minimums? Germany has, in general, adopted the ICAO VFR minimums. All airspace above 2,500 feet AGL is controlled, where 5 miles visibility and a 1,000-foot ceiling applies. Below 2,500 feet AGL in uncontrolled airspace, 1 mile visibility is required and the aircraft must remain clear of clouds.

What is CVFR? CVFR stands for controlled VFR, and is a peculiarity of Germany, Switzerland, and Austria. Major international airports are surrounded by CVFR zones. As the name implies, VFR flight in CVFR zones is controlled by ATC. You must be able to navigate by VOR and follow ATC instructions. You must hold a CVFR rating to enter CVFR airspace, and the aircraft must be equipped with a VOR, an artificial horizon, a turn-and-bank, a VSI, and a clock. A transponder is strongly recommended. A flight plan is required to enter CVFR airspace. You can airfile, at least five minutes prior to entry. Foreigners who do not hold a CVFR license may enter CVFR areas if they have a valid instrument rating, or a UK IMC rating: verify with the local aeronautical authority.

Is night VFR permitted? Yes.

Must I file a flight plan? You must file a flight plan for the following VFR flights: night VFR in controlled airspace; flight in CVFR areas; flights within the ADIZ; and flights at or above 10,000 feet.

Is VFR flight above 10,000 feet permitted? Generally, no. To fly above 10,000 feet, you must hold a CVFR rating, file a flight plan, and have a mode C transponder and the equipment to navigate by radio navaids. The airspace over the German Alps (clearly marked on the aeronautical charts) is exempt from the 10,000-foot restriction; VFR flights are permitted to 20,000 feet.

May I fly the airways VFR? Yes. You must observe the standard ICAO hemispherical heading rules.

Must I maintain en route radio contact with ATC on or off the airways? No, except in CVFR areas.

Is VFR on top permitted? Yes, provided that a VFR descent and landing at the destination is assured.

ADDITIONAL INFORMATION SOURCES

Get a copy of *Flying Under VFR Within the Federal Republic of Germany* from the Bundesanstalt für Flugsicherung (address in VFR QUESTIONS & ANSWERS).

The Deutsche Aeroclub's annual *Flieger-Taschenkalender* is a handy pocket guide packed with a wealth of information for the VFR pilot, much of it in English as well as German.

Good sources of current information, if you understand German, are the following magazines available at most newsstands:

Flieger Magazin is published monthly, for the private recreational pilot. It contains many "how-to" articles, flight test reports, and favorite fly-outs, including exotic flights, such as a trip by G-109 motorglider from Germany to visit the pyramids of Egypt.

Aerokurier is another monthly of great interest to the recreational pilot. In addition to articles for pilots, it also covers flying for the nonpilot aviation enthusiast who likes to read layman oriented articles about commercial and military aviation.

7

Pilgrimage to
the Wasserkuppe

WE CAME OFF THE WEST RIDGE AT REDLINE, in a blur of barren grassland and evergreens racing along the deck toward a little knoll across the valley. Stick back as the knoll rose to meet us . . . blue sky, left rudder, and suddenly at that fraction of a moment on the top of every wingover when the world stands still, the entire canopy was filled by the Wasserkuppe.

Ghostly forms of gliders long gone, hovered for an instant over the ridge: Kronfeld's *Wien*, Hirth's *Minimoa*, Dittmar in the *Fafnir*, Nehrig in the *Darmstadt*; and on the ground near the hilltop, the primaries, one wing down, waiting patiently for the wind to diminish. But as the magic spell broke and we picked up speed, they all vanished as quickly as they had appeared with only the massive military radar domes remaining, peering suspiciously eastward. The Berlin Wall was yet to collapse, and the Iron Curtain's hideous barbed wire barrier that kept East Germans imprisoned for four decades still scarred the border ten miles to the east.

The Wasserkuppe. The pioneering days of soaring. Its name has always held a Wagnerian mystique. Visions of pilots launching boldly into the unknown turbulence of the steep ridge; frail untested craft of sticks and linen creaking and groaning against the violent gusts; flights measured in minutes and seconds, not hours; the apprehension on upturned faces as delicate sailplane meets thunderstorm for the first time ever in the darkness above; the monument to fallen flyers; and later, graceful wooden cross-country machines, their fabric-covered wings translucent against the pale blue sky, setting off on flights that would end more than 300 miles away. More had happened at the Wasserkuppe in the 1920s and '30s than anywhere else to make soaring what it is today, and the ugly green radar domes notwithstanding, the legacy is kept alive.

Hans Gutermuth and Berthold Fischer were high school boys from Darmstadt when they stumbled on the Wasserkuppe in 1911. They were searching for the ideal spot to test their makeshift gliders, inspired by the flying machine, then

The monument to fallen flyers.

taking the European imagination by storm. The road from Frankfurt is not well marked and it is easy to imagine how they must have appraised every ridge and hilltop as they searched deeper and deeper into the Rhön mountains. You ask for directions, scan every rise, and finally, as you drive around one last clearing of trees, you know you have found it even before you see the sign; the perfect location; acres of windswept barren slopes in every direction. In the summers of 1911 and 1912, the boys from Darmstadt and their friends tested more than 30 gliders here, mostly broomstick and bedsheet affairs. Their biggest accomplishment was a 2,700-foot glide off the north ridge by Gutermuth, lasting 1 minute and 52 seconds.

The road rises from the south looking up at the gentle primary slopes where thousands took their first tentative slides in Zoeglings, SG-38s and other assorted primaries. As you approach the hilltop, the shallow east slope is on your right. The most level ground on the Wasserkuppe, it has served powered aircraft since 1924, and is the main airport today. The short paved runway cuts a path through the pine forest at the end, and an assortment of gliders, towplanes, and motorgliders of the Segelflugschule Wasserkuppe busily come and go on any decent day. But I arrived at noon, and the "Mittagessen" is serious business, not to be forsaken for a merely decent day. Flying had to wait until after lunch and so I wandered up to the soaring museum, a comfortably crowded exhibit in a small hangar that contains few original gliders, among them an SG-38 primary, a Falke, and a DFS Olympia. The museum also has a vast collection of photographs and soaring memorabilia.

In the doorway is a large bust of Oscar Ursinus, often called the father of the Wasserkuppe. The editor of *Flugsport*, he wanted to see aircraft development through advances in aerodynamics instead of sheer increases in power. He spared no energy to rekindle interest in gliding after World War I, when the Treaty of Versailles forbade the flying of power planes in Germany, and he was instrumental in organizing the first soaring meet on the Wasserkuppe in 1920. For many years he remained the father figure, setting tasks and announcing prizes, all designed to encourage the development of performance.

I walked on in a stiff breeze, past the overbearing radar domes where the summer encampments used to be. A few more strides, and then I saw it, dropping steeply toward the valley, the main slope of the Wasserkuppe, the famed west ridge, facing into the prevailing wind.

It was here that Klemperer made the world's first bungee cord launch in the *Black Devil* during the 1920 gathering. A modest glide of a little more than a mile that took all of 2 minutes and 22 seconds, the only real accomplishment of that first fragile meet.

In 1921, the *Vampyr* appeared. Designed by the Technical Institute of Hanover, it was the first true sailplane. Forty-four other gliders showed up that year, among them the *Blue Mouse*, an improvement of the *Black Devil*. Interest in gliding was on the increase. Klemperer kept the *Blue Mouse* aloft for 13 minutes but the *Vampyr*, flown by Martens, outdid him with 15 minutes and 40 seconds. Not much today, but a new world record then.

Modern glider is towed aloft at the historic Wasserkuppe.

The breakthrough came at the 1922 meet. First, Martens kept the *Vampyr* aloft for 1 hour and 6 minutes, and then Hentzen, also in a *Vampyr*, worked the lift for 2 hours and 10 seconds, and then for an unheard of 3 hours and 6 minutes. The sailplane had learned to use the ridge. Flight time was no longer measured in minutes alone. It wasn't unusual that year to see several gliders soaring the ridge at any one time.

There were human costs. The machines varied greatly in quality, and little was done to test them structurally. A wing failed here, an elevator there, and in 1923 they erected the memorial to the fallen flyers, an eagle cast in bronze, somber and determined, looking far into the valley beyond the west ridge from his perch of rocks. He guards a shield proclaiming (in loose translation): "We, the fallen flyers have prevailed, for we have tried. People, fly on, and you will prevail because you try." Fresh flowers and a silent figure or two at the memorial's base are a common sight.

"Mittagessen" was just about over and I strolled back to the modern launch site to arrange for the best seat in the house, the one above the Wasserkuppe. In short order, Karl Reinl and I were zipping along in a C-Falke motorglider, but instead of the historic slopes, we were heading straight for East Germany. Karl had started to fly on the old Wasserkuppe, and now he delighted in experimenting with how close he could come to the ugly brown line of plowed earth that at the time was the border, without actually straying across. Having no success in attracting SAMs, we meandered over to the west ridge and I finally saw the Wasserkuppe through the eyes of Dittmar, Nehrig, and all the others who once flew here.

After the Rhön meet of 1922, the art of ridge soaring was perfected at the Wasserkuppe and elsewhere. "Bubi" Nehrig was especially adept at ridge running. But the way off the ridge remained unclear until 1926 when Max Kegel was accidentally sucked up into a thunderstorm. Recognizing his big chance, he made a mad downwind dash to a safe landing and a new world record, 35 miles away. From then on, encouraged by Professor Georgii of Darmstadt University's Aeronautical Meteorology Department, pilots began to experiment with lift under the cumulus clouds. The results came fast in the sleek, new, high-aspect-ratio machines.

Kronfeld—in the *Rhöngeist*, in the summer of 1928—must have circled under a cloud just like the one approaching us now above the west ridge, and used the altitude he gained to drift over to the Himmeldank, a few miles off our wingtip. Here he went down into ridge lift only to start circling again when a suitable cloud appeared, gaining enough altitude to glide back to the Wasserkuppe. And what was more important, he had utilized lift that was independent of the ridge.

The next year, in his graceful *Wien*, Kronfeld raced along a front's leading edge for 84 miles, and in 1931 Gronhoff (in that most beautiful of gliders, the *Fafnir*), Hirth, and Kronfeld all exceeded 100 miles, flying on thermals alone. In 1934, Heini Dittmar soared 234 miles in the *Fafnir*.

Modern soaring really came into its own during the Rhön meet of 1935. Four pilots flew 313 miles and an astonishing 209 flights exceeded the magic 100 kilometer mark. Ludwig Hoffman soared a *Rhönspreber* for 296 miles to Czechoslovakia and upon his return immediately took off again, this time landing in Belgium 200 miles to the west.

Distance and altitude were now the name of the game. No longer were gliders tied to the ridge, no longer was it relevant to measure endless hours spent sitting in ridge lift. The 1938 Rhön meet saw a pilot reach 21,393 feet over the hilltop and 40 flights exceeded 13,000 feet, all in towering cumulii. By now the Wasserkuppe, though still prominent, was only one of many soaring sites. The discovery of thermals, the use of the winch, and Peter Riedel's perfection of the aerotow made flatland soaring a way of life and records were being challenged everywhere. But the Wasserkuppe had done the most to make it all possible.

It was time to land. We turned final as a Rallye towed out the Segelflugschule Wasserkuppe's ASK-13, flown by a visiting Englishman, and we came to a stop well before the East German border. I was about to leave when Frank Emmel, a new-found friend, said I must see something before I left. He led me to an old garage on the premises of the radar base, and inside was a brand new, sparkling, SG-38 primary. The Wasserkuppe Oldtimer's club had just finished building it. It was waiting to be bungeed off the ridge for the first time that coming weekend, when the antique sailplane rally would be in town. In the corner, still in pieces, was the Oldtimer's next project, a DFS Habicht.

As I started back to Frankfurt, I paused for a final look. The sun was setting behind the west ridge, and when I blocked out the ugly green radar domes with the palm of my hand, and only the ridge was visible, I could distinctly make out the silhouette of the *Blue Mouse* silently floating to and fro . . . .

8

Austria

Country rating: **Easy**

ONC Charts: **E-2 and F-2**

Rental cost range:

  2 seat trainer **$85-120**

  4 seat fixed gear **$125-150**

  4 seat retractable **$145-200**

QUALIFICATIONS AND LICENSE VALIDATION

Austria requires temporary validation of foreign licenses, but the government aviation authorities issue validations for recreational VFR flying routinely to holders of licenses issued by ICAO member states. No flight or written test is required. Once your license is validated, expect a thorough checkride from the commercial school or aeroclub where you intend to fly, given Austria's demanding, mountainous terrain. Holders of Swiss and German licenses need no validation because there is a reciprocity agreement between Austria and these countries.

Validation is available in one stop for a fee from Air Traffic Control (Flugsicherung) offices at six airports, and Auxiliary Aeronautical Information Units at eight airfields (apply in person upon arrival): (airports) Wien-Schwechat, Salzburg, Linz, Innsbruck, Klagenfurt, and Graz; (airfields) Bad Vöslau, Trausdorf, Kapfenberg, Punitz-Gussing, Wels, Zell am See, St. Johann/Tyrol, and Hohenems.

The validation fee must be paid in government fee stamps (Bundesstempenmarken) that are readily available at any corner tobacconist (Tabak-Trafik). Fees are subject to change and are at the mercy of exchange rate fluctuations; therefore, obtain the current amount from the appropriate office and obtain necessary fee stamps prior to applying for validation.

Temporary validation is in effect for three months, but may be renewed if you remain a nonresident and continue to fly for private purposes only.

IFR ratings are only validated if issued by countries that reciprocally validate

The Austrian Hoffman Dimona motorglider is popular worldwide.

Austrian IFR ratings. Applicants from other countries (including United States pilots, at present) must take written and flight tests to fly IFR in Austrian registered aircraft.

The N-number option

Pilots holding a United States license may fly N-registered aircraft in Austria without validation of the license. N-registered aircraft are available for rent from Jorg Stefenelli Aviation at Bad Vöslau airfield outside Vienna.

DOCUMENTS YOU SHOULD TAKE

Pilot license
Current medical
Logbook

Notarized photocopies of the license and medical and relevant logbook sign-offs such as complex checkout and most recent biennial is sufficient. (To be on the safe side, originals are always advisable.)

USEFUL FLYING ORGANIZATIONS

Austrian Aero Club
Prinz Eugen Strasse 12
A-1040 Wien
AUSTRIA
Telephone   0222 65 11 28

The country's umbrella organization for recreational flying. A good source for information and guidance.

AOPA Austria
Postfach 114
A-1171 Wien
AUSTRIA

WHERE TO FLY, WHAT TO FLY

Austria is small enough to be traversed full circle in a Skyhawk or a Warrior in approximately five hours of flying time. Yet there are few places in which such an overwhelming dose of mountain scenery can be found in such short a time, as in the Austrian Alps. Yes, the Danube valley and the plains along the border with Hungary are also nice, but for a real thrill head for the Alps. Alpine flying is a speciality in Austria, and if you are a flatlander, some concentrated instruction on how to fly the mountains might be time better spent than staying at a prudent distance from them on your own.

Another exciting local speciality is Alpine soaring. If the weather is right, you owe yourself an hour or two of soaring the ridges with an expert, whether or not you have set foot in a sailplane before. To have the best of both worlds (purists excepted), get checked out in an Austrian motorglider of exceptional grace, the H-36 Hoffman Dimona.

Austria is also the imperial elegance of Vienna, the Salzburg of Mozart, and the centuries old ski town of Innsbruck. And the chance to fly is never far. Below are the airports in and around the most popular destinations. All have aeroclubs or commercial schools offering a good selection of light aircraft for rent. In addition to the usual American-made fleet, French Robins, Tobagos, and Trinidads are also popular.

Bad Vöslau, (02252/7 83 71), is the best airfield for recreational flying near Vienna. A few miles to the south of the city, it offers power flying, soaring, and parachuting. It is also homebase for Jorg Stefenelli Aviation, where you can rent N-registered aircraft without having your United States license validated.

Wiener Neustadt, (02622/36 45), is just south of Bad Vöslau and is the home of the Hoffman Dimona motorglider factory. Call to arrange a demonstration flight.

Salzburg, (06222/4 02 57), (the) airport is an excellent jumping off point to do some serious Alpine flying after you have had your fill of the enchanting town it serves. Pilots who are music lovers can always combine some flying with the annual Mozart Festival.

Zell am See, (06542/72 25), is perhaps the most picturesque of Austria's airfields. Quite near Salzburg, it is on a lake surrounded by steep mountains, and is also a major gliding center.

Innsbruck, (05222/8 23 25), (the) airport is bordered on one side by a vertical rise of more than 6,000 feet. A good location for combining mountain flying with ski resort fun and the pleasures of an 800-year-old town.

Niederöblarn, (03684/420 or 419), in the Styrian Alps is mainly a glider field, but also offers one of the best mountain flying courses in powered aircraft.

Hohenems, (05576/21 70), is on the Rhine a few miles from where the river flows into Lake Constance in the westernmost corner of Austria. The lake is inviting, Switzerland and Germany are a stone's throw away, and the wine (after you have finished flying for the day) is all you have heard it is.

Krems, (02179/601), is an ideal location for scenic flying over the vineyards and castles bordering the Danube.

TOURING

All the airfields above are within comfortable reach of each other. It is easy to plan daytrips and shorter flights among them, returning to your original point of departure if your time is brief. If you have had your license validated and are properly checked out, you can plan a trip of several leisurely days combining aerial and groundbound sightseeing. Plan your track not only over sites of great natural beauty but also picturesque towns and castles made by man over the centuries, for they are a special treat of flying in Europe. An interesting flight is through the Alpine VFR corridor into Italy. Stay away from the bigger airports and their unnecessarily cumbersome European CVFR procedures. And above all, treat the Alps with the greatest respect. Be especially alert for rapidly changing weather conditions and always have an out.

Flying into Hungary has recently become possible, and is an interesting option once you have had a chance to get around Austria. The best jumping off spot is Bad Vöslau, only one and a half hours of flying time by Skyhawk from Budapest, Hungary's capital. You must file a flight plan with Vienna ATC 24 hours before departure. They will also give you a good procedures briefing (all flying to and from Hungary is via airways only). If you leave early enough, you could conceivably do a one-day round-trip, but you will have precious little time to see this city of faded grandeur, hilly Buda on the Danube's west bank, sprawling Pest on the east. Better to stay at least overnight.

VFR QUESTIONS & ANSWERS

What are good sources for VFR regulations? The Austrian AIP.

How do I get a weather briefing? Many airports have weather briefing offices. Teletype and phone briefings are available at airports without weather offices. GAFOR is available for specific routes. Volmet can be received on a VHF radio, and international Volmet can also be called on the telephone. Check at the local airport for current numbers. Some knowledge of the German language might be required for some of these services.

What are visibility and ceiling minimums? In controlled airspace, 5 miles and 1,000 feet; in uncontrolled airspace, above the higher of 3,000 feet MSL or 1,000 feet agl, 3 miles and 500 feet; at or below the lower of 3,000 feet MSL or 1,000 feet agl, 1 mile and clear of clouds, in sight of the ground. Restrictions apply above congested areas. Check the Austrian AIP for specifics.

Is night VFR permitted? Yes, but only controlled VFR, except for pattern practice at uncontrolled airfields. Some restrictions apply. Check the AIP.

Must I file a flight plan? Flight plans have to be filed only for controlled VFR flight. It is advisable to file a flight plan for flights over rugged, sparsely populated terrain.

May I fly the airways VFR? Yes. You must observe the standard VFR cruising altitudes for given directions.

Must I be in radio contact with ATC en route, on or off the airways? Contact is required only on controlled VFR flights and within certain border areas.

ADDITIONAL INFORMATION SOURCES

Flugsportzeitung (in German) is the periodical for Austrian sport aviation, available at the bigger newsstands.

AustroFlug (in German) is a general interest flying magazine covering everything from commercial to recreational aviation in Austria and abroad. Available at newsstands.

OAeC is the Austrian aeroclub's quarterly magazine. It is available by subscription only, but can be usually read at the local flying club.

All the magazines listed for Germany are also readily available in Austria.

9

Switzerland

Country rating: **Easy**

ONC Chart: **E-2**

Rental cost range:

  2 seat trainer **$100-150**

  4 seat fixed gear **$120-190**

  4 seat retractable **$200-250**

QUALIFICATIONS AND LICENSE VALIDATION

You must get your license validated by the Swiss civil aviation authorities to fly a Swiss-registered aircraft on private VFR flights in Switzerland. If your license is issued by an ICAO member state, validation is an administrative procedure, handled by the Bundesarmt für Zivilluftfahrt, the civil aviation authority in Bern, the country's capital. You can apply for validation through the mail at least three months prior to your departure for Switzerland. You can also apply in person. Call for specific arrangements on arrival. Switzerland is small and Bern is within easy reach from most parts of the country. If you apply in person expect at least a few days for the paperwork to be completed. No theoretical or flight test is required by the authorities. Expect a thorough checkride at the local school or aeroclub. Validation is in effect for two years.

For the validation of your IFR rating you must pass a written test on Swiss air laws and regulations.

Austrian and German licenses are recognized without validation under a reciprocal agreement.

DOCUMENTS YOU SHOULD TAKE

Pilot license

Current medical

Logbook

Radio operator license (if separate from pilot license)

One Swiss aeroclub's toys.

All documents except your medical must be presented at validation. Send photocopies if you apply through the mail. You will, of course, need your medical to fly solo. Bring your original documents.

USEFUL FLYING ORGANIZATIONS

Bundesamt für Zivilluftfahrt
Inselgasse
CH 3003 Bern
Attn: Mr. Ernst Hofstetter
Telephone   31 61 59 44

Switzerland's civil aviation authority. Handles license validations.

Aero Club de Suisse
Lidostrasse 5
CH 6006 Luzern

Oversees all branches of sport aviation in Switzerland. Unresponsive to mail inquiries, but you might have better luck in person or over the phone.

AOPA Switzerland
Rietstrasse 35
CH 8152 Glattburg
Telephone   1 810 3343

Helpful to all visiting general aviation pilots, especially to AOPA members.

WHERE TO FLY, WHAT TO FLY

When you mention Switzerland, most pilots immediately think of the Alps. Switzerland's share of these grand mountains is greater than any of its neighbors, and the chance to fly over them is the country's main attraction for visiting recreation pilots. But there is more to flying in Switzerland than the mountains.

Flights over the colorful patchwork of fields and villages in the country's rich, flat farmland are also a picturesque way to spend a sunny day, and there are good opportunities for specialty flying.

Aircraft to watch for

Soaring and motorgliding, which the Swiss take as seriously as the Germans, is especially popular. A powered airplane of Swiss manufacture worth looking out for is the side-by-side, two-seat, aerobatic Bravo. Piper J-3 Cubs, and their military L-4 version sold surplus in large numbers by the United States armed forces in the aftermath of World War II, are a low cost alternative to more modern machines. Switzerland also has a lively antique and homebuilt movement. With a bit of persistence, a flight in a Buecker Jungmeister should not be difficult to arrange. The Swiss do not make their own motorgliders, but flights or checkouts in the German Valentin Taifun, Grob G-109, Falke C, and the Austrian Hoffman H-36 Dimona are highly recommended.

Airports

Switzerland is dotted with recreational airfields, and given the country's small size, you are never far from one. Commercial air traffic is sufficiently light (except in the summer at Zürich International Airport), and the civil aviation authorities sufficiently flexible, to allow VFR recreational flying from even the busiest airports. Below is a sample selection of airfields chosen for location, equipment, and helpful service.

Birrfeld, (056 94 82 87), is an excellent general aviation airfield a short drive on the autobahn west of Zürich. The floor of the Zürich TMA is 5,500 feet MSL, leaving plenty of space underneath. The flying school at the field is well-equipped with a fleet of Cessnas, Pipers, Robins, and Falke C and Dimona motorgliders. Birrfeld is also a busy soaring center, home of four gliding clubs, and has vintage aircraft and homebuilts including at least three VariEzes.

Buttwil, (057 45 11 90), is south of Zürich. It is harder to find than Birrfeld because most rental car maps do not show the village of Buttwil, only the larger town of Muri, a few miles to the east, but is well worth looking up. The airport is a grass strip high on a ridge amidst farms and cow pastures. The Eichelberger family flying school offers a Cessna fleet, Varga Kachinas, a Piper J-3 Cub, and Valentin Taifun motorgliders. The field is also home of the Zürich Gliding Club and the Skylark Gliding Club. The floor of the Zürich TMA over Buttwil is 7,500 feet MSL.

Geneva Cointrin, (022 98 24 00), is apparently the only major international airport where a Cessna might be on final side by side with a jumbo jet as it lands on a ribbon of concrete and the Cessna is headed for the parallel grass strip. The local commercial operator has a diverse light aircraft fleet. The airport is also a stone's throw from pretty Lake Geneva, and Mont Blanc is a short flight away.

Lausanne Airport, (021 36 15 51), in contrast to Geneva is only a small grass strip. Also on the shores of Lake Geneva, it is an ideal staging point for flights to the Alps or north over flatter ground toward Bern.

Grenchen, (065 85 507), in the Bern area is a general aviation field, especially busy on the weekends. The local flying school is well equipped, and gliding activity is also high. Grenchen is a popular fly-in spot for area pilots.

Sion, (027 22 24 80), in the western Swiss Alps in a deep valley is one of Switzerland's premier mountain airfields. A favorite destination for weekend pilots who do serious mountain flying, it is also an important staging point for Alpine soaring flights. Local flying is available through the flying school on the field.

Samedan, (082 65 433), is Switzerland's highest airport and another well-known alpine field in the eastern part of the country. It also serves the fashionable resort of St. Moritz. It is the ideal destination for transalpine flights, especially from the Zürich area (to be attempted only by experienced mountain pilots). Samedan was a principal stop on transalpine races in the early 1900s. Fly locally with the flying school.

Locarno, (093 67 13 86), on Lago Maggiore, and Lugano (091 59 19 33) on Lago Lugano are two nice airports on the Swiss Italian border. They are good locations for flying the Alps from the south. If your license has been validated by the Swiss authorities, you might also find it advantageous to rent Swiss airplanes here for flights into Italy because the availability of rental aircraft in Italy for solo flying by visitors is minimal.

TOURING

Many good touring opportunities are available in Switzerland, mostly in and around the Alps. Well established scenic routes extend from the airports along the Geneva-Bern-Zürich line. Most major Alpine peaks are approachable without the need to fly deep into the mountains. Among the peaks easy to get to are the Wildstrubel, the Eiger, the Jungfrau, and Tiltis. Get a Swiss 1:500,000 ICAO chart and determine at the departure airport those scenic routes that would be the most suitable.

The creme de la creme of Alpine flying is crossing the range. To allow you to do any flying through the Alps, most operators will want to give you a transalpine checkout and the Swiss authorities validating your license might also require it (for the Swiss private license, student pilots have to cross the Alps on several flights, dual and solo). It is well worth the effort. The subsequent thrill of crossing the Alps on your own will be a highlight of your flying career.

There are four main routes through the Alps, and on several segments the autobahn is under you to make navigation easier as you carefully tick off your checkpoints. These recommended VFR routes are marked on the Swiss 1:500,000 ICAO chart.

- From the eastern edge of Lake Geneva you can follow the Rhone river and the parallel autobahn to Martigny. Here you can continue south to Liddes and through the St. Bernard pass to Aosta in Italy. Alternatively, at Martigny you may continue to follow the Rhone and the autobahn to Sion.

- From the Bern area you should fly to Thun, and south down the valley through the Gemmipass between the Wildstrubel and the Balmhorn. Beyond the pass you intercept the Rhone. A turn west brings you to Sion. A turn east leads you to Brig and then southeast through the Simplon Pass to Domodossa and into Italy.

- From the Zürich area you should head to Altdorf close to the southern tip of Lake Luzern and continue south along the autobahn to its terminus near Goschennen. Continue through St. Gotthardpass. Pick up the autobahn where it starts again near Airolo and follow it all the way to Locarno or Lugano.

- The route to Samedan from the Zürich-Boden See area starts at Bad Ragaz. Follow the autobahn to Chur, then head south along the valley to the Julienpass. On the way you fly past ski lifts at Churwalden, Lenzerheide, and Savognin. Turn east to slip through the Julienpass, and soon you are over St. Moritz just this side of Samedan.

The greatest threat to fine Alpine flying is poor or rapidly deteriorating weather. Get the proper training before you venture out on your own, and conservatively apply the techniques and rules of the local operators.

If you are not in the mood for mountains, you can lark about over the wine country along Lake Geneva, west of Bern, or over the Boden See.

VFR QUESTIONS & ANSWERS

What are good sources for VFR regulations? Consult the Swiss AIP and *VFR in Switzerland* published by the Swiss Aero Club.

How can I get a weather briefing? You can get briefings in person at the met offices in Geneva, Zürich, and Basel, or you can call these offices over the phone. Teletyped weather information, including GAFOR, is available at most smaller fields. You may also call a prerecorded GAFOR briefing (German and French) or listen to VOLMET on your aircraft radio. Get the phone numbers at the local airfield.

What are VFR visibility and ceiling minimums? Switzerland has adopted the ICAO minimums.

Is night VFR permitted? Limited night VFR might be possible with special ATC permission, but as a rule it is not permitted.

Must I file a flight plan? Flight plans are generally not required for VFR flights that do not enter airspace requiring ATC services. In some remote mountain areas flight plans are mandatory for search and rescue purposes. Check in the Swiss AIP and with a local flight instructor for the procedures to enter TMAs, CVFR areas, and Control Zones.

May I fly the airways VFR? Yes. Maintain standard ICAO hemispherical cruising altitudes.

Must I maintain en route radio contact with ATC on or off the airways? No contact is required unless the airway goes through a TMA, CVFR area, or Control

Zone, or you wish to enter such controlled airspace from an off-airway position.
Is VFR on top permitted? No.

ADDITIONAL INFORMATION SOURCES

Swiss general aviation magazines are *Fliegermagazin, Cockpit,* and the Swiss Aero Club's *Aero Revue.* Also worth getting is *VFR in Switzerland,* available free from the Swiss Aero Club at the previously mentioned address.

10

Alpine afternoon

THE HEADWAITER RECOMMENDED THE ROAST GOAT with saffron rice and we both had smoked salmon to start. But Rudi waved the wine list aside and ordered mineral water instead. The spring sky had just cleared, and after lunch, our business done, Rudi and I had a date with a Piper Cub at his flying club. I have yet to miss a date like that, and by 3 p.m. we were lifting off from the tiny grass strip that the red-and-cream J-3 called home. As we chugged out of the pattern, I glanced to the left and caught my first glimpse of our afternoon playground. A mere 15 minutes from our gourmet restaurant, as the Cub flies, were the Alps, covered in snow, as if a mad glutton had lined up every whipped cream desert he could find in Switzerland's many pastry shops.

It was the kind of flying most Swiss do, who don't fly for a living: fun flying. Excessive licensing and maintenance regulations and avgas at $3.50 a gallon have placed even the most basic form of reliable IFR transportation out of reach for all but a well-heeled minority. The light airplane's role in getting from A to B efficiently is further dampened by the Alps' capricious weather and an excellent network of inexpensive railways and toll free autobahns that on most trips beats the airplane door-to-door given Switzerland's short distances. So the alibi of "urgent business in distant places neglected by the airlines" is seldom heard. General aviation is mostly sport aviation and its focal point is the local aeroclub.

European aeroclubs have long been a way to ease the high costs of aviation. For many, they are the difference between flying and dreaming about it. Members pitch in with volunteer work, and instructors donate their time. Even so, expenses mount quickly. The Swiss have obsessively high technical standards and require costly 50-hour and 100-hour inspections on all aircraft, regardless of use, on top of a picky annual. By the time you push back from the fuel pumps it all adds up; in the case of a Skyhawk, to about $130 per hour even at the aeroclub. Commercial rates of $170 per hour for the average VFR four-seater are not uncommon, and the standard 40-hour private pilot license goes for approximately double the United States rate. Licensing fees are outrageous and pilots have to be retested periodically to retain their license. (Every six months in the case of an IFR ticket.)

The Central Alps from an aeroclub Piper Cub.

But there are ways to keep flying costs down and oddly enough they are often the more exotic alternatives. Rudi and I were droning toward the Eiger's lofty summit in the Cub for a mere $40 an hour. The Cub hardly drinks, nostalgia is free, and even the Swiss are hard put to obsess over the simple ragwing airframe and the Stone Age engine. A whole fleet of immaculate Cubs, Champs, and Voyagers is on the loose throughout Switzerland, and to get a private license in one is not uncommon.

All this is not to say that private owners are nonexistent. A popular form of private ownership is a syndicate of three or more partners, who often retain close ties to their local aeroclub. On the high end of the scale, Switzerland does have its share of Bonanzas, Barons, Saratogas, and the like, and there are even expensive warbirds in private hands.

VFR flying is simple, save for an unreasonable degree of noise regulations. Rudi and I did not have to file a flight plan for our Alpine sortie, but we had to fly around every little village for noise abatement. The Cub also sported a special set of extra-quiet mufflers, a required modification on virtually every imported airplane. Pattern practice is prohibited between noon and 2 P.M. to let the "burghers" devote their undivided attention to the serious matter of lunch (the day's big meal). A single departure or arrival per airplane is allowed. Most pilots take village dodging seriously. It breaks up the monotony of straight and level, and keeps them on the better side of the local authorities who control most airport leases.

For most pilots, including me, the biggest attraction of flying in Switzerland is the Alps. Very few places in the world offer such a majestic and forbidding creation of nature so close to cosmopolitan population centers such as Zürich and Geneva. Where else can you leave the office in the afternoon to practice glacier landings, and be back in time for an evening of Bach?

Our J-3 felt more and more vulnerable as the first snowy ridge slowly filled the windshield. Despite our huffing and puffing 65-hp Continental, we were still too low to cross. "Head for the upward slope," said Rudi, and soon we felt a reassuring surge of lift. We slope-soared in figure eights, sailplane fashion, steadily gaining on the ridge. When we had sufficient margin, we slid over the top, bisecting the ridge line at 45 degrees, sinking on the lee side in the burbling downwash on our way to the next upwind slope across the deep and narrow valley.

The lack of horsepower need not be a deterrent to Alpine flying. We didn't aspire to look down on the summits of the Eiger and the Jungfrau and countless other peaks from 15,000 feet. It was far more spectacular to loiter in the ever present ridge lift amidst the slopes and look up at the towering peaks.

Ski runs slid by below, the tiny dots of skiers scurrying across the blinding powder. Then we were over impossible crevasses never touched by man, and then an alpine village on the banks of a gushing glacial stream, well below the snow line, the wooden dollhouses sparkling in the freshness of spring.

The abundance of ridge lift, mountain waves, and thermals makes the Alps a motorless pilot's paradise. Soaring and hang gliding are practically national sports. Experienced sailplane pilots often embark on cross-country flights exceeding 300 miles, and hang glider pilots and their long telltale canvas bags are frequent one-way passengers on the cable car lines to the highest summits.

Typical Swiss weekend fuel pump traffic jam. The Robin is equipped with a composite four-blade extra-quiet propeller.

As in all mountains, the pilot's biggest bugbear in the Alps is the weather. Even on good days, the peaks can quickly create their own miniweather systems if the wind pushes unstable air up the slopes. Passes can close in a flash. The weather was CAVU when Rudi and I took off, but already the higher peaks were disappearing in cloud. There are official VFR corridors through the Alps, and GAFOR (general aviation forecast) letter codes indicate if they are open, closed, or marginal. But as Rudi likes to say, "You better have a well devised fallback, no matter what they tell you."

Somewhere along the way we sensed movement on our left, and checking our wingtip, saw an Alouette helicopter of the famed Swiss Air Rescue pull into close formation. The service was founded by the legendary Herman Geiger who pioneered Alpine glacier flying with his Super Cubs in prehelicopter days. The choppers are operated by private companies, earning their keep with mountain resupply flights, but when the call comes in on the crews' portable radios, which are monitored 24 hours a day, everything is interrupted to fly the rescue mission.

Most of our newfound wingman's rescue work is evacuating injured or stranded climbers, often from spots that would depress a mountain goat. But it was reassuring to know that he was there for us too, should we need him. Today he was just enjoying the sun on a routine flight, and as we set course for home he veered back toward the mountains.

Rudi and I gave the Cub a thorough washing before we put it in the club hangar. "If you want to fly in something really exotic, go to Dubendorf," said Rudi as he fussed with the airplane logs. "It is one of Switzerland's oldest Air Force bases, near Zürich, and the museum there sponsors a nostalgia flight of three Tante Ju aircraft—the only Junkers 52 trimotors in the world still flying with the original BMW engines. They give scenic rides over the Alps."

Rudi was right. Only he didn't know that you have to book a whole year in advance. But I was content just to watch the lumbering old transports come and go in slow motion among the supersonic Mirages and F-5s. If you are lucky enough to get a seat it should cost approximately $130 for one hour, which is the same as a Skyhawk at the aeroclub.

A few days later, on a Saturday afternoon, I was on the terrace of the airport cafe at Grenchen, pondering the ways of the Swiss, and the flying they do. A 1940s vintage Pilatus P2 military trainer was rolling on takeoff. A Rallye was climbing out from the parallel grass with a sleek, white glider in tow. Overhead, a Laser 200 was practicing an aerobatic routine, its nimble silhouette crisp against the lazy blue sky; a Super Cub, skis retracted, was returning from the mountains; all this flying, in spite of the overzealous regulators, the noise-conscious "burghers" and the exorbitant avgas prices, landing fees, and licensing costs.

I thought of our problems back home, and decided there will always be a way. A friend arrived in a spotless yellow Buecker Jungmeister and spoke enviously of the acres of "reliable transportation" at my homebase on the East Coast of the United States. I pointed out that I don't spend my Saturdays in a Jungmeister. "It is no big deal," he said "I am only renting it." See what I mean?

11

Italy

Country rating: **Moderate**

ONC Charts: **F-2 and G-2**

Rental cost range:

  2 seat trainer   **$120-200**

  4 seat fixed gear   **$160-220**

  4 seat retractable   **$240-280**

QUALIFICATIONS AND LICENSE VALIDATION

The Italian aviation authorities require temporary validation of your license for private VFR flying. If your license is issued by an ICAO member state, validation is an administrative procedure. Your license will be validated upon presentation at the Direzione Centrale Del L'Aviazione Civile, the civil aviation authority in Rome, or any of its district offices, the Direzzione Circoscrizione Aeroportuale at all the big airports. Apply in person and have patience with minor delays such as erratic office hours. You will also have to pay a small fee in revenue stamps that you can buy at any tobacco shop (Tabacchi).

    The validation also covers your IFR rating, and is in effect until the expiry of your license.

DOCUMENTS YOU SHOULD TAKE

Pilot license
Current medical
Logbook
Radio operator license (if separate from pilot license)

For validation you need not present your medical, but you will need it to fly solo. Notarized photocopies are sufficient at present for validation, but take your original documents just in case.

USEFUL FLYING ORGANIZATIONS

Ministero Transporti
Direzione Generale Del l'Aviazion Civile
Servizio Navigazione Aerea
Via Cristofo Colombo
I-00145, Roma

The country's national civil aviation authority. It has district offices at all the major airports.

Aeroclub d'Italia
Viale Maresciello Pilsudski 124
I-00197, Roma
Telephone   879 641

A good source of information for the visiting recreational pilot.

AOPA Italy
Aeroporte Urbe
Via Salaria 825
I-00138, Roma
Telephone   6810 8871

Might provide assistance or advice concerning license validation in case of difficulties. Can also give general advice on recreational flying. Located at Urbe Airport, Rome's main general aviation airport only 20 minutes from downtown.

WHERE TO FLY, WHAT TO FLY

Italy is rated moderate because, although license validation is easy, you will find it difficult to rent an airplane once validation is in your hand, due to the structure of private flying in the country. Private, recreational flying is readily available, but primarily through a nationwide network of self-supporting aeroclubs. Or, if you are well to do, you can buy your own airplane. A few commercial flying schools, which might be willing to rent to visitors on short notice, are to be found mostly around Rome. A floatplane operation on Lake Como, the Aero Club Como, is also willing to rent solo to qualified visitors.

As a rule, the aeroclubs do not offer temporary memberships to the short term visitor, but flying with a local safety pilot is easy to arrange. On a long term stay, you can join your local aeroclub, just like any Italian, and do all the flying you want.

The widespread application of a peculiar form of airspace restriction also hampers private, recreational flying. Many large airports and also a surprising number of small airfields are either entirely off limits to private aircraft not based there, or are accessible by prior permission only. Many of them you cannot even list as a legal alternate on IFR flight plans. The rules tend to change arbitrarily, and the airfield guides might not always list this restriction, so always call ahead. When you call, also check fuel availability. It can be spotty.

The villages of Tuscany have changed little over the centuries.

As a result of the restrictions, the highest avgas prices in Europe, and the associated high costs of flying, most aeroclub flights tend to stick close to home base and last, at most, a few hours. However, depending on location (consider Venice, or the medieval villages of Tuscany), even local flights can be highly rewarding.

If you want to do extended aerial touring in Italy, you might be best off, as suggested by some Italian aeroclub officials, to rent an airplane in another European country where it is easily arranged, and fly it to Italy.

Below is a list of Italian airports, and some suggestions of scenic flying you can do around them. Get your license validated, and look up the local aeroclub. Expect to fly with a safety pilot, but try hard for a temporary membership, and a checkout. The worst they can say is no, and bear in mind that, like Argentina, much of Italy also works on the "amigo principle."

Roma Urbe, (06 8120290), is Rome's general aviation airfield, a twenty minute drive from downtown. Here is the headquarters of AOPA Italy. There are commercial schools on the field that might be willing to rent to short term visitors solo.

Bresso-Milan, (02 6101625), is the field of Aero Club di Milano, a particularly well equipped club. Among the fleet of over twenty airplanes are Piper Cubs, CAP 10 and CAP 20 aerobatic airplanes, and an Italian Parentavia P-68 twin.

Unfortunately this friendly place does not provide temporary memberships, but flying with a safety pilot is easy to arrange and might be worth it. Head for the Po Valley, and perhaps for a day trip to the Alps and the nearby lakes.

S. Nicolo di Lido-Venice, (041 5260808), is on a small slip of land at the feet of the famed city on water. You will be thrilled by extravagant aerial views of Venice if you fly from here.

Aero Club Como, (031 57 44 95 or 55 98 82) is a floatplane club in the heart of Como on the lakeshore next to the city soccer stadium. Lake Como, at the base of the Italian Alps only a short drive northwest of Milan, is one of Italy's most picturesque recreational areas. The club has been in operation since 1930 and currently flies float-equipped Cessna 172s, Super Cubs, and a Lake Amphibian. It is one of few places in Italy willing to rent solo to qualified short-term visitors, and also offers floatplane instruction and ratings to all comers.

Ampugnano-Siena, (0577 349150), is in the heart of Tuscany, perhaps the most picturesque part of Italy. Fly over a lovely patchwork of fields, forests, vineyards, and medieval villages little changed over centuries.

Aosta, (0615 362442), is an excellent airfield at the base of the Italian Alps toward the border with Switzerland and France. It is a good staging point for local mountain flights as well as flights across the Alps into Switzerland (or, more likely a destination for flights from Switzerland).

Salerno, (089 301186), near Naples, is a good general aviation airport near Naples, which is restricted to aircraft based there. Fly with the local aeroclub along the Mediterranean and around Mount Vesuvius.

Excellent soaring centers at the base of the Alps are **Rieti** (0764 49218), and **Valbrembo** (035 528093).

VFR QUESTIONS & ANSWERS

What are good sources for VFR regulations? Refer to the Italian AIP. Get assistance at the local school or flying club.

How can I get a weather briefing? You may get comprehensive weather briefings in person or over the telephone from the met offices of the major airports. Get phone numbers at your local airport. GAFOR is also available. Language might be a problem over the phone. English is not as widely spoken as in some other parts of Europe. Line up an Italian speaker on your end before you call.

What are VFR visibility and ceiling minimums? Italy has adopted the ICAO VFR minimums.

Is night VFR permitted? No.

Must I file a flight plan? You must file a VFR flight plan if your flight crosses an IFR boundary, or if both your departure and arrival airports are controlled.

May I fly the airways VFR? Yes.

Must I maintain en route radio contact with ATC on or off the airways? Yes. You must check in with the appropriate ATC facility even if you have not filed a flight plan, and must make position reports as requested. These requirements sound onerous, but in reality the system works well and doesn't overburden the VFR pilot.

Is VFR on top permitted? Yes. You must be assured of a VFR descent and landing.

ADDITIONAL INFORMATION SOURCES

Volare is a good general interest aviation magazine for the private pilot, available on newsstands. *Aerofan* is a start-up Italian sport aviation quarterly that has been published irregularly in the past; it is currently being published and hopefully will continue.

12

Spain

Country rating: **Moderate**

ONC Charts: **F-1 and G-1**

Rental cost range:

   2 seat trainer **$50-60**

   4 seat fixed gear **$70-90**

   4 seat retractable **$110-120**

QUALIFICATIONS AND LICENSE VALIDATION

The Direccion General de Aviacion Civil in Madrid routinely validates foreign private licenses issued by ICAO member states. The country is rated moderate because the bureaucracy of validation might take more time than you have on a short-term visit. Most sport flying in Spain is done through a network of non-profit aeroclubs that offer temporary memberships, some more readily than others. Flying with a safety pilot is easy to arrange, and the countryside is beautiful and varied.

You may try to get validation in advance through the mail by submitting photocopies of your documents and three passport photos, but this might prove less reliable than applying in person. If you do apply through the mail, do it at least 90 days before your trip.

DOCUMENTS YOU SHOULD TAKE

Pilot license

Current medical

Logbook

Radio operator license (if separate from pilot license)

Three passport photos

Take your original documents, and also have photocopies that the Direccion

General de Aviacion Civil can keep. Copy your logbook's biographic section and the last five pages of flight records.

USEFUL FLYING ORGANIZATIONS

Direccion General de Aviacion Civil
Avenida de America 25
E-28002, Madrid

This is the civil aviation authority responsible for validating foreign licenses.

Real Aero Club de Espana
Caerrera de San Jerinimo 15
Madrid

The umbrella organization that supervises all sport flying and aeroclubs in Spain. It is very friendly to visitors, and a good source of information. Responds to simple mail queries.

AOPA-Spain
Mallorca 264/3/2
E-08008, Barcelona
Telephone   34 3 215 6855

The local AOPA, which can provide good information to visitors, especially AOPA members. They do not respond to mail queries, due to minimal staff; call instead.

WHERE TO FLY, WHAT TO FLY

Sun drenched Spain has long been a favorite refuge of Europeans from the frigid North. Many such refugees arrive in private light airplanes. Their flights to the Mediterranean coast across Spain's rugged and sparsely inhabited mountains are fine adventures. But there is also a lot of recreational flying to be had through Spain's many aeroclubs, scattered throughout this historic and relaxing land. The ATC staff are used to dealing with foreigners in English, but the aeroclub people are not, so some ability to speak Spanish is strongly recommended.

Although there are a lot of small airports in Spain, many require prior permission by users not locally based, even in Spanish-registered aircraft. Be sure to check in advance.

Good areas for recreational flying are the Mediterranean coast, the Moorish triangle of Seville-Cordoba-Granada, and Madrid and its environs. Give the Real Aero Club de Espana a call for an update on the current status of the aeroclubs at the airports listed below.

The coast

Costa del Sol, Costa Blanca, Costa Brava, constitute one large costa de fiesta, and it is dotted with airports from the French border to Gibraltar. **Castellon de la**

Plana is a pleasant and unhurried general aviation field approximately 30 miles up the coast from Valencia. It is a good staging point for coastal flights in either direction. There is a local aeroclub, and the sea is just across the road from the airport. To the north along the Costa Brava there are recreational flying opportunities at **Genora Airport**, approximately 50 miles up the coast from Barcelona, and **Ampuriabrava**, a resort airport exclusively for nonscheduled, noncharter light aircraft. The Balearic islands of Mallorca and Ibiza are within easy reach of these airports by light aircraft, but special overwater rules and regulations might apply. Check with the locals before you set your heart on an island flight in a Spanish registered aircraft.

Along the Costa del Sol, check out **Malaga** for recreational flying.

Moorish Spain

Close by air to Malaga is a triangle formed by the cities of Seville, Cordoba, and Granada, from where the Muslim Moors ruled their kingdom of Al Andalus for eight centuries. It is picturesque, mountainous terrain and the relics the Moors left behind are worth seeing from above. Best among them from the air is Granada's famed Alhambra palace. All three towns have airfields, and are also easily reached in good weather from the coast. To the west just outside Granada are the Sierra Nevada mountains towering above 10,000 feet.

Madrid

The Aero Club de Madrid outside Madrid, the country's capital city, is a good staging point for flights around central Spain. Aerial attractions easily reached on a local round-robin flight are Toledo, little changed for the last four centuries, Segovia and its Roman aqueduct, and the ancient city of Salamanca.

VFR QUESTIONS & ANSWERS

What are good sources for VFR regulations? Consult the Spanish AIP.

How can I get a weather briefing? There are good met offices at the bigger airports. There is also a comprehensive GAFOR system that covers Spain in 34 sectors.

What are VFR visibility and ceiling minimums? Spain has adopted the ICAO VFR minimums.

Is night VFR permitted? No.

Must I file a flight plan? Yes. Flight plans must be filed for all VFR flights in Spain.

May I fly the airways VFR? Yes, as authorized by ATC. You must maintain assigned IFR altitudes within the airways. The hemispherical ICAO VFR altitude rule applies outside the airways.

Must I maintain en route radio contact with ATC on or off the airways? Yes. You must give periodic position reports.

Is VFR on top permitted? No.

ADDITIONAL INFORMATION SOURCES

An excellent information source for VFR flight, if you can read Spanish, is Fernando Bujarrabal's *Manual de Aviacion General Espana*. It is available locally (inquire at the Real Aero Club de Espana, address on page 67). It includes airport diagrams, several regional maps, and a wealth of regulatory and facilities information.

13

Rally 'round the world

WOULD YOU LIKE TO CLIMB INTO a four-seater somewhere in France or Germany, wing your way across Greece, and circle the pyramids of Egypt? Or, perhaps you would like to fly up beyond the Arctic Circle into the land of the midnight sun, or south to explore the mysteries of the Sahara and the Casbah. Are you deterred by the customs hassles, and the logistics of crossborder flying?

There is an excellent alternative to going it alone. It is the international air rally, a recreational flying package tour for groups of light aircraft and their crews. The organizers lay out the route, arrange all the paperwork, customs clearances, refueling, and accommodations, and hand over a complete navigation package to each participant. You simply show up with your airplane, attend the daily pilot briefing and go flying.

The roots of rally flying are in the great international air races that departed Europe for Australasia and Africa during aviation's golden age in the early 1930s. The races opened the world for the airplane, showed the potential of this then-exotic new machine, and established international air routes soon to be commercialized. Today's rallies retain the convenience of organized mass flight without the pressures of the high stakes race. Rally flying is popular not only with private airplane owners, but also with aeroclub members who often team up to share the costs and end up with an exotic flying vacation they could otherwise not afford.

There are all kinds of rallies in Europe throughout the year, advertised in the calendar of events of the national flying magazines. At the most informal level, aeroclubs or type associations often organize weekend rallies. It is quite common, for example, for a British flying club to put on a weekend cross-channel rally to some nearby continental destination. Club members who have signed up in advance divide the club aircraft among themselves, decide how to share the flying duties, get a briefing from someone charged with operations for the rally, and off they go. With some planning it isn't too difficult for you to participate in one of these events as a visitor.

At the other end of the spectrum are the elaborate, long distance, one of a kind events, such as a vintage rally from Great Britain to Australia. Participation is open to all qualified entrants (qualifications defined in the entry forms), but the expenses are enormous and finding an airplane to share if you don't have your own is difficult. Most participants manage to get commercial sponsors to help with the expenses in exchange for ruining their airplanes' paint jobs with company and product logos.

Between these extremes is the international rally lasting from a week to two weeks, arranged and run by a professional rally organization such as the Paris based RAID International Association, or by a commercially sponsored volunteer rally organization such as the Organizing Committee of the Annual International Air Rally of Malta. These events are aimed at the recreational pilot, and except for trips in areas renowned for bad weather, are designated as VFR rallies. It might take up most of your time in Europe, and you must start making arrangements long before you leave home, but with careful planning you might participate in one of these rallies on a visit. You could rent an airplane for the rally from a commercial operator in a European country where such rentals are relatively easy to arrange (France and Britain come to mind), or you could connect with European participants in search of someone to share the expenses. If you contact the rally organizers well in advance, there is a good chance that they might help you find someone with whom to share the flying, or might suggest airplane rental alternatives.

RAID has been organizing air rallies for years (they also put on vintage car rallies). One year they arranged rallies lasting between one and two weeks to Egypt, Greece, Morocco, the Soviet Union, and into Scandinavia beyond the Arctic Circle. Participation is high in these rallies. Groups of 40 to 50 aircraft, ranging from modest Cessna 172s to Piper Navajos, are common.

For each rally, RAID designates a departure airport, easily accessible from most points in Europe, where participants are asked to assemble by a certain date. RAID's services begin from this airport on the rally's official start date. RAID provides each pilot in command all the maps, airport diagrams and approach plates for the trip. The association arranges all flight permits to enter national airspace, customs clearance, refueling, and aircraft parking. Participants are expected to fly well-maintained aircraft, but mechanics accompany each rally for unanticipated glitches.

Among the RAID staff are pilots speaking French, English, and German to advise less experienced participants and conduct the pilots' briefings before each leg. In addition to the flying arrangements, RAID also takes care of all the usual group tour services, such as hotel accommodations, transfers between the hotels and the airports, guided tours, interpreters, evening entertainment, and an occasional formal group dinner.

RAID charges a registration fee per aircraft, and a per person cost for the accommodations and land arrangements. Pilots pay fuel and user fees separately. The organization can often get some charges, such as landing fees, waived, which might amount to a considerable chunk of change. You must pay 30 percent of costs upon registration, and the balance six weeks prior to the rally's start date. Refund policies are similar to landlubber tour rules. If you cancel five weeks before the rally, you will receive a 50 percent refund. If you cancel fewer than five weeks before the rally, you will get a refund of the registration fee only. RAID is merely passing on to the participants the terms that the organization is given by the hotels for the land arrangements. (All rules are subject to change; therefore, carefully read the fee schedule of any tour contract before signing.)

RAID's rallies are touristic. As much emphasis is placed upon visiting the destinations as there is placed upon the flying: no competitions en route. Courtesy prizes are awarded in such categories as the entrant from farthest away, the lowest powered aircraft, and the most unusual aircraft.

Let's look at a typical package for Egypt, or as RAID calls it, the Air Rally of the Nile. It is a 15-day VFR rally. It starts at Kerkyra Airport on the island of Corfu, Greece, where participants are expected to arrive by the first day. The first official rally leg is flown on the next day to Alexandria, Egypt, via a refueling stop at Crete's Heraklyon Airport. Total distance for the day is 750 nautical miles. The following day is a 150-nautical-mile flight to Cairo, where rally participants fly over the pyramids and stay for the next two days to see the sights. Next is a 200-nautical-mile leg flown into the Sinai Desert to visit St. Catherine's monastery. Then it is on to Luxor on the Nile 200 nautical miles away and more ancient history in the Valley of the Kings. There is a full day at Luxor, then a 320-nautical-mile flight, first farther up river to Abu Simbel, and then back down to the Aswan Dam. Another full day is spent at the temples around Aswan, and then comes a 350-nautical-mile flight to Alexandria for a final gala night. The rally ends the following day with a flight back to Corfu to conclude the rally and everyone flies home.

RAID has no restrictions on the type of participating aircraft, but requires a minimum 650-nautical-mile range for the trip to Egypt. The brochure recommends a miniannual before departure, advises you to bring engine oil and a pint of hydraulic fluid, a spare tire and inner tube, and a few spark plugs. You are also reminded that vacuum pumps with more than 500 hours usually fail sooner rather than later.

You are assured that all hotels are top quality (most are Hiltons and Sheratons), and that the food is chosen for the international palate. You are cautioned not to drink the water, and to bring a flashlight "which will be most useful in the tombs." You are told that the security conscious Egyptians will want the serial numbers of all your cameras. And with true Gallic care for your well-being, you are advised that "the wines are fruity, but with a high alcohol content and fairly costly. We recommend the beer sold in large bottles."

The cost for the rally in U.S.-dollar terms at a June, 1990, exchange rate was $1,125 per aircraft and $2,125 per person double occupancy, plus fuel for the airplane.

Judging by the 45 participants of a rally and their enthusiastic reports of circling the pyramids and flying down the Valley of the Kings at 300 feet, when it comes to seeing Egypt, RAID's Rallies of the Nile are the best way to go for pilots. And imagine the trials of trying to arrange such an aerial tour on your own.

The Annual Malta Air Rally, now in its twenty-third year, is quite different from the rallies organized by RAID. It is basically a five-day international fly-in with a greater emphasis on competition and less group flying. Participants are instructed to make their own way to the Mediterranean island of Malta (a popular tourist destination for Europeans, especially Britons), and are assigned arrival times, which they must hit ± 10 minutes to be evaluated for the arrival competition. Everyone starts with 600 points. The most precise arrival time forfeits the fewest points and wins. A flight planning competition is held among flight logs submitted within 30 minutes of arrival. For the next three days there are timed section competitions over closed courses, spot landings, and a lot of tourism on this fortress island made famous by the Christian Knights of Malta. On the last day there is a big banquet, lots of prizes are awarded, and a lot of northern Europeans fly home a little less depressed at the thought of facing another winter.

You might well get hooked if you fly a rally or two in and around Europe. And who knows, you might even be ready for the transatlantic rallies organized out of Montreal, or the next air rally from Paris to Beijing.

14

Portugal

Country rating: **Moderate**

ONC Charts: **F-1 and G-1**

Rental cost range:

  2 seat trainer **$55-60**

  4 seat fixed gear **$80-90**

  4 seat retractable **$100-110**

QUALIFICATIONS AND LICENSE VALIDATION

Portugal's director general of Civil Aviation will validate foreign licenses issued by ICAO member countries for flying Portuguese-registered aircraft on noncommercial VFR flights. Apply by mail well in advance of your visit, or in person. The country rating is moderate because action on your mail application for validation is uncertain, and if you apply in person, the paperwork might take longer to grind its way through the system than the time you will be spending in Portugal on a short-term visit. Once the validation is in your hand, you can make arrangements with the local aeroclubs for temporary membership. If you choose not to validate your license, flying with a safety pilot is easy to arrange, and is well worth the effort over this attractive land.

DOCUMENTS YOU SHOULD TAKE

Pilot license

Current medical

Logbook

Radio operator license (if separate from pilot license)

Four passport photos

Bring your original documents, and also have numerous notarized photocopies, including the relevant sections of your passport, to leave with the validating authorities. They thrive on keeping records.

USEFUL FLYING ORGANIZATIONS

Direccao General de Aviacao Civil
Avenida de Liberdade 193
1298 Lisboa
Telephone   571110, 573517

The civil aviation authority that handles license validation.

Aeroclub de Portugal
Avenida de Liberdade 226
1298 Lisboa

The authority supervising recreational flying and the individual aeroclubs. It should be your first point of contact on arrival to get a list of aeroclubs and an update on license validation and flying opportunities for visitors. You are better off making contact in person because Aeroclub de Portugal is unresponsive to mail queries.

WHERE TO FLY, WHAT TO FLY

Portugal is a pretty country, and in certain respects less overrun by tourists than its eastern neighbor, Spain. For aviators, a point of interest is the legacy of the Portuguese Prince Henry the Navigator, who established for his fifteenth century seafarers many of the navigational principles and techniques that we still use in the VFR cockpit today.

Recreational flying activity centers around the Algarve, Portugal's southern coast, and Lisbon, the capital. The country is small enough to be conveniently toured by light aircraft from any local airport you choose as homebase. You will get by with English with ATC and at the bigger tourist spots, but some knowledge of Portuguese would be most helpful.

Faro is the main city of the Algarve, and its airport is home of the **Aero Clube de Faro**, (2 38 46), run by some of the local air traffic controllers. This aeroclub is accustomed to foreign visitors. It grants temporary membership, and arranges license validation in advance if you send photocopies of your documents. Cessnas and an Aero Commander are available.

The Algarve coast is approximately 150 miles long, and Faro is conveniently at its midpoint. Accommodations from pensiones to luxury resorts abound. The more interesting and wilder terrain is west of Faro. You can fly all the way west to Sagres and circle Prince Henry's school of navigation. Along the way is Lagos, a quaint fishing village, and **Lagos Airport**, (0082 6 29 06). Well-polished short-field skills and a shoehorn are necessary to get into the 1,500-foot dirt strip, but it is worth it.

The Aero Club de Lisboa, **Lisbon Airport**, (881101 or 882591), is the place to arrange flying around the capital and the nearby Portuguese Riviera 20 miles to the west.

Attractive general aviation airfields north of Lisbon are at **Coimbra**, (94 214), a historic university town, and **Oporto**, (94 82141), the port capital of the world (wine, not ships).

VFR QUESTIONS & ANSWERS

What are good sources for VFR regulations? Check the Portuguese AIP.

How can I get a weather briefing? The main general aviation airports have met offices where briefings are available. Be cautious with the weather; in spite of its sunny reputation, the sea and coastal mountains make for a volatile mix, and the weather might deteriorate quickly, for brief periods. Always have options.

What are VFR visibility and ceiling minimums? Portugal has adopted the standard ICAO VFR minimums.

Is night VFR permitted? No.

Must I file a flight plan? For internal VFR flights, you need not file flight plans, but you would be well advised to do so over the country's wilder areas.

May I fly the airways VFR? Yes, provided that you obtain permission from the responsible ATC unit. Maintain the standard ICAO hemispherical VFR altitudes.

Must I maintain en route radio contact with ATC off the airways? Generally, no.

Is VFR on top permitted? No.

15

Greece

Country rating: **Easy**
ONC Charts: **F-3 and G-3**
Rental cost range:
  2 seat trainer **$100-120**
  4 seat fixed gear **$120-150**
  4 seat retractable **Prices not available**

QUALIFICATIONS AND LICENSE VALIDATION

You may fly Hellenic-registered aircraft within Greek territory without license validation as long as it is issued by an ICAO member state. You will only have to take a checkride prior to solo flight, a requirement not of the civil aviation authority, but of the flight school from which you will rent. For recreational flying, there is no local time limit on the validity of your license as long as it is valid in the issuing country.

DOCUMENTS YOU SHOULD TAKE

Pilot license (and evidence of validity if not on license)
Current medical
Logbook
Radio operator license (if separate from pilot's license)

Take original documents.

USEFUL FLYING ORGANIZATIONS

The National Aero Club of Greece
2A, Chanion Street
112 57 Athens, Greece
Telephone 822 8394
Facsimile 823 7901

Coordinating organization for Greek sport aviation. Just moved into new quarters. Best source for information on recreational flying in Greece. Call them for information if response to a written query is delayed.

Ministry of Transportation
Civil Aviation Authority
P.O. Box 73751
Athens
GR-16604, Greece

WHERE TO FLY, WHAT TO FLY

Greece is the cradle of European civilization and a land of magical, Mediterranean islands with the sights to match. It is a favorite destination of European VFR pilots who fly aircraft here from their home countries. It is also popular with nonpilot tourists, and the Greek government has developed an excellent network of airports on the islands that also greatly benefit recreational pilots. Greece also has a network of aeroclubs where visitors are welcome. Temporary memberships cost approximately one to three hours worth of flying time.

All Greek airspace is controlled, so you must stick to published VFR routes unless permitted to deviate by ATC. Popular VFR routes extend from Athens to the Aegean Islands, the Ionian Islands, Crete, and northern Greece.

Below is a list of airports, some of which have aeroclubs and all of which are popular with visitors flying into Greece. A good bet is to rent on the mainland and fly out to the islands. Same-day round-trip scenic flights to islands close to the mainland are popular.

Fuel is not always available on the islands, so plan carefully, seek local advice before departure, and carry enough fuel, if possible, to get you back.

Dekeleia and Marathon are airports outside Athens where you will find flying clubs and recreational flying opportunities. You might want to call the National Aero Club first for an update.

Skopelos is an Aegean island north of Athens to which daytrips are popular. No avgas.

Kephalonia is a picturesque island on the Ionian Sea, a nice flight of approximately 150 nautical miles west from Athens along the Gulf of Corinth. The airport is on the island's southern coast bordered by steep mountains. No avgas.

Kerkyra Airport serves the island of Corfu up the west coast of Greece beyond Kephalonia near the Albanian border. Active aeroclub.

Mykonos is a well developed, busy island only 80 nautical miles from Athens along a chain of other islands. You might find it too crowded for a longer stay, but it sure is pretty from aloft, and is an ideal daytrip destination. No avgas.

Mikra Airport serves Thessaloniki in northeastern Greece and has an active aeroclub.

Heraklion Airport serves the large and rugged island of Crete. It has one of the more active aeroclubs in Greece.

Samos is approximately 150 nautical miles east of Athens off the Turkish coast. You may island hop all the way, and the scenery doesn't get much better.

Karpathos is approximately 250 nautical miles southeast of Athens, near the better known, touristy island of Rhodes. Karpathos is still mostly off the beaten track, well worth a visit. Avgas might not be available.

VFR QUESTIONS & ANSWERS

What are good sources for VFR regulations? Consult the Greek AIPs.

How can I get a weather briefing? International airports have met offices. At most other airports, teleprinters will provide basic weather information, and telephone briefings are possible.

What are VFR visibility and ceiling minimums? Five miles visibility and a 1,000-foot ceiling in controlled airspace and one mile visibility and clear of clouds under the higher of 3,000 feet MSL or 1,000 feet agl in uncontrolled airspace.

Is night VFR permitted? ATC permission is required, but is usually granted.

Must I file a flight plan? Yes, for all cross-country flights, which must keep to controlled airspace (airways). ATC might grant permission to fly in uncontrolled airspace.

May I fly the airways VFR? Yes. Cross-country flights must be along the airways unless ATC grants special permission to deviate.

Must I maintain en route radio contact with ATC on or off the airways? Yes, VFR position reporting is required.

Is VFR on top permitted? No.

ADDITIONAL INFORMATION SOURCES

Two aviation magazines are published in Greece, *Sport Aviation* (the National Aero Club's magazine), and *Flight*. Of course, you not only have to be able to speak Greek but also have to know the Greek alphabet to read them.

16

Take your camera

A GREAT WAY TO RELIVE your foreign aerial adventures once you are back in the hum-drum routine of home and office, is to settle into your favorite easy chair and browse through the photographs you took. You will once again bank steeply over that fairy-tale castle, scoot over the beach and palm trees, or glide onto the rough mountain strip ringed by glacial peaks. You will again sense the sounds, the speed, the tranquility, but only if the pictures are good.

It takes only a few poorly shot rolls of film to convince you that you will never take a picture like the pros unless you commit yourself to arduous months of photographic study. Such thoughts are a big mistake. The basics of aerial photography are easily reduced to a few key elements. Follow them with today's easy-to-use cameras and excellent film, and you will get good pictures every time, without ever having to bury yourself in a hefty "how-to-shoot-great-pictures" book that menaces a coffee table's weight and balance.

In simplest terms, picture quality depends upon five basic elements: your camera, your lens, your film, and your ability to compose and employ the proper techniques to overcome the specific challenges posed by individual shots.

WHICH CAMERAS?

The fundamental question is whether you can get away with one of the pocket-sized fully automatic cameras with one fixed lens, or if you need an SLR (single lens reflex) camera with through-the-lens viewfinder and interchangeable lenses. Your choice depends upon the flexibility you want in taking pictures. The fixed lens, fully automatic pocket cameras use the same size film as the SLRs, and their lens is of very high quality, so they will take outstanding pictures. Their big limitation is the size of the lens, usually 35 mm (a moderately wide angle). They are excellent for the average portrait and the panoramic landscape, but are useless when you need a telephoto lens to bring images closer, as is often the case in aerial photography.

An SLR's big advantage is that it gives you a wide choice of lenses. Practically any SLR body will do, but your best choice is one that, in addition to being fully

Fill the frame with the principal subject. Pan the moving airplane to avoid blurring. Shoot at a fast shutter speed (1/250) if you have the option, but not too fast to "freeze" the prop.

automatic, gives you control over setting the shutter speed (the amount of time the shutter is open when you press the button). This feature is important when shooting from an airplane or shooting an airplane in motion. Avoid SLRs with an overwhelming choice of fancy features. Spend the extra money on lenses.

Another option is the automatic camera with a built-in zoom lens. This might be a good choice, but on the telephoto end, the zoom lenses might be too short (they usually go to 85 mm) for most aerial shots requiring a telephoto lens.

WHICH LENSES?

If you do go the SLR route, you will have to decide which lenses you need. The issues are image quality and flexibility in composition. The heart of technical picture quality is the lens and the film. The camera body only controls the amount of time for which the film is exposed through the lens to the image. If the lens does not project the truest and sharpest image possible onto the film, or if the film does not reproduce the greatest detail and truest colors, you will end up with a set of disappointing pictures. Get brand name lenses to ensure image quality.

In air-to-ground and airplane photography you are faced with photo opportunities that require a wide variety of lenses, from wide-angle to telephoto. A good selection of individual lenses is 28 mm and 35 mm wide-angles, a 50 mm normal lens, and 105 mm and 200 mm telephoto lenses. It is, however, cumbersome to switch back and forth between these lenses. An excellent compromise is to get two zoom lenses that cover the whole wide-angle-telephoto range between them. The ideal combination is a 28-85 mm and an 85-205 mm zoom. These lenses have become practically as good as the nonzoom lenses they cover. Unless you are gunning for six-by-eight-foot murals, you will be hard put to tell the difference on the prints. Buy a zoom lens of recent design rather than a decade-old bargain lens that has been languishing in a warehouse.

Do not get a telephoto lens longer than 205 mm for air-to-ground photography. The focal length of anything larger requires absolute stillness (usually a tripod, even on the ground) for sharp focus. The airplane's engine vibration alone will throw a lens larger than 205 mm out of focus.

WHICH FILM?

You are faced with a number of choices and compromises in selecting film: prints or slides? High speed (400 ISO) or low speed (25 ISO)? Prints or slides is a matter of personal preference. Prints are less expensive to enlarge because the lab does not have to make an internegative of the image. Slides are easier to store, and fade less over time.

A more complex question with greater trade-offs is film speed. In short, the ISO number (formerly referred to as ASA) tells you how quickly a film absorbs light (the image it sees). The higher the number, the faster the rate at which the film absorbs light (the image). Thus, a 400 ISO film needs less time to absorb the same amount of light than a 25 ISO film. This means that you might still get a good picture with a 400 ISO film when there is no longer enough light for a 25 ISO film. Great, let's load up on 400 ISO. Unfortunately, the 400 ISO film pays a stiff price for absorbing light so fast; it absorbs less detail. In photo language, it has less resolution. This might be fine for a wallet-size picture, but the slightest enlargement of the print will be grainy and disappointing.

Slow films, on the other hand, give excellent resolution: a very high amount of detail if you use a good lens. Drawbacks are that in low-light, you might have to shoot a moving target at such a slow shutter speed (long exposure) that the target will be blurred, and you will run out of light all together when the guy next to you is still merrily firing away with higher speed film.

Ultimately, good resolution should win out whenever it can, because it will give you superior image quality. A good rule of thumb is to use the slowest-speed film possible for any lighting condition. If you really want professional-quality shots use 25 ISO whenever possible (the best aerial photographers refuse to use anything else), but you will also be quite well off with 64 and 100 ISO. Don't expect great results with anything faster, but carry a few rolls of 400 ISO for those unforgettable moments at dusk.

COMPOSITION

Composition is the key to taking shots like the pros. There are two major errors committed by inexperienced photographers, which most often make the difference between a magazine-quality photograph and a disappointing snapshot. One common mistake is failing to make sure that the main subject fills the viewfinder. The result is a big snapshot with a teeny-weeny castle somewhere in the middle. The other frequent error is failing to avoid background clutter around the main subject. The result in this case is a picture in which the nice antique airplane that you were shooting is surrounded by tiny modern rental cars, or the antique has telephone poles growing out of a wing, or is besieged by half-naked people in stereo headsets and running shoes.

"How did that biplane get so puny in the picture? It positively loomed in the camera when I snapped it," you say. "And when did those guys in the fluorescent Bermuda shorts sneak into the frame?" The source of both problems is that the camera is dumb (it records everything coming through the viewfinder), and you have not learned to "see" like the camera.

Camera lens and human eye are often compared. They do see the same things. But to stop there is to ignore a fundamental difference: your eye might see everything, but it notices only what your brain tells it to see; the camera on the other hand, records everything it sees.

Look up right now. Don't concentrate on any one object but without moving your eye, take a few seconds to notice all the objects you really see. A lot more than you first "saw," right? This is what your camera would record. Now concentrate on the biggest object in your field of vision. Notice how the things around it are no longer being registered by your brain. But if you were to take a picture, the camera would still record everything, because all the other junk is still there.

To get a full-frame image of the object in the viewfinder, you would have to move closer. To get rid of all the junk, you would have to change your vantage point so that only an unobtrusive background is visible with the object. To really

Avoid clutter. This aircraft was surrounded by dozens of people attending an air show.

get the hang of composition, pick up your camera and spend a lot of time carefully looking at individual images through its viewfinder. Analyze the size of the center of interest. Notice the vast emptiness or clutter-filled spaces around it. Devise ways to frame what you would want to see on the printed picture; visualize what you want the slide or print to show. Remember, what you see in the viewfinder is what you will get in the print.

Basic composition is the ability to fill more than 50 percent of the viewfinder with the center of interest and concurrently avoid distracting clutter. If these are the only two points you learn and put into practice from this chapter, you will immediately see a dramatic improvement in the pictures you take.

TECHNIQUE

It is worth keeping a few technical points in mind beyond composition, to get the most out of your pictures. Lighting, bracketing, and shutter speeds are important.

Lighting

Three basic factors must be considered: how the subject is lit, what is the time of day, and how to handle backlighting problems. For good, basic aerial photography, shoot subjects when they are lit from an angle, preferably in quartering frontal light. This condition throws the best light on the details and accentuates form to give the picture more life. Full frontal light from a high angle makes the subject flat.

If at all possible, shoot early in the morning or late in the afternoon on sunny days when the light's low angle gives the greatest accent to form, and color saturation is richest. Put the camera away between 10 A.M. and 4 P.M. If you must shoot on overcast days, look for the most colorful subjects you can find, and you will not be disappointed.

Backlighting might cause a problem when strong light behind a subject fools the camera into underexposing the subject and causes it to be too dark on the print. The easiest way to get around backlighting is to use a flash attachment to throw extra light on the subject. On cameras that you can adjust manually, you may go extremely close to the center of interest, take a true light reading, and reset the camera accordingly.

Bracketing

Bracketing is a technique you may use on cameras that can be set manually, which reduces the chances of lighting error. Take a picture at the setting the camera tells you to use, and then snap one at one aperture setting above and one aperture setting below the recommended setting. Professionals widely use this technique when in doubt.

Look for evidence of interesting local customs.

Boats are always a good subject.

Shutter speed

For best results, it is important to have a camera on which you can manually set the shutter speed. When you take pictures from airplanes in flight, the airplane's vibration might blur any shots taken at shutter speeds slower than $1/250$ of a second. When you shoot airplanes in motion, you might also have blurring if you expose slower than $1/250$ of a second.

SHOOTING AIR-TO-GROUND

Air-to-ground photography presents two special challenges: the camera platform (airplane) is in constant motion and the distance between camera and subject is much greater compared to the distances when taking pictures on the ground.

For reasons of safety, you should never do the flying and the photography. While you shoot, it is imperative that you hand over control to another pilot. You should also continue to strictly observe all regulations while you shoot.

Composition. Your greatest composition challenge in air-to-ground photography is to fill the viewfinder with the center of interest if it is a building or some similar sized object. Even the largest castle might look tiny in the viewfinder from a legal minimum altitude. A telephoto lens is indispensable if you want such detailed shots, and is usually well worth the effort. Wider, panoramic shots are easier, but here, too, make sure you fill the viewfinder. A good trick to capture the mood of the moment is to take a few shots that include, in an understated fashion, a wingtip or other suitable hint of the airplane.

The pilot and photographer should discuss in advance how close the pilot will fly to the subject and they should also discuss a prescribed flight path. Usually the best strategy is to circle the target so that the photographer can see all angles and available light and can shoot all the way around during subsequent circles.

Plan the flight path so that the angle of vision relative to the subject is 45 degrees or lower. Structures look more dramatic at shallower angles.

Technique. Decisions are required whether to use a high-wing or low-wing aircraft and whether to shoot through plexiglas or to open the window. For air-to-ground shots high-wing airplanes are usually better. You have a greater range of downward visibility. Always shoot through an open window instead of through plexiglas whenever you can. Although picture sharpness is not affected if you shoot through plexiglas with lenses smaller than 105 mm, color quality suffers, and the plexiglas throws a hazy hue on the pictures.

Your primary subject will look best in low quartering frontal light; therefore if at all possible, shoot in the morning or late afternoon in sunlight.

If you can adjust shutter speed on the camera, shoot at a shutter speed of at least $1/250$ of a second to avoid blurring due to high frequency airframe vibration caused by the engine.

Look for unusual activity. This T-1040 is refueling with kerosene from a drum at an African bush strip.

SHOOTING AIRPLANES

Besides recording what you see from the cockpit, you might want to take pictures of the airplanes you encounter, especially the ones you are unlikely to find at home. Don't haphazardly shoot pictures while on the run across the airport tarmac. With a little effort, you might easily get magazine-quality shots of airplanes on the ground.

Air-to-air photography is beyond the scope of this guide. It is a highly specialized form of photography that requires precision flying skills, and should not be practiced without extensive prior training.

Static portraits

Static portraits are the most popular airplane photos, and the easiest to take. All you have to do is visit a busy airfield at the right time (request permission before you go near the airplanes), and frame your shots with attention to detail.

Composition. Quartering frontal shots are the most effective. The biggest problem is avoiding clutter. Airplanes are often crowded together and tied down. Be patient and experiment with angles. One very effective way to edit clutter is to shoot slightly up at the airplane from a kneeling position. This approach also gives a dramatic picture. Be careful not to crop off the landing gear.

Filling the viewfinder is also very important. A static airplane should fill at least two thirds of the viewfinder. Otherwise it will be infuriatingly small on the prints. This might mean cropping out part of a wing, especially in a quartering frontal shot. Crop the closer wing.

Center your composition on the cockpit area, even if this means cropping the closer wing. The natural tendency is to compose so that the wingtips are at the two edges of the frame. This will result in the cockpit area being too far forward; the developed print will look awkward.

Technique. Lighting is the primary concern. Always choose the side of the airplane that is lit. Light under the typical open airport skies is strong, so avoid backlighting because the airplane will be too dark. Take backlit shots only at dawn or dusk for dramatic silhouette effect, or use filler flash.

Airplanes in action

These shots are more dramatic than the static portraits, but more difficult to take. You are most likely to take two general types of action shots: ground activity and ground to air.

Composition. Static portrait composition rules also apply to photography of ground activity. You will get the best results if you can get close enough to capture the turning propeller and the cockpit area with the crew as the main detail. *Watch out for propellers!* An effective and relatively clutter-free opportunity is when an aircraft is taxiing past, on a taxiway with a clear background. Bracket the shutter speed to select the most attractive appearance of the propeller blur; recall that an extremely fast shutter speed will freeze the prop and cancel the illusion of action.

Your ground-to-air shots will be effective only if you take them with a telephoto lens, and only if you can get close enough to fill the viewfinder with the airplane. The most common error of ground-to-air shots is that the subject is too small. The best vantage point for ground-to-air shots is near the runway threshold where you can photograph landing aircraft.

Technique. Backlighting and movement are problems. For ground activity, frontal lighting is essential, especially good light on the people in the picture. If their faces are dark, the picture will be impersonal. Ground-to-air shots are best taken during the early morning or the late afternoon, with the sunlight striking the side of the airplane in the picture. At other times of the day, your ground-to-air shots will be especially flat with little or no contrast.

To get the sharpest image possible of a moving airplane, use a high shutter speed such as $1/250$ of a second, which is ideal. It is fast enough to give you a good chance at freezing the image of the moving airplane, yet it is not fast enough to freeze a turning propeller and ruin the shot. If your automatic camera does not allow you to set the shutter speed at $1/250$ second, and you suspect that it is using a slower shutter speed, you might still get satisfactory results if you pan especially carefully.

Panning is a very important technique that can be used to overcome the problem of a blurred image due to a moving airplane. You must pan at any shutter speed if the airplane is taxiing faster than a walking pace, or if it is in flight. Track the airplane with your camera, and keep it stationary in the viewfinder; keep the same point on the airplane in the same spot in the viewfinder. Keep your legs slightly apart and slightly bent. Twist your body from the waist up to

Get as close as safely possible to achieve the best framing desired, especially for excellent air-to-ground photography.

follow the airplane. Keep your arms stationary relative to your upper body. Gently squeeze the shutter at the correct moment, without stopping your panning motion. Beyond a sharper center of interest, panning at a slower shutter speed yields a streaked background that conveys the feeling of speed on the final print or slide. Blurring from panning is negated by any shutter speed faster than 125th of a second.

Abstract details

The photography of abstract details is an often overlooked but very rewarding aspect of airplane photography. Airplanes are laden with interesting curves and shapes, and often bear attractive insignia. An abstract detail might be more effective in evoking flight or the mood of an era or place than a formal portrait. A well kept secret is that these shots are very easy to take.

Composition. Clutter is easy to avoid, and your abstract shots must be absolutely free of it. The minute an external object sneaks on the print, the shot is no longer abstract. The ideal abstract shot has only airplane, or airplane and sky in it. Even the ground is eliminated. Your imagination is the limit, but the following themes are popular:

- Vertical, close to the aft fuselage, looking forward.
- Horizontal, aft quartering, wing, nose, cockpit, and sky.
- Detail of insignia, airplane's surface fully filling the image.
- Tail and sky, shot from down low, looking up.
- Nose art on warbirds, fully filling the frame.

Technique. Generally make sure that the photographed part is well lit, with light falling on it directly. This will avoid the backlighting problem where the sky is also showing. Bracket if you have any doubts about backlighting. Closeups where only the aircraft surface is showing should not be a problem as long as the light is uniform, because the camera's automatic meter will take a uniform reading.

BEAR IN MIND

Be sure to take extra batteries for the camera, and have them ready when you shoot air-to-ground, especially if you fly in cold weather. Weak batteries that work well on the ground give up the ghost quickly when the temperature aloft drops.

Get an ultraviolet filter for all camera lenses. Ultraviolet light is stronger aloft, and the filter also protects the lenses from scratches, dust, and other contaminants.

A polarizing filter is useful to cut through haze and bring out most of the colors in the viewfinder, especially if you must take pictures in the middle of the day when the sun's angle is undesirable.

Always tape an elastic strap on eyeglasses to hold them firmly on your head when shooting through or outside an open window for air-to-ground photography. It would be disheartening to watch glasses sail majestically toward the medieval fortress you are trying to photograph.

Don't waste film, but don't be a miser either. Be especially liberal with the shutter on air-to-ground shots, where you never know until the film is back from the lab, which was the best shot, and often it is the one you least expected.

A motor drive is helpful, especially in air-to-ground photography.

17

Netherlands

Country rating: **Easy**

ONC Chart: **E-2**

Rental cost range:

  2 seat trainer   **$80-100**

  4 seat fixed gear   **$100-120**

  4 seat retractable   **$130-160**

QUALIFICATIONS AND LICENSE VALIDATION

The Netherlands does not require the validation of licenses issued according to ICAO standards and used for personal VFR flight in Dutch-registered aircraft within the country. If you want to fly a Dutch aircraft out of the Netherlands, you must get your license validated. It is an easy, administrative process. No theoretical or flight tests are required by the government in either case, as long as the gross weight of the aircraft you intend to fly is fewer than 4,400 pounds. However, you will have to pass the usual checkride required by the flying establishment renting you an airplane.

DOCUMENTS YOU SHOULD TAKE

Pilot license

Current medical

Logbook

Radio operator license (if separate from pilot license)

Take the original documents.

USEFUL FLYING ORGANIZATIONS

Luchtvaartinspectie
Saturnusstraat 71
Postbus 575
2130 AN, Hoofddorp
Netherlands
Telephone   02503-63131

The branch of the civil aviation authority responsible for licensing and license validation (necessary only if you plan to fly a Dutch-registered aircraft out of the country).

AOPA-Netherlands
Dorphuisstraat, 10
9663 GG, Nieuwe Pekela
Netherlands

Represents local general aviation interests. Member of IAOPA. Has a computerized information database on general aviation flying.

Koninklijke Nederlandse Vereniging voor Luchtvaart
Josef Israelsplein 8
Den Haag
Netherlands

The aeroclub of the Netherlands (try saying it in Dutch). Coordinating body for sport aviation.

WHERE TO FLY, WHAT TO FLY

Holland is a small, flat country of canals, tulip fields, coastal resorts, dikes, and land reclaimed from the North Sea. It is easily covered in one day by light aircraft. Flying has longstanding traditions in Holland, dating back to the pioneering routes developed by KLM Royal Dutch Airlines to Indonesia and beyond, during the 1920s and 1930s. Anthony Fokker—whose legacy as an aircraft designer lives on in the factory and the airplanes that bear his name—was also Dutch. Recreational flying is popular in Holland and easy to arrange for the visitor. Practically everyone speaks fluent English.

Below is a selection of good general aviation airfields and the attractions around them. Go airport hopping or fly into one destination and explore the neighborhood. Take care to stay out of the Schiphol TMA and don't forget that flying the airways VFR is not permitted in Holland.

Rotterdam-Zestienhoven serves Rotterdam, Europe's largest port. It is a busy airport with a lot of light airplane flying. A number of commercial flying schools and aeroclubs are based here. Nearby, toward the coast, is Delft, perhaps the most picturesque old Dutch town, crisscrossed by a maze of canals. It is famous for china, inspired by the porcelain brought back from China by the ships of the Dutch East India Company centuries ago. Farther toward the coast is the Hauge, capital of Holland and seat of the World Court. Northeast of Rotterdam and not far from the airport is the town of Gouda, famous for its cheese. One of the prettiest aerial sights in the spring is the colorful sea of tulip fields around Rotterdam.

Midden Zeeland in the southwest corner of Holland is an outstanding sport airfield serving the coastal town of Middelburg. In addition to power flying, soaring and parachuting are also practiced. Nearby is a large inland lake popular with campers and the sailing crowd.

Leliestad is an interesting small airfield 13 feet below sea level on land that was, until recently, the Zuider Zee. Antique aircraft are based here. It is an ideal place to see firsthand Holland's famous land reclamation efforts.

Texel is on an island on the other side of the main dike that blocks off the Zuider Zee from the North Sea. It is a relaxing destination with good beach walking among the sand dunes.

Teuge is a pleasant general aviation airfield in the eastern part of Holland, not far from Arnhem and the notorious "bridge too far" of World War II fame.

Groningen in northern Holland, is a busy, but friendly airfield. It is home to a number of aeroclubs and flying schools, including a central state flying school.

VFR QUESTIONS & ANSWERS

What are good sources for VFR regulations? Consult the "Netherlands VFR Flight Guide," extracted from the Dutch AIP.

How can I get a weather briefing? At one of four met offices in person or over the phone. Briefings are available from any of these offices in Dutch, English, French, and German. Recorded GAFOR is available in Dutch.

What are VFR visibility and ceiling minimums? The Netherlands adheres to standard ICAO minimums.

Is night VFR permitted? No.

Must I file a flight plan? You must file only for certain flights within controlled airspace. Check the AIP.

May I fly the airways VFR? No, not even to cross the airways. A VFR flight must descend below the floor of an airway to cross.

Must I maintain en route radio contact with ATC flying VFR? Contact is required only if you want permission to enter a control zone.

Is VFR on top permitted? No.

ADDITIONAL INFORMATION SOURCES

It is worth getting a copy of the "Visual Flight Guide to the Netherlands," available locally or through the mail from N.V. SDU, Christoffel Plantijnstraat, P.O. Box 20014, NL-2500 EA, The Hauge. There is a charge.

A wide selection of English, German, and French aviation magazines is available on the newspaper stands.

18

Belgium

Country rating: **Moderate**
ONC Chart: **E-2**
Rental cost range:
  2 seat trainer **$90-110**
  4 seat fixed gear **$110-140**
  4 seat retractable **$140-180**

QUALIFICATIONS AND LICENSE VALIDATION

Belgium is rated moderate because according to the Royal Aero Club of Belgium, validation of a foreign license to fly Belgian registered powered aircraft solo is not possible. You must get a Belgian license, for which you have to pass a written test on Belgian air laws and regulations, and pass a flight test. Flying with a safety pilot is readily available. For holders of an American license, an option to fly solo in Belgium without having to get a Belgian license and take the tests is to find an N-registered aircraft for rent. Call the Royal Aero Club of Belgium for advice on where to find one. If you have a glider rating you may use it without validation, but plan to allow extra time for the respective glider club to verify the exact terms with the Civil Aviation Authority.

DOCUMENTS YOU SHOULD TAKE

Pilot license
Current medical
Logbook
Radio operator license (if separate from pilot license)

Take the original documents if you plan to get a Belgian license or fly an N-registered aircraft. Otherwise, photocopies are sufficient to show a safety pilot a record of experience.

USEFUL FLYING ORGANIZATIONS

Royal Aero Club of Belgium
1 Rue Montoyer
B-1040, Brussels

The Aero Club coordinates all sport flying in Belgium. It can give advice on getting your Belgian license, finding N-registered aircraft, and places to fly.

AOPA-Belgium
Fruithoflaan 107/B 73
B-2600, Berchem, Antwerpen
Telephone   32 3 449 0722

AOPA is helpful to visiting pilots, but the small staff is busy, because the vice president also acts as AOPA's EEC liaison. The best bet is a brief phone call.

Administration de l'Aeronautique
Communication Centre Nord
Rue Vooruitgang 80
B-1210, Brussels

Belgium's civil aviation authority; handles licensing.

WHERE TO FLY, WHAT TO FLY

Belgium is a small country, approximately 200 miles west to east and 100 miles north to south. It is an attractive land to fly over, the terrain changing from the flat, densely populated, coastal farmland in the north and west to the rolling, thickly forested Ardennes to the southeast. Medieval market towns dot the countryside, little changed from a bird's eye perspective over the last five centuries. Sections of Ghent, Bruges, and Liege are particularly attractive from the air. The whole country is easily covered in an airplane such as a Piper Warrior in a leisurely day-long cross-country flight. Belgium has its share of general aviation airports with its flying schools and aeroclubs, and soaring is also popular. Below is a selection of airports near places most likely to be on the visitor's itinerary.

Brussels-Grimbergen is the general aviation airport serving Brussels, Belgium's capital. The city is also host to NATO headquarters and the office of the European Economic Community. The airport is north of Brussels, under the TMA, and is home to numerous flying schools and aeroclubs. It is a good staging point for flights to the coast and elsewhere, if you are visiting Brussels and your time is short.

Deurne a pleasant general aviation field on the Scheld River, serves Antwerpen. The city is famous for its diamond merchants (you can see the polishers at work), and Rubens, whose house you can visit.

Oostende on the English Channel serves the beach resort town of the same name. It is a busy training field and is also a common destination for cross-channel pilots. The French towns of Dunkerque and Calais are a short distance down the coast. Bruges is a short flight inland, to the east.

Kortrijk-Wevelgem has become popular with flyers from Ghent because airports closer to that city have succumbed to developers. It is near the French border along the main highway out of Ghent to France. There are numerous flying schools and clubs on the field.

Namur-Temploux sometimes also known as Suarlee, is an outstanding sport airfield on the northeast outskirts of Namur and a short distance east of Charleroi. Here you will find not only touring opportunities, but also soaring and aerobatics.

St. Hubert is a large flying and gliding center deep in the Ardennes. The surrounding countryside is a visual feast. The ghosts of two world wars are also nearby for those who remember Bastogne and the Battle of the Bulge.

Spa-La Sauveniere is a delightful little airport in the Ardennes, north of St. Hubert and close to the centuries-old town of Liege, famous for its lace. Spa still makes the mineral water that was the tonic of nineteenth century health nuts. The Battle of the Bulge museum is in town and Malmedy is nearby. More beautiful countryside.

VFR QUESTIONS & ANSWERS

What are good sources for VFR regulations? The best source is the Belgian AIP.

How can I get a weather briefing? The major airports have met offices also reachable by telephone, English is spoken. Get the phone numbers at the local airport.

What are VFR visibility and ceiling minimums? Belgium has adopted the ICAO VFR minimums.

Is night VFR permitted? Only local flying in close proximity to the airfield is permitted for night VFR.

Must I file a flight plan? Flight plans must only be filed for flights requiring ATC services. Under certain conditions, air filing is acceptable. Check the AIP.

May I fly the airways VFR? Yes. You must maintain radio contact with ATC and provide position reports.

Must I maintain en route radio contact with ATC off the airways? No, as long as you remain outside terminal control areas and control zones.

Is VFR on top permitted? Yes, as long as a VFR descent and landing at the destination is assured.

ADDITIONAL INFORMATION SOURCES

Vade Mecum is the publication of the Royal Aero Club of Belgium. The popular French and English aviation magazines are available on the newsstands.

19

Denmark

Country rating: **Easy**

ONC Charts: **D-2 and E-2**

Rental cost range:
   2 seat trainer   **$90-120**
   4 seat fixed gear   **$130-150**
   4 seat retractable   **$160-190**

QUALIFICATIONS AND LICENSE VALIDATION

Denmark does not require validation of a pilot license for flying Danish-registered aircraft on noncommercial VFR flights within Danish airspace if you meet the following criteria: not a Danish citizen, permanent residence is abroad, staying in Denmark for fewer than 90 days, have flown at least 10 hours in the previous 12 months, and have passed an appropriate annual or biennial flight review in the preceding 12 months. Make sure you meet these requirements and head for the nearest aeroclub or flying school where you will be given the usual checkride for that facility.

If your license is from a country with which Denmark has a mutual validation agreement (presently Norway and Sweden), you may also exercise your instrument rating privileges provided you have passed an instrument currency check to the standards of Danish, Norwegian, or Swedish regulations within the last six months.

Pilots planning to live in Denmark beyond 90 days need to validate their licenses. Validation for noncommercial flying is a simple process. No written test or government-administered flight test is required. You must meet the recent proficiency check requirements outlined above and you might need a letter from your own civil aviation authority describing the extent of your flight training. Check with the Danish Civil Aviation Administration prior to departing for a stay exceeding three months.

DOCUMENTS YOU SHOULD TAKE

Pilot license
Current medical
Logbook
Radio operator license

You will also have to show your passport. Bring your documents in the original.

USEFUL FLYING ORGANIZATIONS

Civil Aviation Administration
Ellebjergvej 50
DK-2450 Copenhagen SV
DENMARK
Telephone   31 48 44 44

This is the Danish government aviation authority responsible for all licensing and regulations.

AOPA-Denmark
Roskilde Lufthavn
DK-4000, Roskilde
DENMARK
Telephone   42 39 11 55

Helpful to visiting pilots, especially AOPA members.

WHERE TO FLY, WHAT TO FLY

Denmark is an exceptionally flat country of more than 400 islands and a finger-like peninsula extending north of Germany. The highest terrain is barely 600 feet, and the flying environment is hospitable to visiting pilots. Besides a handful of airports where rental aircraft are available through commercial flying schools and aeroclubs, there are many small grass strips throughout the country.

Roskilde-Copenhagen is the capital's general aviation airport, approximately 15 miles west of Kastrup, the main international airport. The city of Copenhagen is just down the road. Roskilde's own main point of interest is the Viking ship museum, housing five original ships of these great navigators of old.

Odense airport on the island of Funen is in fairy tale country, more precisely in the land of Hans Christian Andersen. The Andersen museum is the town's main attraction.

Tirstrup on the east coast of Jutland is the airport serving Aarhus, famed for its September town festival. Just outside Aarhus is a popular prehistoric museum.

Aalborg airport in north Jutland serves a city with a particularly charming old section.

Esbjerg airport is a good choice if you are spending time in southwest Jutland.

TOURING

Flying cross-country in Denmark is a lot of fun, especially among its countless islands. Navigation is not difficult, given the many opportunities to simply follow shorelines. Round robin flights taking up a day or less are easy to arrange among various combinations of the airports listed, depending on your point of departure. Make sure you also include a grass strip or two along your route. Get suggestions from the locals.

A particularly pleasant excursion during the summer beach season is a flight to the tiny island of Anholt, half way between Denmark and Sweden in the Kattegat. It is within easy striking distance from Copenhagen, Funen, and eastern Jutland. Bathing is mostly au naturel. Keeping airplane noise to a minimum is expected, by arriving and departing promptly, without any low level aerial lingering over the village and the beaches.

Flights to nearby Sweden are tempting, but visitors who do not obtain license validation cannot fly Danish-registered aircraft outside Danish airspace. A visit to Sweden in the company of a Danish pilot might be a worthwhile option.

VFR QUESTIONS & ANSWERS

What are good sources for VFR regulations? The Danish AIP.

How can I get a weather briefing? In person or over the telephone from the meteorological offices at the following airports: Copenhagen-Kastrup, Aalborg, Odense, Ronne, and Tirstrup (get phone numbers and operating hours from the airport where you will fly). In Danish, there is also a recorded airport weather forecast and a recorded GAFOR system. In flight, you can listen to Volmet.

What are VFR visibility and ceiling minimums? In controlled airspace above the higher of 3,000 feet MSL or 1,000 feet agl, 5 miles, and 1,000 feet; at or below the higher of these altitudes, 3 miles and 1,000 feet. In uncontrolled airspace above the higher of 3,000 feet MSL or 1,000 feet agl, 5 miles and 1,000 feet; at or below the higher of these altitudes, 1 mile and clear of clouds. For current details check the Danish AIP.

Is night VFR permitted? No.

Must I file a flight plan? Flight plans must be filed only if the route enters the Copenhagen TMA and selected control zones.

May I fly the airways VFR? Yes.

Must I maintain en route radio contact with ATC on or off the airways? No. Contact must be maintained only during those sections of a flight that are within TMAs and control zones.

Is VFR on top permitted? No.

ADDITIONAL INFORMATION SOURCES

AOPA-Denmark suggests the magazines *Flyghorizont* and *Flyv*, both in Danish.

20

Sweden

Country rating: **Easy**

ONC Charts: **C-2, D-2, and E-2**

Rental cost range:
  2 seat trainer   **$100-130**
  4 seat fixed gear   **$130-170**
  4 seat retractable   **$150-200**

QUALIFICATIONS AND LICENSE VALIDATION

The Swedish civil aviation authorities are among the most liberal when it comes to the recognition of pilot licenses issued by foreign states. All private pilot licenses issued by ICAO member states are accepted automatically, without validation, as long as the holder's stay in Sweden is one year or less. To use an instrument rating, you must first pass a short, routine checkflight with a CAA examiner. If your stay in Sweden is longer than one year, you must get the license validated at the end of the first year through a simple administrative procedure. The aircraft rental facility will require the usual checkride.

DOCUMENTS YOU SHOULD TAKE

Pilot license
Current medical
Logbook
Radio operator license (if separate from pilot license)

This documentation will need to be reviewed only by the operator renting you an aircraft. Take the original documents, to be on the safe side.

USEFUL FLYING ORGANIZATIONS

Royal Swedish Aero Club
Box 200 81
S161 02, Bromma
Telephone   08 292 912

The aeroclub coordinates all sport flying in Sweden. It is a good source of information if you have specific questions about flying in a particular area of the country or about specialty flying, such as gliding or aerobatics.

AOPA-Sweden
Flygplatsinfarten 39
S-161 69, Bromma
Telephone   08 295 000

Helpful to all general aviation pilots, especially AOPA members.

WHERE TO FLY, WHAT TO FLY

Sweden is a land of thousands of lakes, millions of acres of forest, and the midnight sun. It is also a highly developed industrial nation with a history dating back more than a thousand years. Distances are vast, the airplane is a natural mode of transportation, and recreational flying is popular. Be on the lookout for a Saab Safari, not the latest in nordic automotive technology, but something far more delightful, a side-by-side two-seat midwing bubble-canopied all-metal trainer/touring aircraft powered by a 200-hp Lycoming engine. Many airports are located close to some of the larger cities and places of particular interest to the visitor. With the exception of Kiruna to the far north, aerial touring between some or all of these destinations is practical on most short-term visits.

Bromma is the general aviation airport serving Stockholm, Sweden's capital and principal city on the Baltic Sea. The airport is only six miles from the charming medieval streets of the city center. Bromma is also home for the Royal Swedish Flying Club and AOPA-Sweden. Stockholm is surrounded by an archipelago of more than 20,000 islands, an especially rewarding sight from the air. In addition to commercial flying schools, Bromma is also home to several flying clubs.

Barharby, a smaller airfield outside Stockholm, is Sweden's EAA and homebuilders' center.

Save is a pleasant airport serving Gothenburg, which has been a trading and shipping center of long standing on Sweden's west coast. Save is a good staging point for flights along the scenic western coastline.

Dala Airport, approximately 100 miles northwest of Stockholm is central to Sweden's picturesque folklore country near Borlange and Lake Siljan.

Optand Airport serves Ostersund in Sweden's central mountain region, a favorite haunt for nature lovers, as attractive from above as from the hiking trails on the ground.

Kiruna in the extreme north is the true land of the midnight sun. It is 100 miles north of the Arctic Circle. Go in June, rent an airplane from the local flying school at midnight, and view 7,000-foot high Kebnekajse, Sweden's highest mountain, and the glaciers around it, as the sun never sets.

VFR QUESTIONS & ANSWERS

What are good sources for VFR regulations? Consult the Swedish AIP. The Swedish Civil Aviation Authority also publishes a pamphlet, *VFR Flying in Sweden*.

How can I get a weather briefing? Weather briefings are available in person at the main airports. You may also call a number of met offices. Get the phone numbers at the local airport. A recorded VFR forecast is also available over the phone in Swedish.

What are VFR visibility and ceiling minimums? Sweden has adopted the ICAO VFR minimums.

Is night VFR permitted? Yes. ATC permission is required in controlled airspace, but is usually granted.

Must I file a flight plan? Flight plans are not required for VFR flight except in the northern mountainous areas, but are strongly recommended everywhere.

May I fly the airways VFR? Yes. Flight in airways above 8,500 feet MSL requires a CVFR rating and the pilot must maintain ATC contact and give position reports. Below 8,500 feet MSL, you may fly the airways uncontrolled. In both cases, maintain the standard ICAO hemispherical VFR cruising altitudes.

Must I maintain en route radio contact with ATC off the airways? No.

Is VFR on top permitted? No.

ADDITIONAL INFORMATION SOURCES

Get a copy of "VFR Flying in Sweden" from the Civil Aviation Authority, Fack, S601-79, Norrkoping (011 192 000).

Local and regional flying magazines recommended by the Royal Swedish Flying Club are *Flygrevyn*, *Mach*, and *Flyghorizont*.

21

Across the Atlantic

FOR THE VAST MAJORITY OF US, the most convenient and economical way to fly in a foreign country is to rent an airplane when we get there. But who among us hasn't dreamt of flying a light airplane, preferably our own, across oceans to our ultimate destination, and touring in it at our leisure? The long-distance adventure many private pilots in America often think of is a transatlantic flight to Europe. It is a route laden with lousy weather and romantic aviation history. It was the first great aerial leap from continent to continent across a forbidding ocean. It claimed its victims, created its heroes, and it remained a challenge through World War II, when technical advances in the design and construction of multiengine aircraft finally made transatlantic trips routine. But for pilots of single-engine light airplanes, it remains the great adventure.

It is a flight not to be taken lightly even by the most experienced private pilots, and if you don't have an instrument rating, the regulations won't let you try. But with the right skills, equipment, preparation, patience, and financial resources, it is a dream readily turned into reality. Every year, dozens of light aircraft make their way safely across the Atlantic. Most are on delivery flights, flown by professional ferry pilots, but more of them than you might think are in the hands of instrument-rated private pilots who have done their homework and set the compass on "E," for Europe.

The total distance across the Atlantic, depending upon the route you take, is equal to or less than the 2,500-nautical-mile flight across the United States from coast to coast. Along the extreme northern scenic route across the pond, which many people call the Atlantic, the longest leg is only 480 nautical miles. This distance is within the range of even a Cessna 150, and some intrepid pilots have made transatlantic crossings in these modest little aircraft. You will most likely want more airplane, but it need not be much more than a four-seater with a 180-hp engine and a cruising speed of approximately 120 knots.

Other factors you should consider carefully are your piloting skills, the weather, the route you should choose, and survival, in case of trouble. The introductory overview below gives you a basic idea of what you will face if you are bitten by the transatlantic bug, and points you in the right direction. The two publications that you should get immediately if you decide to take the leap, are Transport Canada's *Transatlantic Flight Requirements*, available free of charge from the Canadian Atlantic regional office (506 851 7220) and the FAA's *North Atlantic International General Aviation Operations Manual*, available from any Government Printing Office for $2.25 (Document number 050007008864). Two excellent books should be referenced (though they should be updated for navigation by Loran-C and global positioning satellites): *Ocean Flying* by Louise Sacchi, and *Long Distance Flying* by Peter Garrison. Sacchi was a transoceanic ferry pilot for light aircraft manufacturers for decades in the days Loran-C and satellite navigation were not available to the general aviation pilot. Garrison, a popular aviation writer and contributing editor of *Flying*, built Melmoth, his own single-engine design, and roamed the world in it.

SINGLE-ENGINE AIRCRAFT—CANADIAN STOP

All single-engine aircraft crossing the Atlantic must first stop in Moncton, New Brunswick, Canada, where they are inspected by Transport Canada, and if it is your first crossing, you must pass a friendly oral examination on transatlantic flight. Transport Canada's pamphlet mentioned elsewhere in this chapter outlines the requirements for the oral exam.

PILOT SKILLS

You owe it to yourself to be honest about your abilities, and you should be experienced and current in the specific skills you need for the crossing. Experience means "having done many times," not "having read all about it."

Regulatory Requirements. As far as the regulations are concerned, in addition to a private pilot license and the qualifications required for aircraft type, you must also have an instrument rating to fly as pilot in command of an aircraft crossing the Atlantic.

Navigation and IFR Skills. You must be highly proficient in long-distance navigation, especially dead reckoning and pilotage, and the associated flight planning. You must have spent many hours finding your way around on the gauges, not under a hood with a safety pilot watching for traffic, but alone when all outside was a blanket of gray, and water streaked the windshield. You must have encountered airframe ice (not just the threat of it) often enough to feel comfortable dealing with it. You will find VORs only at certain points of departure and arrival; therefore, thousands of hours following VOR needles in visual meteorological conditions doesn't count; several hundred recent hours of pilotage and actual instrument time does, especially if the last hundred hours or more was in the airplane you intend to use for the crossing. You will encounter long-range NDBs; know how to operate and interpret the ADF. If you get a Loran (and you should), make it your business to know everything about it, but use it only to confirm and fine-tune your primary means of navigation.

Flight Planning Abilities. A key element of a successful crossing is good flight planning. It is also great fun for the novice. Choose your route, get all the charts, and spend a lot of time carefully planning all the legs, honing your planning skills. The types of charts you will use are different from the familiar sectionals and low altitude en route charts, so you will have to spend some time becoming familiar with them. They are also available for your local area, so you might want to use them on training flights.

Practice Flights. If you don't have the experience, set up a systematic program for yourself to become more experienced. Spend your weekends going on progressively longer IFR cross-country flights in actual instrument meteorological conditions. Get up there when the freezing level is low, initially with a pilot who is experienced in such conditions. Dead reckoning on the gauges is not practical because you have to fly IFR in the system, so dead reckon 500 to 600 miles at a time under the hood, in visual meteorological conditions with a safety pilot, to hone your dead reckoning skills.

Physical Condition. The long legs of a crossing, and a heightened sense of tension felt by all first-timers to some degree takes its toll on the body, so it truly pays off to be in good physical shape. This also goes for any passenger you plan to take. If you don't exercise regularly, start exercising three to six months before the crossing.

THE AIRPLANE

The airplane you choose is usually determined by the size of your bank account, and, to some extent by the challenge you want to pose yourself. An important element you should consider is your airplane's cruising speed. Although pilots have crossed the Atlantic even in motorgliders, a common selection criteria is an ability to cruise at least at 120 knots. This speed means approximately six to seven hours of flying per day on a typical crossing itinerary, which should be a comfortable load for the novice. Many pilots prefer an airplane with a cruising speed of approximately 150 knots, which makes the legs quite comfortable but doesn't reduce the sense of adventure.

Single or Twin? The cliche question. Statistically your chances are equal. Twins have more engine failures than singles, and a fully loaded twin with extra ferry tanks in the early stages of a leg might not be able to sustain level flight on one engine. Twins are also more expensive to feed and maintain, but they can carry more. Ultimately, your choice is a matter of personal preference.

Aircraft Condition. The airplane should be in unquestionably good mechanical condition. Have a mechanic do a thorough annual several months before the crossing. It is important that you put on a good number of hours after the annual or any important mechanical repair to make sure that everything was put together correctly.

A very important item of which you must be absolutely sure is the engine's oil consumption. Depending upon the length of the individual legs in your itinerary, you might have a problem in an airplane that consumes a higher than average amount of oil. Engines with chromed cylinders, babied engines, or just plain vanilla engines might consume more than a usual amount of oil. Conduct careful test flights to monitor oil consumption. If you have a problem and the engine is not high time, several long flights at high power and high rpm will often cure the problem by properly seating the piston rings.

An item usually not covered by an annual is the radio stack. Here a good rule is to leave well enough alone, but get all the glitches fixed (including small ones), and perhaps have the ADF bench tested by your radio shop. Also, make sure that the ADF has a Beat Frequency Oscillation (BFO) switch to receive frequencies that might not be in use in the United States. Allow enough time prior to departure to put a few hours of use on any repair or test.

Another must-do item is swinging the aircraft compass. Take your time and do a thorough job. Find someone who has experience swinging compasses to help you. Do it with the engine throttled up to cruise power. The Canadian authorities require that the compass be swung within 30 days prior to your departure.

Do yourself a favor if your airplane does not already have an autopilot and purchase at least a wing leveler. Hundreds of miles from land is not the place to find out that manually holding an accurate heading for hours is torture.

Beyond these steps, there is little else you can do, except set yourself conservative engine time thresholds. Many pilots will not attempt the crossing if the airplane's engine has fewer than 200 hours on it, or is past the midpoint of TBO.

SPECIAL EQUIPMENT

A lengthy list of special equipment must be considered for a transatlantic flight. Several items are required by regulations, but many optional items might also be deemed essential for safety and convenience.

Extra Fuel Tanks. Extra tanks are not required if the aircraft has the range for the proposed route, including a three-hour fuel reserve requirement per leg. Most pilots choose to install them because the extra range enables them to fly longer, more direct legs instead of the scenic route to the far north. Much can be said for having the flexibility of more fuel than required, when the destination fogs in and the next airport is 500 to 700 miles away.

You should use the services of a professional shop specializing in ferry tank installations. Three such outfits are Globe Aero (813 644 2451) at Lakeland Airport in Florida (they deliver most of Piper's aircraft overseas), Wiggins Airways (617 762 5690) at Norwood Airport just south of Boston, Massachusetts, and Aerofusion (207 945 3561) in Bangor, Maine. Several types of tanks are available off the shelf and are simple to install and remove (for the specialty shops). The installation is officially a ferry tank installation and is documented by an FAA Form 337 (major alteration). Another FAA document you get with the installation is an authorization to operate your airplane a specified percentage above gross weight with all the extra fuel on-board. The shop will complete all the paperwork, but double-check the Federal Aviation Regulations on your own to verify that documentation has been properly prepared and displayed. It is of utmost importance that you are fully trained in fuel management and fuel system operation following the ferry tank installation.

Additional Navigation Equipment. Though you might think it would be silly in this day and age not to have a Loran, solid coverage will not be available over northern Canada and Greenland, and will be marginal on portions of the direct route between Canada and Reykjavik. Nevertheless, you should take a Loran for the coverage it will give you on the rest of the route. Program all way-points in the flight planning stage, and have a knowledgeable manufacturer representative verify the programming. A neat trick is to get an independent dry cell and have a radio shop wire the Loran so that you can plug it into the dry cell in case of an alternator failure. Not every type of dry cell is suitable, so consult with a radio shop and the manufacturer.

By the early 1990s, prices for global positioning system receivers were becoming competitive with Loran-C receivers. It might be worthwhile to consider becoming a pioneering user of a global positioning system receiver in light aircraft on a transatlantic flight, but make it a priority to thoroughly understand the limits of the system before purchasing a receiver.

A requirement of the Canadian authorities on all routes north of Prins Christian Sund at the extreme southern tip of Greenland is a second, independent ADF. An inexpensive, battery-powered marine ADF no longer meets this requirement.

On the Goose Bay to Reykjavik route via Prins Christian Sund, a Loran-C receiver may be substituted, according to Canadian regulations, for the second ADF. On the Gander to Shannon route (not recommended for the novice because of the extreme nonstop distance), a Loran is a regulatory requirement.

A somewhat cumbersome regulatory requirement for all routes is an HF radio. It is an expensive and not particularly reliable piece of equipment, and the airlines are happy to relay your position reports anyway. You can rent one from an avionics radio shop.

Another Canadian requirement, if any portion of the flight is to be made at night, is two landing lights, or one bulb with two filaments.

EMERGENCY AND SURVIVAL EQUIPMENT

Here is where you have to meet some stringent requirements, and can go to town for more. The Canadian authorities have a long laundry list of required survival equipment. The big items are a second, battery operated, water activated, floating ELT; a life raft (made by a recognized manufacturer) sufficient to hold all occupants and with certain minimum provisions, such as emergency flares, sail, fishing equipment, signal mirror, paddles, pump, water desalination kit, and other items; authorized life vests for all occupants; and a watertight immersion suit (dry-suit) for all occupants. If you go into the frigid drink you will survive in a dry suit on average for about eight hours compared to about one hour in a wet suit and minutes in anything else. They are cumbersome. The way to wear one is to get into it up to your waist and arrange the remaining part around you in the cockpit (it is a one-piece suit) ready to be donned and zipped up in an instant. If you have macho tendencies, just consider that every light aircraft ferry pilot wears one religiously.

NAVIGATION

If the airplane is in good shape and you are comfortable on instruments, the largest potential problem will be a mistake in navigation. It is imperative that you become thoroughly versed in the nuances of transatlantic navigation.

Flight Planning Techniques. Flight planning techniques for the individual legs are essentially no different from basic VFR flight planning, but given the long distances, you have much less margin for error. A mistake might put you not 10 or 20 miles but 100 or 200 miles off course. Be especially careful to properly consider magnetic variation, which can be as much as 50 degrees! Also check and double-check fuel usage calculations.

One difference from flight planning over land is having to specify your own checkpoints over the featureless water with latitude-longitude coordinates at approximately 100-mile intervals along the great circle route between point of departure and destination; enter the checkpoints into the Loran-C receiver. A good technique is to fill out the flight log for each leg with the information not dependent on the weather forecast (the inspector at Moncton will want to see this), and complete the log after you get the weather briefing.

Charts. Given the vast distances, you will have to use one of the small-scale 1:5,000,000 aircraft position charts for planning and to track your overwater position. This is perfectly fine because the primary use for a larger scale is easier identification of landmark details, which is not an issue over the Atlantic's watery wastes. The aircraft position charts for the Atlantic crossing are numbers 3071 and 3097. A helpful chart feature is their Lambert projection, which means that any drawn straight line is the great circle route, the shortest distance between any two points on the chart. (The line between two points on a sectional chart is not the shortest distance between them, given the projections used to draw the sectionals, but the difference is negligible over the short distances on which these charts are usually used.)

Overland legs require the appropriate ONC or WAC charts. Also, get the relevant IFR charts and the related supplements. AOPA's chart department can provide all the charts you need, and the staff is very knowledgeable and helpful.

WEATHER

Horrible and capricious are kind words to describe the rapidly changeable weather that can rage over the Atlantic at any time of the year. But often it can also be calm and clear and predictable for the duration of your daily leg. The best period is during the summer months of June, July, and August, when a succession of high pressure zones tends to dominate southern Greenland. At this time, low pressure movements through the route are less frequent and fronts move through quickly, usually reducing waiting time on the ground to a few days. For the novice transatlantic pilot, a crossing at any time other than June through August is not recommended, although ferry pilots cross over in small, single-engine airplanes throughout the year.

The big bugbear of the North Atlantic is icing. The freezing level can be down to the surface, even in the summer, and must be greatly respected.

Weather forecasting over the Atlantic is excellent, especially at Goose Bay and Gander. You get a full weather folder with all the information you would ever want, and it is usually quite accurate, even the winds.

ROUTES

Three common northern routes cross the Atlantic Ocean. The best choice will most likely depend upon aircraft range. The direct Canada-to-Europe routes bypassing Iceland, and the southern route through the Azores are not outlined here, because they require nonstop flights of up to 15 hours even in the fastest single-engine airplanes and are likely to be of little interest to the novice transatlantic pilot.

Northern Route. (Fort Chimo, Canada; Frobisher, Canada; Sondrestrom, Greenland; Kulusuk, Greenland; Reykjavik, Iceland; Faroe Islands; and Glasgow, Scotland) The longest segment on this route is 480 nautical miles between Frobisher and Sondrestrom. Cessna 150s take this route. The Greenland icecap extends up to 10,000 feet. United States registered aircraft require 30 days prior permission to land at Sondrestrom, an American airbase. An alternative to Sondrestrom is Godthaab, a civilian airport to the south.

Central Route I. (Goose Bay or Gander, Newfoundland; Narssarssuaq, Greenland; Reykjavik, Iceland; and Prestwick, Scotland) The longest leg is 740 nautical miles from Reykjavik to Prestwick. Most single-engine aircraft will require a ferry tank, especially considering a three-hour reserve requirement. A segment of this route over Greenland has a minimum en route altitude of 11,000 feet. Prior permission is required from the Canadian military to use Goose Bay.

Central Route II. (Goose Bay or Gander, Newfoundland; Reykjavik, Iceland; and Prestwick, Scotland) The typical one-stop Atlantic crossing flown by the airliners when they still had propellers. From Goose Bay, Reykjavik is 1,330 nautical miles; from Gander, 1,420 nautical miles. All single-engine light aircraft will need ferry tanks, but perhaps it is worth the effort for the most direct crossing. The route touches the southernmost tip of Greenland at Prins Christian Sund, where there is a powerful NDB.

22

Ireland

Country rating: **Easy**

ONC Chart: **E-1**

Rental cost range:

  2 seat trainer **$60-110**

  4 seat fixed gear **$90-170**

  4 seat retractable **$150-210**

QUALIFICATIONS AND LICENSE VALIDATION

Ireland does not require the validation of licenses issued by ICAO member states for noncommercial VFR flight. To rent an Irish registered aircraft, all you have to do is show up at the local aeroclub or flying school with current documents, and take a checkride. If it only were so easy everywhere else!

Recognition does not extend to an instrument rating; a written and flight test are required; written tests are administered on fixed dates four or five times a year.

DOCUMENTS YOU SHOULD TAKE

Pilot license

Current medical

Logbook

Radio operator license

You must present the original documents.

USEFUL FLYING ORGANIZATIONS

AOPA Ireland
Loughlinstown Rd, Celbridge
Co. Kildare
IRELAND
Telephone   (353) 1 571824
Facsimile   (353) 1 571509

AOPA-Ireland takes an active role in recreational flying and is a good information source. The organization publishes an annual *Fly in Ireland* booklet covering most topics of interest to the visiting recreational pilot.

Irish Aviation Council
38 Pembroke Rd, Ballsbridge
Dublin 4
IRELAND
Telephone   (353) 1 874474

The Irish Aviation Council is the governing body of sport aviation in Ireland. As an umbrella organization for a variety of aviation associations, it is a good source of information about specialized flying, such as gliding, ballooning, and aerobatics.

WHERE TO FLY, WHAT TO FLY

In Ireland you will see more shades of green than anywhere else, and the best vantage point is from the air. The country's reasonable aviation regulations make it one of the easiest places in which to fly. Dublin's busy airspace aside, the pace is relaxed, the skies uncrowded. Dublin, Cork, and Shannon are the main public airports. There is also a wide selection of smaller airfields, many of them grass strips, most of them privately owned. If you fly into a private strip, you will need prior permission so the owner can "prepare the appropriate welcome," say the Irish.

Practically all airfields have one or several local flying clubs, and the larger airfields also have commercial flying schools. It is easy to arrange dual flying anywhere, but self-hire availability might vary, so check around.

Dublin-Weston, (01 280435/280659), has become a good alternative general aviation airfield because Dublin Airport has become progressively busier. A great advantage to Weston is that it is in uncontrolled airspace, keeping procedures pleasantly simple.

Dublin Airport, (01 379900), is Dublin's main international airport. It has all the bells and whistles, and several well established flying organizations offering airplane rental. Commercial traffic has increased and its control zone requires a special VFR clearance, which is usually granted routinely, traffic permitting. Delays might occur.

Cork, (021 313131), is the main airport for the southwestern part of the island, and an excellent staging point for local scenic flights.

Kerry, (066 64644), is a short flight from Cork near the Killarney Lakes.

Shannon, (061 61444), is a major airport near the town of Limerick. In earlier days it was a major refueling spot for transatlantic flights, and is still an important transit point across the pond for aircraft constrained by range. There are more than 900 castles, ruined and restored, in its immediate vicinity.

Galway, (091 55569), a hop north of Shannon, is the gateway to Ireland's haunted, lonely Northwest. Great salmon fishing is also nearby.

Sligo, (071 68280), north of Galway, serves the nearby seaside resorts. Sligo is also the burial place of the poet Yates, and outside the town, at Rosse's Point, is a famous golf course.

Speciality airports near Dublin are **Gowran Grange,** (045 97326), which is a glider field, and **Clonbullogue,** (045 30103), a parachuting center.

TOURING

Ireland is small enough for all its airports to be within easy reach of each other. Daylong or half-day out and return flights in a four-place aircraft can comfortably cover a third of the island at a time. Or you can take a few days to leisurely cover the entire country. A good example is a circular route.

Leave Dublin toward Cork to the southwest over horse country. Fly over the 200-foot high Rock of Cashel on the way (where St. Patrick supposedly picked the shamrock to explain the Trinity, and gave Ireland its national symbol). Take an aerial look at the medieval fortress of the next town, Cahir.

On the second stage, fly northwest from Cork toward Kerry and then turn northeast to the Limerick-Shannon area and north to Galway. This route takes you over the spectacular Killarney Lakes, and scores of ancient castles in the Limerick-Shannon area. Plan the route carefully with local assistance to get the best views.

On the third stage, fly up north to Sligo over the remote countryside before turning southeast for the flight back to Dublin.

A strongly recommended alternative is splitting this circular itinerary into three local daytrips.

The ever changeable weather can play havoc with longer trips, so have plenty of time built in for rain delays. Before you do any flying, get a good initial briefing from a qualified aviation meteorologist at one of the met offices about general weather patterns and the areas to particularly watch for sudden change. Get a detailed weather briefing before every flight, and always know where the nearest airport is, in case you need it quickly.

VFR QUESTIONS & ANSWERS

What are good sources for VFR regulations? The Irish AIP, available for use at all public airports and many flying establishments.

How can I get a weather briefing? In person or by telephone from the Meteorological Offices at Dublin, Cork, and Shannon airports. In addition to a general briefing, you can preorder a specific route forecast. It is also possible to access weather information by telex, a service of particular use to flying establishments in the more out-of-the-way locations.

What are VFR visibility and ceiling minimums? Five miles and 1,000 feet within controlled airspace, and above the higher of 3,000 feet MSL or 1,000 feet agl in uncontrolled airspace. Two miles and clear of clouds in visual contact with the ground below the higher of 3,000 feet MSL or 1,000 feet agl. Check the AIP for current details.

Is night VFR permitted? No.

Must I file a flight plan? For flight in controlled airspace and overwater flights of 100 nautical miles or more, a flight plan is required.

May I fly the airways VFR? Yes. You must observe ICAO standard altitudes for given directions of flight.

Must I maintain en route radio contact with ATC on or off the airways? No.

Is VFR on top permitted? Yes, but visual descent must be assured.

ADDITIONAL INFORMATION SOURCES

Fly in Ireland is AOPA-Ireland's annual publication, full of addresses, airport and airspace diagrams, and other useful information.

Irish Air Letters is Ireland's journal of current and historic aviation.

All major British aviation magazines are also available at the larger newsstands.

23

Glide above
the great white horse

YORKSHIRE IS FAMOUS FOR QUAINT VILLAGES, where time has stood still;
James Herriott, the literary veterinarian; Castle Howard, where they filmed
Brideshead Revisited; the North York Moors; and pigs. But what is better than
trudging from the veterinary surgery, to the villages, to the castles, and the scenic locales one by one? Seeing them all at once from a glider, of course.

A few miles west of Thirsk, the town made famous by Herriott, an escarpment called Sutton Bank rises sharply out of the surrounding fields. At its southern end is one of Britain's best soaring sites, home of the Yorkshire Gliding Club,
where I managed to slip in a visit during a vacation that was full of nature walks.

The first thing we saw after takeoff on an orientation flight was one of Yorkshire's most unusual landmarks: an enormous white horse carved into the
escarpment wall just off the airfield's south end. The schoolmaster and his students, who laid it out in 1857, have unwittingly made Sutton Bank the most easily recognizable grass field in the world, and created a lifetime trademark for the
gliding club.

We floated over the horse, explored the ridge facing the prevailing westerlies,
and circled Castle Howard, the ruins of 750 year old Rievaulx Abbey, and the burial place of Oliver Cromwell. It was a sunny, picturebook morning and I chatted
with club instructor Tony Hirst as we made our leisurely way over the pastoral
Yorkshire countryside. Ridge lift and wave are common throughout the year, and
in the summer months, thermal conditions can also be excellent despite
England's reputation for foul weather.

The absolute club glider altitude record of 30,200 feet was established after a
winch launch in the summer. Only a few days prior to the orientation flight several people had flown gold distance/diamond goal flights—186 nautical miles
over a predetermined course that, if documented by a sealed barograph and
turnpoint photos taken by a sealed camera, is recognized as an official achieve-

This airport is hard to miss on a fine day.

ment by the national soaring authority and the Federation Aeronautique Internationale. The gliders on these flights reached 20,000 feet at times.

The winch is an economical alternative to launching sailplanes. It is a big engine, usually a converted bus or truck engine, on a stand with a drum of cable bolted on the vehicle's axle where the wheels used to be. The winch is at one end of the glider field. The cable is drawn across the field by a car or tractor, and is hooked up to a glider. The cable is then reeled in at high speed by the winch, launching the glider, which climbs steeply before releasing the cable. Launches that rise to 1,200 feet are normal.

I learned that the Yorkshire Gliding Club not only welcomes visitors from afar but in large measure depends on them for its commercial existence, offering a wide range of soaring activities on excellent equipment to novice and expert alike.

Many British clubs offer week-long gliding vacations for beginners. The Yorkshire Gliding Club has courses starting every Monday from April to October. They are designed to be a concentrated introduction to soaring, and weather permitting, most participants are close to soloing by week's end. Not only are the courses ideal for students attending on their own, but they are also a great way to get nonsoaring members of the family started in the sport while an experienced pilot enjoys some serious flying in the club's single-seat aircraft.

Each course is limited to 10 people, ensuring ample stick time for each student in the two ASK-2ls and the Falke motorglider used in the course. "We have no hard-and-fast rules about using the Falke, but it is an excellent teaching aid in concentrated courses like ours," says part-time instructor Tony Hirst. "I usually like to take my students on several glider flights to teach them coordination, and then put them in the motorglider to practice landings. I position the motorglider on downwind and cut the throttle. The student then glides to touchdown, and off we go for another try. An hour or two of that will get in about two dozen landings and then it is back to the gliders again."

Henryk Doktor, the club's CFI, and his assistant, Mike Wood, have decades of soaring experience between them and teach the course full time. They are helped out by several part-timers like Tony. "We teach the students not only to glide . . . if conditions are appropriate, they also learn soaring flight right from the start, be it ridge lift, thermals, or wave."

The club has three towplanes and employs two full time tow pilots who double as winch operators on good ridge days. Aerotows are to 2,000 feet, and if there is lift, each flight lasts approximately 45 minutes. Depending on the weather, students can expect to log approximately 10 hours of flying during their week.

Course participants are put up from Sunday night through Friday evening at the Yorkshire Gliding Club's enviable clubhouse. They eat breakfast, lunch, and dinner in the club restaurant, do ground school in the common rooms, and sleep in double bunk rooms in the residential wing. The club also has a fully licensed bar.

Although the gliding course is a commercial venture, it is run like a club operation. Participants are expected to appreciate that gliding is a communal sport and everyone takes part in handling gliders and chasing after tow ropes. "Every once in a while we get a bloke who just wants to pop out of the glider after landing and head for the pubs, but that is the exception," according to John Shanley, towplane pilot.

Yorkshire Gliding Club trainer prepares for another launch.

And what about the infamous English weather? It is as changeable as it is dismal; at least part of most weeks will be flyable. Also, you pay in advance only for the food and lodging (the price beats a week's worth of bed-and-breakfast, including meals). Flying is pay as you go, and there are no minimum requirements. And if all else fails, and even the birds are walking, you can explore the earthbound pleasures of Yorkshire.

If you are an experienced glider pilot, you may pick and choose from an impressive lineup of fiberglass sailplanes. A license with a glider rating and a logbook are enough for a checkride in an ASK-21. If you cut the mustard, you will face a more formidable task: deciding whether to fly the Astir, the Pegase, the DG 101, or the DG 200. High-performance checkouts and cross-country instruction tailored to individual needs are also available. Fly for fun in a Ka8 or a vintage Slingsby T-21 open-cockpit side-by-side two-seater.

On a private basis, you may stay as short or as long as desired. Because you will likely mix flying with sightseeing from day to day, you might want to find accommodations away from the field. Bed-and-breakfasts abound and there are charming old-world inns and hotels in the nearby towns and villages. Mrs. Bielby's immaculate bed-and-breakfast is a working farm just down the road from the gliding club. Mr. Bielby tends 600 sheep.

Soaring over Yorkshire's rolling patchwork of fields and pastures, and circling above its many relics from days gone by is a great way to make a good vacation better. And if, at the end of a long cross-country, or after an afternoon of meandering above the green pastures, everything starts to look the same, just mumble a word of thanks to an eccentric Victorian schoolmaster, and head for the great white horse.

North America

24

Canada

Country rating: **Easy**

Charts: **Canadian WAC or VNC**

Rental cost range:

  2 seat trainer **$40-60**

  4 seat fixed gear **$60-80**

  4 seat retractable **$90-120**

QUALIFICATIONS AND LICENSE VALIDATION

Validation of a foreign license is required by Canada to fly Canadian registered aircraft, but for recreational VFR flying by holders of licenses issued by ICAO member states, it is a simple one-step administrative procedure. Present a valid license and medical, and proof of identification at any Transport Canada, Aviation Group regional office. They will issue the validation while you wait. District offices are also able to validate licenses, and might be closer than a regional office. However, district offices are not sufficiently staffed to provide walk-in service. If you prefer a district office, determine the closest one from a regional office and make an appointment. Six regional offices cover Canada:

Pacific; Vancouver, British Columbia (604 666 5851)
Western; Edmonton, Alberta (403 495 3863)
Central; Winnipeg, Manitoba (204 983 4336)
Ontario; Willowdale, Ontario (416 224 3177)
Quebec; Dorval, Quebec (514 633 3262)
Atlantic; Moncton, New Brunswick (506 857 7220)

    License validation is in effect for 90 days, and is renewable.

    Validation does not extend to an instrument rating. Passing an instrument written exam and instrument flight test are required prior to operating in instrument meteorological conditions in a Canadian-registered aircraft.

    The *tourist* license is another category of validation available to nonresidents, which recognizes a license for noncommercial VFR flying, but permits upgrading and additional ratings while in Canada. It requires passing a written test on Canadian airspace regulations. It is valid for two years and its main purpose is to allow licensed foreign pilots to receive additional qualifications at Canadian flying schools.

DOCUMENTS YOU SHOULD TAKE

Pilot license
Current medical
Proof of identification (usually a passport)
Logbook
Radio operator license

Take original documents.

USEFUL FLYING ORGANIZATIONS

Transport Canada, Aviation Group
Ottawa, Ontario
CANADA K1A 0N8
Telephone   613 991 9979
Facsimile   613 996 9439

This group is the Canadian government's aviation regulatory authority. Its Aviation Information Services section provides information, including some free publications, to visitors.

Canadian Owners and Pilots Association
77 Metcalfe St., Suite 605
Ottawa, Ontario
CANADA K1P 5L6
Telephone   613 236 4901
Facsimile   613 236 8646

Canada's AOPA. Helpful to all visiting pilots, especially to AOPA members.

WHERE TO FLY, WHAT TO FLY

When you mention Canadian flying, most visitors conjure up a vision of bush pilots in high-wing floatplanes soaring over vast virgin forests and sparkling lakes, hundreds of miles from the nearest human settlement. Bush flying is there for the asking along the Alaska Highway and over all of northern Canada, but you will also find excellent flying over the tamer south. Except for the wilderness areas, you are never far from an airport, and rental airplanes are easy to find. Canada has FBO/commercial flying schools similar to the United States, with some aeroclubs, too. Below is a sampler of airports around some of the most popular tourist attractions.

Niagara's Horseshoe Falls from the southern turn of the scenic racetrack course.

Toronto-Island Airport, (416 868 6942), is minutes away from downtown Toronto, accessible by what must be the world's shortest ferry ride across a narrow channel separating it from the mainland. The local FBO offers a Cessna fleet. Niagara Falls is just 45 minutes away, if you follow the shore. Enjoy the Toronto skyline. There is a good pilot shop on the field.

Markham, (416 640 4408), **Buttonville,** (416 477 8100), and **Brampton,** (416 543 1503), are three other big Toronto-area general aviation airports where you will find flying schools and airplanes for rent.

Montreal-St. Hubert, (514 462 0346), is Montreal's main general aviation airfield, east of the city across the St. Lawrence River approximately a 45-minute drive away. There are numerous flying schools on the field.

Les Cedres, (514 455 5755), to the southwest of Montreal, and **Mascouche,** (514 474 4133), to the north, are two smaller alternatives to St. Hubert.

Rockcliffe, (613 746 4425), and **Gatineau,** (819 770 1500), are two general aviation airports at Ottawa, Canada's capital. Both have commercial flying schools. The National Air Museum is located at Rockcliffe and Gatineau offers gliding.

Quebec Airport, (418 874 8333), serves Quebec City, Canada's most "old-world" town. The walled-in old city and the French restaurants are exquisite. View the area on a local flight or, better still, stay here for a few days during a cross-country flight.

Charlottetown, (709 896 3185), is on Prince Edward Island, the popular maritime vacation spot. It is an excellent fly-in destination, and you might be able to rent locally (call ahead).

St. Catherines, (416 684 7447), on the Canadian side of Niagara Falls, is the most convenient airport for waterfall sightseeing operations.

Hamilton Airport, (416 679 4151), at Hamilton, Ontario, southwest of Toronto, is home of the Canadian Warbird Heritage. Among the fleet of warbirds is one of only two Hurricanes in the world still flying and a magnificently restored Avro Lancaster bomber.

Vancouver-Boundary Bay, (604 946 5361), south of Vancouver, is the city's main general aviation airport.

Delta Airpark, (604 689 7394), is another Vancouver general aviation field, and a homebuilders' and warbird center. It is a few miles east of Boundary Bay.

Calgary-Springbank Airport, (403 292 8601), is the main general aviation airfield of this oil-and-rodeo town. The Canadian Rockies, Banff, Lake Louise, and Jasper are a short flight to the west. Aerobatic aircraft are available on the field.

Black Diamond-Thompson's Ranch, (403 938 7639), is a glider field south of Calgary. It is well placed for cross-country soaring flights in high-performance sailplanes toward the Canadian Rockies.

Edmonton Municipal, (403 428 3991), serves Edmonton, which is another oil-and-rodeo town.

St. Andrews, (204 983 8407), is the main general aviation airport of Winnipeg.

TOURING

Countless opportunities are found in Canada for aerial touring, ranging from relaxing afternoon jaunts around a particularly picturesque area, to heavy-duty bush flying. Whet your appetite by considering these popular options: historic eastern Canada, Toronto, the Great Lakes and Niagara Falls, the Rockies in the vicinity of Calgary, and the Alaska Highway.

An ideal base for touring around eastern Canada is Montreal, itself a favorite tourist destination. The St. Lawrence River simplifies downriver navigation to Quebec City, approximately 130 miles to the northeast, and upriver navigation and along the shore of Lake Ontario to Toronto, 280 miles to the southwest. Ottawa, Canada's capital, is only 90 miles to the west. Prince Edward Island (PEI), and the rest of the Canadian Maritimes are a bit farther away, about 600 miles east: five hours in a Cessna 172 (watch out for tenacious fog around PEI and points east). Lake Champlain and scenic Vermont and New Hampshire in the United States are within easy reach to the south.

Toronto is a good place for staging flights to Niagara Falls (St. Catherines Airport) and to the Canadian Great Lakes region. Niagara Falls is an easy day-trip including hours of sightseeing. Stop in Hamilton, Ontario, to see the airplanes of the Canadian Warbird Heritage. If you plan to operate from Toronto, a flight along Lake Ontario and down the St. Lawrence River to Montreal is an excellent choice, especially if you can stay for a day or two. Ottawa is also within easy reach. Pleasant aerial tours, which you can make as short or as long as you like, are along the shores of Lake Huron and Lake Superior, especially in the fall during foliage season.

Fly out of Calgary over the Canadian Rockies. Banff, and peaks towering more than 11,000 feet are only 60 to 80 miles to the west. A spectacular flight along the entire range is to Banff and Lake Louise, continuing northwest to Jasper, slightly more than 200 miles from Calgary. Be wary of the mountain weather.

The ultimate in bush flying is flying the Alaska Highway. It is an adventurous, but manageable route for the cautious VFR private pilot with some mountain experience, a healthy respect for the weather, and many long cross-country flights. For visitors unfamiliar with the vast expanse of wilderness leading to Alaska, following the highway is the only recommended route. The distances are formidable. Dawson Creek, the beginning of the highway, is more than over 400 miles northwest of Calgary. The distance to Fairbanks, Alaska, is another 1,526 miles. The main stops along the way are Fort Nelson, Watson Lake, White Horse, and Haines Junction. Distances are between 100 to 600 miles from town to town.

You will have to fly through numerous mountain passes, the highest rising up to more than 4,000 feet MSL. The terrain around you will reach up beyond 7,000 feet. There are good aeronautical charts covering the route, including Transport Canada's Alaska Highway Chart (Air 5099), which covers the segment from Fort Nelson to Northway in Alaska just beyond the Canadian border. Order the chart from the Canada Map Office, Department of Energy, Mines, and Resources, 615 Booth Street, Ottawa, Ontario, K1A 0E9, (613 952 7000). Also get a free copy of *Flying the Alaska Highway in Canada*, from Transport Canada (address at the end of this chapter). If flying along the Pacific coast to Alaska looks more appealing on the map, forget it. The horrible weather along this route makes it impractical for the VFR private pilot.

VFR QUESTIONS & ANSWERS

What are good sources for VFR regulations? Canada's AIP, available for use at FSS facilities and many flying establishments, is published in English and French. Books condensing the regulations appropriate to VFR flight are also available, mostly at airport pilot shops. Make sure the copy you use is current.

How may I get a weather briefing? From the FSS, in person or by telephone. Standard recorded weather forecasts are also available. Get the phone numbers at the airport from which you will fly.

What are VFR visibility and ceiling minimums? In controlled airspace, 3 miles and 1,000 feet. In uncontrolled airspace, 1 mile and clear of clouds. Check the Canadian AIP for details

Is night VFR permitted? Yes.

Must I file a flight plan? Yes, for all flights beyond 25 miles from the departure airport.

May I fly the airways VFR? Yes.

Must I maintain en route radio contact with ATC on or off the airways? No.

Is VFR on top permitted? No.

ADDITIONAL INFORMATION SOURCES

Transport Canada offers several useful publications. Available free are *Air Tourist Information Canada*, which includes a summary of VFR regulations, and *Flying the Alaska Highway in Canada*. You can order both from Transport Canada, Aeronautical Information Services, Ottawa, Ontario, Canada K1A 0N8 (613 991 9970). Also available free from Transport Canada's Atlantic office (P.O. Box 42, Moncton, New Brunswick, E1C 8K6) is *Transatlantic Flight Requirements*, for pilots transiting Canada en route to Europe via the North Atlantic.

If you are going to do some serious solo flying in Canada, an indispensable booklet is a current issue of the *Canada Flight Supplement*, containing airport diagrams and useful flight planning and emergency information, available from the Aeronautical Information Services at the address above.

Canadian aviation magazines are *Aviation Today*, *Canadian Flight*, and *Canadian General Aviation News*.

25

To Niagara Falls

WE BANKED STEEPLY OVER THE RIVER and Niagara's horseshoe falls filled the airplane's right windows. Two visitors from Europe looked down, mesmerized, at the millions of gallons of frothing, thundering water. A few hours before, we were sipping our morning coffee in Boston, and we would be home in ample time for a leisurely evening barbecue.

Talk to foreigners visiting the United States and Canada about what they would like to see, and, invariably, Niagara Falls will be among the first sights they will mention. Most will also do whatever it takes to get there. Unless you fly commercially at great expense, this means a long, boring drive of 8 to 10 hours one way from the popular tourist destinations in the northeast, a few hours at the falls, and another marathon drive back: at least two exhausting days. But in a light airplane you get there in a few hours from anywhere in the northeast, spend three or four hours on the ground at the falls, circle over them to get the full effect, and be home well before nightfall. And you need not have local friends with airplanes, if you are a licensed and current pilot. Get your license validated and rent an airplane from an FBO. It will be the big flying adventure of your trip.

We took off from Hanscom Field at 9 A.M. and climbed westbound to 8,500 feet. It was a cruising altitude where the Piper Arrow would perform efficiently, we would be above the several ARSA's along the way, and the air would still be dense enough to keep our visitors from being drowsy. The direct route is right over Albany, New York state's capital, but it has a busy commercial airport and there is also a lot of incoming IFR traffic toward Boston from the west, so I prefer to fly outbound slightly north of Albany. We aimed for the Cambridge VOR via Keene, and settled down to enjoy the scenery. In contrast to the drive on the turnpike, the flight is quite scenic.

To our north was Mount Monadnock, just across the New Hampshire border near Keene, and after approximately half an hour, we were over the Connecticut River (a good VFR fix), and then the Berkshire Mountains. Emergency landing spots were few and far between, but the rolling hills were pretty in their summer coat of green, and our visitors saw first-hand just how uninhabited so much of

Niagara panorama

this country still is. The barren, rocky peak of 3,500-foot high Mount Greylock showed up on schedule to the south, and then we were out over the Hudson River Valley farmland. The smooth squares of yellows, greens, and browns looked comforting after all those trees. To the south was Albany, and for some time we had been squawking an assigned transponder code and getting traffic advisories from Albany Approach.

We aimed for the southern tip of Lake Saratoga near the famous Saratoga Springs racetrack, and from here on, our navigation would be a "no-brainer." First, we would fly slightly south of the four-lane interstate highway until the Finger Lakes, and then directly overhead all the way out. But the route is busy, and a number of big, commercial airports were still ahead, so it was important to stay in contact with ATC and continue receiving traffic advisories. We flew on course past the Utica VOR, avoiding Griffiss Air Force Base to the north of our track. Griffiss is a SAC base, and the chances of seeing a lumbering B-52 on a long, flat approach are good. We flew on, past Lake Oneonta to the north, a good VFR landmark leading to Syracuse, then south of Syracuse along the Finger Lakes.

The Iroquois Indians say that the Finger Lakes were formed when God reached down and touched the earth with his hand. From the air you are tempted to believe them. The names, Owasco, Cayuga, Seneca, evoke a time when only hawks and eagles saw the lakes as we were seeing them now. Cozy bed-and-breakfasts and Victorian retreats abound in this soothing environment, a favored summer refuge for New Yorkers since the 1800s. You can see a Curtiss Pusher among the many historical artifacts in the Glenn Curtiss museum in

Hammondsport, the aviation pioneer's hometown. A few miles south of Lake Seneca near Elmira is Harris Hill, one of America's first major soaring sites, developed in the 1930s. The excellent National Soaring Museum at Harris Hill is well worth a visit, and the place is still an active gliderport. For a different kind of excitement, there is the Watkins Glen racetrack.

We droned on, over the interstate highway, and somewhere past Syracuse the ground to the north seemed to blend into the blueness of the sky well below where the horizon should have been. We had reached Lake Ontario, first of the vast inland seas that form the Great Lakes. Somewhere not too far ahead, where its southern shore neared its tip, was Niagara Falls. As we flew past Rochester, we had to make a choice. Should we circle the falls first and then land to see them from the ground or should we land first? We decided to land first.

It would be better to take a break from flying, see the falls from the ground, and then fly over them, being more prepared to notice the details. We started the descent into Niagara Falls International, the airport of choice on the United States' side, only a few miles east of the falls, and touched down on Runway 28L 3 hours and 20 minutes after takeoff from Hanscom. Our ground speed had been slowed down by a strong headwind along the 360-mile route, but we would gain it back on the way home.

The Canadian airport closest to the falls is St. Catherines, and Toronto is less than an hour away. The flight from Montreal takes about as much time as the flight from the Boston area. From New York, Philadelphia, and Washington, D.C., Niagara Falls is closer, but the routes go over sections of the Appalachian Mountains, which might create additional locally changeable weather, compared to the flatlands west of Albany. An advantage to flying to Niagara Falls from the east is that the weather systems approach from the west, and you can often scurry home ahead of a system if need be.

We piled into a cab for the 15-minute ride to the falls and looked at them from the United States' side first. The falls are formed as the Niagara River flows over a precipitous drop on its way from Lake Erie into Lake Ontario. Aesthetically beautiful and thundering with raw power, they are truly a wonder of nature. From the United States' side we sensed the power as we stood next to the rushing torrent and donned yellow raincoats to descend along a path for an even closer look. To fully appreciate the view, we had to walk across a bridge to the Canadian side (some non-United States visitors might need a visa to cross over into Canada, and should make sure that they have a United States visa that allows them to return). We soaked up the view, and then it was time for a late lunch, and the "piece de resistance," the aerial view.

We knew we would be practically over the falls as soon as we lifted off from Niagara Falls International westbound, and we confirmed with the FBO the well established procedures for flying over the falls. We had to inform the tower of our intention to circle the falls, and were told to report back on the tower frequency when we were through. There is a racetrack pattern to be flown clockwise, with one turn just south of the Horseshoe Falls, and another one to the north above the railroad bridge crossing the gorge.

Immediately after takeoff, we were cleared to switch to a common "falls traffic" frequency to announce our intentions and to monitor for other traffic. We entered the clockwise pattern at 2,500 feet MSL, which was approximately 1,800 feet above the falls. The recommended altitude for fixed wing aircraft is 2,500 to 3,000 feet; for helicopters, 2,000 to 2,200 feet; and for turboprops and jets with cruising speeds more than 150 knots, 3,200 feet and above. (Respect the altitude recommendations because the area is very noise sensitive.)

Our entry from the United States' side was quite dramatic. We saw no falls while approaching from the southern turnpoint, only an abrupt end to the river. Then, as we turned, the entire falls opened before us, and we picked up the magnificent view from the Canadian side heading for the northern turnpoint. We made a number of circuits, and on each one noticed details we had missed before. When we had our fill, we set course for home, climbed to 9,500 feet over a scattered-to-broken layer of clouds, and were on the ground at Hanscom Field two and a half hours later. Had we gone in a car or a bus, we would have just been arriving in Niagara Falls.

26

United States

Country rating: **Easy**

Charts: **Respective sectional or WAC**

Rental cost range:
  2 seat trainer   **$40-80**
  4 seat fixed gear   **$55-95**
  4 seat retractable   **$70-105**

QUALIFICATIONS AND LICENSE VALIDATION

License validation is required to fly United States-registered aircraft. Holders of licenses issued by ICAO member states face a relatively simple process for validation. Visit one of the Federal Aviation Administration's many flight standards district offices (FSDOs) scattered throughout the country, and present your pilot license, medical, and proof of identification. The documents must be current and the medical must be issued by the same country that issued the license. The FSDO will issue you, on the spot, an equivalent United States license, limited to noncommercial recreational flying. The United States license will be valid until the expiry of the original license.

An instrument rating will be covered by the United States' validation. Radio operator licenses are no longer required. The FAA is very flexible in issuing equivalent licenses, essentially operating on the principle of finding a way to grant a license, if at all possible, rather than looking for excuses to deny one. You can get an equivalent license even if you don't speak a word of English, restricted to flights not requiring the use of English. This sounds odd, but consider the vast number of American aircraft flying without a radio; to fly them, the language in which you read the aircraft manual and receive a thorough preflight briefing matters little.

It is the responsibility of the operator renting the airplane to assess your flying abilities. Expect a thorough checkride, including an instrument proficiency check if you plan to fly in instrument meteorological conditions.

Contact an FAA regional office and request the location of the most convenient FSDO to accomplish license validation and obtain any additional pertinent regulatory information:

Alaska Region; Anchorage, Alaska; 907 271 5645
Central Region; Kansas City, Kansas; 816 426 5626
Eastern Region; New York, New York; 718 917 1005
Great Lakes Region; Chicago, Illinois; 312 694 7000
New England Region; Boston, Massachusetts; 617 273 7244
Northwest Region; Seattle, Washington; 206 431 2001
Southern Region; Atlanta, Georgia; 404 763 7222
Southwest Region; Forth Worth, Texas; 817 624 5000
Western Region; Los Angeles, California; 213 297 1427

DOCUMENTS YOU SHOULD TAKE

Pilot license
Current medical
Logbook (not required by the FAA, but necessary for aircraft rental)

In addition, proof of identity is also required by the FAA, for which the most suitable document is a passport.

USEFUL FLYING ORGANIZATIONS

Aircraft Owners and Pilots Association
421 Aviation Way
Frederick, Maryland 21701
Telephone   301 695 2000

AOPA is an excellent national organization representing the interests of general aviation, including recreational flying. It provides a wide range of services for its membership, including chart and flight planning assistance. *AOPA Pilot*, the monthly magazine, is one of the best and is available to members by subscription only. AOPA is helpful to all visiting private pilots, especially if they belong to an international AOPA. The association is an excellent nongovernmental source for regulatory and nonregulatory information. Depending upon the circumstances, AOPA might also be able to provide advice or assistance if specific difficulties that require special attention arise, such as a violation.

Experimental Aircraft Association
3000 Poberezny Road
Oshkosh, WI 54903-3086
Telephone   414 426 4800

EAA represents the interests of homebuilders, antique aircraft flyers, warbird flyers, and aerobatic pilots. It heavily emphasizes amateur aircraft construction, and restoration. Its annual convention and air show at its Oshkosh, Wisconsin, headquarters is legendary. EAA publishes *Sport Aviation* magazine for its members.

Soaring Society of America
P.O. Box E
Hobbs, New Mexico 88241
Telephone   505 392 1177

This organization coordinates soaring in the United States, and controls and monitors all official badge and record soaring and national soaring competitions. It is an excellent source of information about soaring sites and opportunities in the United States. The society publishes *Soaring*, a monthly magazine available primarily by subscription.

The United States is only one place where Piper Cubs still fly.

WHERE TO FLY, WHAT TO FLY

The United States is where it all began. You can fly into Kitty Hawk and stroll the length of the Wright's first hop, and America is still one of the least restrictive and least expensive environments for the recreational flyer. It is still easy to avoid airspace requiring radio communication with air traffic control and cross the country from the Atlantic to the Pacific without having a radio on board or filing a flight plan. (Realize, though, that filing and activating a flight plan is a proven safety precaution and foregoing a flight plan is shortsighted, if not downright foolish.)

In part, America's open skies are due to a fairly tolerant regulatory attitude, compared to other countries—although the American government also is forever slapping general aviation with additional restrictions, some of which never go into effect due to pilot outcries—and, in part, due to the country's vast, sparsely inhabited spaces. Out West you can be on an IFR flight and not hear a word on the radio for 20 minutes, or you can fly VFR over cornfields for hours.

But the United States is also home for the world's most crowded skies. If you can handle the pace in some parts of the Northeast or Southern California, you will feel comfortable anywhere. The fairly unrestrictive regulations work well in these busy areas too, and the good safety record suggests that perhaps some other parts of the world could also do well with a bit less regulation and a bit more flying.

The backbone of recreational flying in the United States is the fixed-base operator, more commonly referred to as the FBO. The name is a catch-all phrase for an operator that can provide aircraft rental, flight instruction, fuel, maintenance, aircraft sales, and a variety of other services. An airport often has several FBOs, some competing, some complementary. Look for the FBOs with the flying schools and rental fleets and you will be in the right place. FBOs are commercial businesses and advertise in the local yellow pages. Their services and equipment vary in quality, so make it a point to visit a number of them and shop around.

The aeroclub, as it is known in the rest of the world, with its recreational facilities and social events, is uncommon in the United States. References to aeroclub rates at flying schools usually mean a break on rental costs for an annual membership fee. More common are club-like associations created by a specific interest in a special field of aviation, such as homebuilding or flying warbirds or antiques (EAA). Aircraft rental is rarely available from these organizations but you might be able to informally arrange flying in an exotic aircraft owned by the membership. EAA is the best source for information about grass roots flying clubs.

America is warbird country.

New York City

The general aviation airport closest to the city is **Teterboro** (201 288 1775) in New Jersey, across the Hudson River, not far from the George Washington Bridge. It is teeming with traffic, especially on the weekends, but in large measure it serves the private pilot. The New York skyline is a turn out of the pattern. **Lincoln Park** (201 628 8860), also in New Jersey, is a less crowded alternative north of Teterboro. North of New York City in the suburb of Westchester is **Westchester County Airport** (914 946 9000), a big general aviation field with limited airline traffic. On Long Island, close to the city, a good choice is **Farmingdale-Republic** (516 752 7707).

Washington, D.C.

There are a number of general aviation airports serving America's capital. Good choices for the visitor are **Montgomery County** (301 977 0124) to the north in Maryland, **Leesburg** (703 777 9252) to the west in Virginia, and to the southwest near Arlington, **Manassas** (703 361 1882), also in Virginia. Farther west in Maryland, but still within commuting distance is **Frederick** (301 662 8156), home of AOPA. Famous as one of the oldest small airfields in America dedicated to the private pilot (though now no longer providing FBO services, only tiedowns for locally based aircraft) is **College Park,** in Maryland.

Boston

Three large general aviation airfields conveniently ring Boston. To the north is **Beverly** (508 922 4280) near Marblehead. To the west is **Hanscom Field-Bedford** (617 274 7200), and to the south is **Norwood** (617 762 4750). Each has several large FBOs on the field with excellent fleets of rental aircraft, including light twins.

Orlando, Florida

Disney World is the star attraction here, and practically next door to Mickey and friends is **Kissimmee Airport** (305 847 4600). Fly with the local flying school and don't miss the warbird restoration facility and museum of Reilly Aviation (407 847 7477). Owner Tom Reilly is truly one of the masters in the warbird restoration business. **Orlando Executive Airport** (407 894 9831) in the middle of town is another good choice in this area.

Miami-Fort Lauderdale

There is a whole string of airports on this section of the Florida coast, always a favorite vacation spot for Americans fleeing the northern winter chill, and especially popular in recent times with sun-seeking northern Europeans. To the north is **Pompano Beach** (305 786 4135) and **Fort Lauderdale Executive** (305 491 1302). Big general aviation airfields between Fort Lauderdale and Miami are **North Perry** (305 962 5660) and **Opa Loca** (305 688 4462). South of Miami is **Tamiami** (305 238 6093) and the uncontrolled **Homestead General** (305 247 4883).

Chicago

The closest general aviation airport to the Windy City is **Meigs Field** (312 744 4787), practically downtown on the shore of Lake Michigan. Rentals are not available but it is an excellent airport of arrival if you fly into Chicago. It is a favorite of business jets and turboprops, and is open to everyone except student pilots. North of town in the suburbs is **Pal Waukee** (312 537 1200), and farther out is **Waukeegan Regional** (312 244 0055). To the west, a good choice is **Du Page County** (312 584 2211).

Los Angeles

As in most places in the United States, the visitor's choice is made difficult in the Los Angeles area not by too few airports but too many. **Torrance** (213 325 0505) and **Long Beach** (213 421 8293) are well within the limits of this sprawling city, close to the ocean. Farther south along the shore is **John Wayne-Orange County Airport** (714 755 6526). To the north is **Whiteman** (818 896 5271), an uncontrolled field sandwiched between **Van Nuys** (818 785 8838) and **Burbank** (213 840 8830). To the west is **Chino** (714 597 1731), an antique and warbird haven.

San Francisco

South of downtown San Francisco and the international airport are **San Carlos** (415 592 2550), **Palo Alto** (415 856 7833), and **San Jose** (408 277 5246). Out on the Pacific Ocean is the uncontrolled field of **Half Moon Bay** (415 573 3701). Across the Golden Gate, toward wine country, in this land where driving distances take on a whole new meaning are **Gnoss** (415 897 7101), **Santa Rosa Air Center** (707 576 9756), and **Sonoma County** (707 546 2567).

Grand Canyon

The airport serving the Grand Canyon and doing a brisk business in sightseeing trips is **Grand Canyon National Park Airport** (602 638 2446). Call in advance to find out if self-hire aircraft are available. Otherwise plan to rent in Las Vegas to the west, and fly in to view the canyon. The canyon region is an extremely environmentally sensitive area; therefore, check the *Federal Aviation Regulations* for specific Grand Canyon flight rules.

Grand Tetons, Wyoming

The general aviation airfield serving this stunning mountain range is **Jackson Hole** (307 733 7682). Yellowstone National Park is close by, to the north (there are flight restrictions over Yellowstone).

Niagara Falls

Arrange local flights over the world famous falls from **Niagara Falls International** (716 297 4494). Use this field as an airport of arrival when you fly in from elsewhere. The falls are a short taxi ride away. Well established circling procedures are in effect over the falls.

Soaring

Soaring is not as widespread in the United States as it is in Europe, but America's topographical features offer some of the best soaring sites in the world, exceptionally suited for flights of world record standards. Rental sailplanes are available at all sites (call ahead to make specific arrangements).

Ridge Soaring (814 355 1792) in Julian, Pennsylvania (between Williamsport and Altoona) is the prime soaring center along the famed Appalachian ridges where world record flights of more than 1,000 miles have been flown several times. Black Forest Glideport (719 648 3623) near Colorado Springs at the foot of Pikes Peak, is the world's premiere site for high altitude wave flying. Soaring flights to altitudes more than 40,000 feet high have been made here. Some good cross-country soaring sites where you will find outstanding desert soaring are Hobbs (505 392 1177), New Mexico (headquarters of the Soaring Society of America), Minden (702 782 7627 or 7353), Nevada, and Estrella (602 568 3218), Arizona. A picturesque eastern soaring site more akin to what you would find in Europe is Sugarbush (802 496 2292), Vermont, in the Green Mountains only 120 air miles northwest of Boston, Massachusetts. Call the Soaring Society of America for their most recent site listing if you have trouble with the telephone numbers.

TOURING

The United States is the ideal country for cross-country touring. Airplane rental costs are low compared to the rest of the world, and the vast and varied terrain provides limitless opportunities to wing your way over beaches, deserts, mountain ranges, and gentle farmland. Consider the following flights for a flavor of the possibilities.

Bahamas

The closest islands in the Bahamas are only 60-80 miles east of the Miami-Fort Lauderdale area. Once you make initial landfall, the big overwater leg is behind you and you can island-hop for the rest of the trip. There is a wide range of choices in accommodations from glittering resorts in Nassau and Freeport, to hideaway coves on the more remote islands accessible only by airplane. Get one of the good pilot's guidebooks to the Bahamas, available at most pilot shops. Many FBOs along the Florida coast make rental aircraft available for flights to the Bahamas, in spite of the situation with the aerial drug smugglers. The FBO will also provide all the emergency equipment required for the overwater flight and will brief you on United States and Bahamian customs regulations in effect at the time of your flight. This trip is a longtime favorite with visiting foreign pilots.

Experimental Aircraft Association

Wittman Field at Oshkosh, Wisconsin, is EAA's home airport, within easy light airplane range from the Chicago area. A flight to visit the excellent world-class museum is highly recommended and an easy day-trip. From Chicago, head north along Lake Michigan, fly inland around Milwaukee, and pick up the highway to Fond du Lac and Oshkosh. Total distance from Pal Waukee is only about 150 miles. The best time to be in Oshkosh is during the annual EAA convention, but that might not be the best time to fly in because more than 16,000 other aircraft are utilizing airspace and ground facilities. Many visitors prefer to fly in to nearby Fond du Lac or Appleton during this time. If you do decide to fly in or around Oshkosh during the convention, get an information and flight briefing package from the EAA well in advance. Be sure to make accommodations reservations months, perhaps a year or more, in advance. If you can't plan that far ahead, rooms in private homes are usually available up to the last minute. EAA operates a housing hotline for assistance.

Los Angeles, Las Vegas, Grand Canyon

High roller or not, you will find a visit to Las Vegas, Nevada, a rewarding flying experience. Leave the Los Angeles Basin across the San Bernardino mountains to face several choices across the mountains. Along the highest routes, the ground rises beyond 6,000 feet, with the surrounding peaks extending above 11,000 feet. Follow Victor airways or the divided highways. Past the mountains, expect good CAVU desert conditions. Be wary of high winds and density altitude across the mountains, and smog and fog in the Los Angeles basin. Total distance to Las Vegas is approximately 200 miles.

If you haven't bankrupted yourself in Las Vegas, continue to the Grand Canyon, another 120 miles to the east in Arizona. Carefully observe the flight regulations and restrictions when you fly over this stupendous work of nature that renders insignificant anything man can create. Plan sightseeing flights for early morning or late afternoon when the light is at its best. Land at Grand Canyon National Airport to visit the canyon overland.

New England

The New England states have a lot to offer to the visiting recreational pilot ranging from day-trips to leisurely touring. Attractive mountain routes extend over the Berkshires in Massachusetts, the Green Mountains in Vermont, and the White Mountains of New Hampshire. These areas are especially admirable during the fall foliage season, perhaps prettier here than anywhere else. A great variety of trees is in the forests, and the leaves of each species turns a different color, splashing the mountainsides with a blazing display of reds, oranges, and yellows. Sugarbush in the Green Mountains is a scenic destination and an outstanding soaring site, open from April to November.

Popular oceanside destinations are Cape Cod, and the islands of Martha's Vineyard and Nantucket, less than two hours flying time by light airplane from the Greater Boston area, and not much more from New York City. For more coastal pleasure, fly up the rugged shores of Maine to Camden, Bar Harbor, and beyond.

Big Sur

Another scenic coastal flight awaits you on the other side of the continent along the Pacific Ocean, south of San Francisco. Follow the shoreline from immediately south of San Francisco to Santa Cruz, Monterey, Big Sur, and farther until you encounter the divided highway north of San Luis Obispo. It is about 150 miles one way, and some of the most unspoiled coastline around.

Transcontinental

Crossing the United States from ocean to ocean in a light airplane is the ultimate flying adventure for the visitor from abroad. Following a good checkout, many FBOs are quite willing to rent an airplane for the two or three weeks necessary to complete the round-trip. Their only requirement is a minimum number of flying hours per day (usually three), which you are likely to do anyway. The total distance one way will be approximately 2,600 to 3,000 miles depending on the route. In the average four-seater at 120 knots, expect approximately 50 hours of flying time for the round-trip. If you fly approximately eight hours a day (two four-hour legs), you can do it coast-to-coast one way in three days. Given weather delays and sightseeing time, for the round-trip, two weeks might be tight, three weeks is about right, and a month is luxurious. Fifty hours is a lot of flying and requires reliable equipment, so make sure you are dealing with a good FBO. Arrange for the checkout in the airplane that you will take on the trip, and check it out while the FBO is checking you out.

Dogfight fantasy

America is Disney World, a land of extremes where more fantasies come true than anywhere else, if you can foot the bill. Entrepreneurs specialize in bringing to the layman experiences that elsewhere are only dreamed about, and air combat and a P-51 Mustang checkout are among them at surprisingly reasonable prices for what you get. The dogfight fantasy has titillated nonmilitary pilots since the earliest days of air combat, and now you can finally know if you could have, had you been given the chance.

Two companies specialize in teaching air combat, both using military trainers in which you fly against opponents and try to shoot them down with an electronic or laser gun, in an honest-to-goodness dogfight. Place an opponent into the gunsight, squeeze the trigger, and if you score, the electronic or laser gun sets off a smoke generator and your enemy goes down in flames.

Air Combat USA (P.O. Box 2726, Fullerton, CA 92633, 714 522 7590) out of Fullerton Airport in Southern California operates Siai Marchetti SF 260s. Sky Warriors (404 699 7000 for recorded information and a brochure) operates out of Fulton County Airport in Atlanta, Georgia, and flies ex-Navy Beech T-34s. Both schools are modeled on the U.S. Air Force and Navy air combat schools and are run by ex-military pilots, many of whom have combat experience. They are serious places of learning with strict safety standards and rules of engagement, but are open to pilots with any level of experience, and even nonpilots who want a demonstration. Both offer several learning modules from basic to advanced where they teach the combat maneuvers and then let you fight it out with an opponent. Each session consists of approximately one to one and a half hours of flying and extensive preflight and postflight briefings. The whole flight is videotaped and the tape is presented to you. Cost per session was approximately $500 at both schools in late 1990.

But what if you missed World War II and the P-51 Mustang that should have had your name written on it? You can have it now, all 2,000 horsepower, if you call Doug Schultz or Lee Lauderback (407 846 4400). Based at Kissimmee Airport in Florida, next to Disney World, this is no namby pamby ride in a cramped jumpseat where the radios and armor used to be. This Mustang has full dual controls and you do all the flying. You receive instruction just like in a Cessna 172, and you find out once and for all if you could have done it, had you been born at the right time. The two partners in the Mustang are both professional jet pilots, and Schultz flew two tours in Vietnam in Phantoms and is a graduate of the famed Top Gun air combat school. Their Mustang goes for approximately $1,000 per hour. Book well in advance.

A word of caution. Fantasies do come and go. There is every reason to believe that these firms will be in business for a long time to come, but you never know. Should you not find them, others will surely have stepped into their place. America's quest for fantasies-come-true is never ending. Seek and ye shall find.

VFR QUESTIONS & ANSWERS

What are good sources for VFR regulations? The *Federal Aviation Regulations* and *Airman's Information Manual* are government documents that cover regulations and procedures. Pilot shops at airports and aviation mail-order houses carry publications extracting the pertinent information for private pilots. Be sure the information is current.

How can I get a weather briefing? The most common method is to call the flight service station (FSS) covering your area, for a verbal briefing. A recording will tell you what information to have ready for the briefer. You can also get a recorded briefing for your local area. Every airport has the telephone numbers you need. Selected FBOs have equipment for a briefing via a computer terminal, which might be free or cost a nominal fee.

What are VFR visibility and ceiling minimums? Three miles and 1,000 feet in controlled airspace. One mile and clear of clouds in uncontrolled airspace. Refer to the FARs and AIM for full details on VFR minimums.

Is night VFR permitted? Yes, there is no differentiation between day and night VFR traffic rules and minimums.

Is single-engine IFR permitted? Yes.

Must I file a flight plan for VFR flight? No. A flight plan serves to mobilize a search-and-rescue effort in case the flight is overdue; therefore, it is always advisable to file a flight plan, especially because an international visitor might become disoriented over unfamiliar terrain.

May I fly the airways VFR? Yes, provided you adhere to the specified hemispherical VFR altitudes and have a current altimeter setting from within 100 miles of current position.

Must I be in touch with ATC en route, on or off the airways? No, unless you are flying in airspace requiring radio communication, such as a terminal control area (TCA).

Is VFR on top permitted? Yes.

ADDITIONAL INFORMATION SOURCES

AOPA's *Aviation USA*, published annually, is a densely packed manual with all the aviation information the visiting recreational pilot would want. The book is a combination of the popular handbook and airport directory, which were formerly published separately. The handbook portion is essentially an abbreviated pilot training manual with enhanced material on aviation regulations and the airport directory is an excellent guide to public-use airports, including airport diagrams, frequencies, and nearby lodging.

Private Pilot is a monthly magazine for recreational flyers. It focuses on flight test reports on production, experimental, and antique aircraft, how-to and technique articles, write-ups on places to fly, and aviation product reviews. Available on newsstands.

Flying covers a wide range of topics, from sport aviation to flight test reviews of business jets. Each issue contains a good mix of articles drawn from divergent segments of aviation. It is widely read by pilots and nonpilot aviation enthusiasts. Available on newsstands.

Air Progress is another magazine with an emphasis on pilot reports, antiques, and some military aviation. Available on newsstands.

Plane and Pilot is also for the recreational pilot, covering type reviews, product news, and technique. Found on newsstands.

AOPA Pilot is the association membership magazine, covering general aviation from trainers to business jets. It also summarizes the latest in new product and legislative news.

Sport Aviation is the EAA's monthly magazine, emphasizing pilot reports on homebuilts and antiques, coverage of building projects and techniques, and membership news. Available by subscription only as part of the EAA membership fee.

Soaring is the monthly magazine of the Soaring Society of America, available primarily by subscription.

A telephone book's yellow pages in all cities and towns have a wealth of FBO listings.

27

A low-level dash past Manhattan

IT WAS A FRESH SPRING MORNING along the entire East Coast, perfect for a day of aerial wandering just to watch the ground go by. My friend John, who lives and flies in Europe, was in town and I was wondering where to fly, what experience would he most remember back home. I considered the hills, the forests and river valleys, the Atlantic Coast and the islands around my home base near Boston. They would all be fun, but there were plenty of such destinations where he flew. Then my eyes settled on what at first glance looked like the most forbidding airspace on the map: the New York TCA. That was the place . . . . The day was ideal for one of the greatest visual feasts still available to private pilots in our age of crowded skies: a VFR flight past the Manhattan skyline below the tops of most skyscrapers.

At first, John thought I was kidding, but he took a closer look at the New York Terminal Area Chart and saw it himself. Woven in under the restricted airspace of the city's three major airports, JFK, La Guardia, and Newark, routed over the Hudson River slipping past Manhattan, was indeed a corridor allowing VFR flights to transit the area under the TCA, below 1,100 feet. Examining the elevations of obstacles on Manhattan's southern tip, he also noticed that we would be looking up at the top of the World Trade Center.

The VFR corridor survives because it is primarily over water—American airspace regulations are still motivated by common sense—and the unsuspecting citizenry on the ground in New York and New Jersey is safe from airplanes falling out of the sky. In spite of the best efforts of some overzealous bureaucrats, more regulation is usually imposed only if the aviation community fails to live up to the trust placed in it to fly responsibly and professionally under a minimum amount of rules and restrictions necessary to assure safe flight. The corridor's excellent safety record has so far proven the regulators right. The only extra equipment needed is a transponder with altitude encoding capability (Mode C), required within 30 miles of any TCA, tuned to the 1200 code for VFR flights.

The World Trade Center from the VFR corridor.

Most rental aircraft based near TCAs are likely to be transponder equipped. Of considerable surprise to some visitors is that you don't even need a radio to fly the corridor if your departure and destination airports are uncontrolled. At or below rooftop level among reinforced concrete skyscrapers VHF reception is spotty at best.

As with any other flight, the key to viewing the skyline safely is thorough preflight planning. At first glance the TCA's many circular sectors might appear intimidating, but a careful look reveals that flying through the VFR corridor is a fairly simple exercise. It requires intercepting the Hudson River well north of the city or where it meets the Atlantic, depending upon the direction of arrival, and following it at or below the altitudes prescribed for the various segments.

John and I would approach New York from the northeast. We charted our 150 mile route along the VORs and planned to approach the Hudson on a heading from the Carmel VOR, 14 miles north-northeast of Westchester County Airport. This would put us over the water 20 miles north of midtown Manhattan just outside the New York TCA with plenty of time to set up our run along the river. We carefully studied the VFR corridor on the map, strapped ourselves into my Piper Arrow, and set course for the Big Apple.

We climbed to 8,500 feet en route, navigating with ease in the unlimited visibility. We could see the Atlantic roughly 30 miles to the east, paralleling the course all the way, and could even make out Long Island's narrow smudge off the left wingtip as we approached Hartford, Connecticut.

Approximately 25 miles from Carmel we set up a shallow descent to put us over the VOR at 3500 feet and took another good look at the New York TCA Chart. The Hudson's silvery ribbon appeared across the windshield, and at the 11 o'clock position, thin, densely packed spikes jutted skyward on the horizon: Manhattan.

Over Carmel we altered course to 255 degrees and continued descending. The Tappan Zee Bridge, the first prominent VFR landmark along the northern approach to New York City, came into view left of the nose. Two miles north of the bridge was the boundary of the TCA. We would have to be below 3,000 feet to slip under it. We made it comfortably, turning southbound along the river at 2,500 feet. Traffic over the Hudson keeps to the right as on a road, so we edged to the side. The landing light was also illuminated to make the aircraft more visible. Power was reduced to 65 percent for a slower speed, safely creating additional reaction time and happily prolonging the experience.

We monitored Westchester Approach but did not contact them. They were probably too busy to provide VFR traffic advisories and, at any rate, as you approach the river, they usually just tell you to watch yourself and call them back on the way out if retracing the route to depart the area.

We continued the descent, crossing the Tappan Zee Bridge. Approximately six miles downstream we had to descend to 1,500 feet, and in another five miles we had to be at or below the final descent altitude of 1,100 feet. We estimated the 1,500-foot mark in relation to a small swivel of land jutting into the river on the west bank beyond the bridge. On the left was Yonkers, a sea of densely packed residential brownstones, dwarfed by the skyscrapers now looming ahead. The George Washington Bridge stretched across the Arrow's nose, and a mile this side of the bridge was the 1,100-foot stepdown boundary and the northern tip of Manhattan Island. We chose to be conservative and two miles before the bridge the aircraft was straight and level at the final cruising altitude of 800 feet, picked for comfortable margin below the bottom of the TCA. Then, with the best intentions, all that remained was to hold altitude very precisely, watch for traffic like a hawk, and try not to be overwhelmed by what was about to come.

That last intention never quite works for me. The George Washington Bridge flashes by close enough to touch, the altitude below seems to shrink all of a sudden, and the teeming, massive concrete canyons dwarf the aircraft and strike me with awe, no matter how often I run the gauntlet.

On the first pass it is difficult to notice the details apart from the two most obvious landmarks, the Empire State Building and the World Trade Center. John and I gazed at the whole busy skyline, establishing our bearings, and beginning to consider what to look for on the way back. We also picked out the traffic flow over the water and established our place in it. The informal system worked well. There was a steady procession of light aircraft and sightseeing helicopters in each direction, all flying at approximately the same speed.

The aircraft carrier is a museum, the cruise ships still sail.

It was vital to be aware of all traffic in the area, but the most important reference point, and the easiest way to slip into the flow, was to keep an eye on the airplane immediately ahead of us (the guy who couldn't see us). We matched its speed and quickly developed a sensation of driving down a highway. A string of landing lights identified the oncoming traffic on the other side.

Flying north to south was advantageous, providing enough time to anticipate the first specific sight we wanted to see off the southern tip of Manhattan,
the Statue of Liberty. The grand old lady in oxidized green stood out well against
the water and looked quite delicate from above. At her feet was Ellis Island, the
processing center from where, in another time, so many immigrants took their
first long, uncertain look at Manhattan before being let in or sent back by the
immigration inspectors. It is a nicely restored museum now, a cornerstone of the
American experience well worth a visit. We were careful to keep the lady to our
west to avoid intruding into Newark's airspace. The TCA floor in the narrow strip
between the statue and the New Jersey shore descends to 500 feet, and immediately on shore it extends to the ground, but to the east we were safe up to 1,100
feet.

Ahead, the water widened out into a bay and beyond it, sharply outlined
against the open Atlantic was the Verranzano Narrows Bridge connecting Brooklyn and Staten Island. For pilots flying the VFR corridor the bridge is the southern gateway, the initial landmark northbound, and the exit point for southbound
aircraft.

John and I could have cared less about the glitter of Atlantic City's casinos or
a short flight south along the New Jersey shore. Besides, we hadn't yet had
enough of Manhattan. Our pass downriver had been but a fleeting glimpse. We
rolled into a standard left turn over the bay, and as we completed the 180, we
found ourselves staring straight at the world of global high finance (high dun-
cery?) at approximately the level of the 50th floor. The massive cluster of banks in
the Wall Street area at Manhattan's southern tip, dominated by the twin towers
of the World Trade Center, is a formidable sight. We also saw the East River
branching off to the right, and spanning it, the Brooklyn Bridge, built in the
1880s (the first of the three nearest bridges seen when looking upriver). The
water below was dotted with the frothy wakes of ships of all sizes. Dozens of
light aircraft and helicopters darted on their way in our immediate vicinity. A
well-choreographed procession of jetliners filled the sky above, and tiny cars
crawled along like ants on Manhattan's cluttered streets. Frenetic activity, reminiscent of being on Fifth Avenue at rush hour.

We slipped into close formation with the World Trade Center's twin towers to
set course back up the Hudson. We had dined atop one of the towers, on the
107th floor in the Windows on the World restaurant, which is twice as high as the
northbound altitude. Daredevils had parachuted off them, climbed them from
the outside like mountains, and one had walked across a tightrope stretched
between their summits.

Then they were gone, and the Empire State Building towered above us,
bringing black-and-white visions of a rampaging King Kong. We could also easily
identify the delicate art deco Chrysler Building, the glossy white Citibank Building with its top sliced off at a sharp angle to make it look distinctive, and Rocke-
feller Center and Trump Towers at the upper end of Fifth Avenue near Central
Park.

Below us, tied up at the passenger docks, was an ocean liner. At another berth by 44th Street, was a boat that catches the eye of every pilot flying the corridor, a retired aircraft carrier, now serving as an aviation museum. To our layman's eyes the flight deck looked ridiculously small even for the Arrow, let alone the Navy jets that catapults once launched daily over distant seas.

The carrier turned our thoughts to the options we had if the fan stopped. At the base of the unattractive escarpments on the Jersey side we saw quite a few flat, open spaces, mostly rail depots serving the port. Some of the docks on the New York side could have also been useful in a pinch. The aircraft probably would have been wrecked, but the chances of walking away from an emergency landing appeared to be good. A few years ago, a pilot put a small plane on one of the docks without a scratch when the engine quit. A more sanguine option for less urgent emergencies is New Jersey's Teterboro Airport, four miles west of the George Washington Bridge.

Banishing thoughts of bellying in, we droned past Central Park and on beyond Harlem. Then we were over the George Washington Bridge once again, in a gradual climb, bound for home.

We were lucky that day: unlimited visibility, hardly any wind, and too early in the spring for bone-rattling thermal turbulence. I never fly the corridor unless the visibility is at least 7 miles. That is approximately the length of Manhattan, and might sound conservative, given the 3-mile VFR visibility minimum, but the corridor is too crowded for any distance less than 7 miles, especially on weekends. Fortunately, New York has done a good job of pollution control since the 1970s and most of the time the weather is sufficiently changeable to produce a reasonable number of clear days every month.

Turbulence is sometimes hard to avoid. Often a bumpy ride is the price for

A gift of France, a lasting symbol of America.

the good visibility brought by the passage of a cold front. The prevailing westerlies take some of the bumps out of the ride, placing corridor traffic upwind of Manhattan's concrete when they blow. But on particularly windy days the lee side of the Jersey escarpments will also throw off strong turbulence that can be thoroughly unpleasant and even dangerous. On days of strong gusty crosswinds the corridor is best avoided. One way to reduce the risk of flying in turbulence is to fly through the corridor early in the morning or late in the afternoon. Late afternoon on a CAVU day is best because Manhattan is magical then, glowing in the setting sun's orange warmth.

The VFR corridor is readily accessible from any airport within a 150-mile radius from Manhattan, requiring at most a half-day commitment for the flight. In addition to the usual sectional charts in use for VFR flying, the detailed New York VFR Terminal Area Chart is essential equipment for the uninitiated pilot. It is also a good idea to study a detailed Manhattan street map to help identify and anticipate the specific sights you want to see.

Visitors to New York can easily make arrangements for rental airplanes with FBOs at a number of area airports. Perhaps the most suitable airport is Teterboro in New Jersey, only a few miles from the George Washington Bridge. It can be reached even by bus from the Port Authority of New York. An alternative toward the north is Westchester County Airport, the home of several well established FBOs. On Long Island, Republic Airport near Bethpage is a good choice, easily reachable by rental car on the Long Island Expressway.

The quickest and perhaps the safest way to experience the skyline flight is to do it with a local instructor. But if you are in a position to get checked out thoroughly in the New York airspace environment and have plenty of time to carefully plan a VFR corridor flight on your own, go it alone. And whatever your choice, be sure to take plenty of film.

Central and
South America

28

Mexico

Country rating: **Moderate**

ONC Charts: **H-22, H-23, J-24, and K-25; WAC charts with radio frequencies preferred.**

Rental cost range:

  2 seat trainer **$60-80**

  4 seat fixed gear **$70-100**

  4 seat retractable **Prices not available**

QUALIFICATIONS AND LICENSE VALIDATION

The Mexican civil aviation authorities will validate a foreign license for noncommercial VFR flight in Mexican registered aircraft, but require the applicant to pass a written examination in Spanish on Mexican air laws and regulations. In addition, your medical must be validated by CENMA. The logistics required might take more time than you have on a short visit, and not everyone who would like to rent aircraft in Mexico speaks Spanish.

These conditions would make it difficult to arrange flying in Mexico, were it not for the ready availability of rental aircraft in the United States for flights into Mexico. However, before they turn you loose toward Mexico, the United States FBO might want more pilot/renter information, compared to an FBO elsewhere in America, due to drug smuggling. Considering all these factors, Mexico is rated moderate.

DOCUMENTS YOU SHOULD TAKE

Pilot license
Current medical
Logbook
Radio operator license (if separate from pilot license)

Have all the original documents with you.

USEFUL FLYING ORGANIZATIONS

Director of Civil Aviation
A. Universidad, No. 70-5 Piso
Mexico 12, D F Mexico

This government agency is responsible for general aviation matters, including license validation. Inquire here about the procedures to validate your medical.

WHERE TO FLY, WHAT TO FLY

Mexico has long been a favorite destination of recreational flyers from north of the border. Remote beaches, fine resorts, deep-sea fishing, Mayan ruins, and tales of pirates, rustlers, miners, and missionaries, are all attractive draws. The present problems with aerial drug smugglers have tightened border crossing procedures (you have to land on both sides of the border to return to the United States), and fuel in Baja California is available at controlled airports only, but these are minor inconveniences.

Approximately 50 of the largest airports in Mexico are government run and services at them are handled by the Aeropuertos y Servicios Auxiliar (ASA). The availability of fuel is more certain at these airports than at private fields, and is also less expensive. Fuel in Mexico is 80/87 to 100/130 octane. It is advisable to take engine oil.

There are three general areas for recreational flying: the West Coast, Baja California, and the Yucatan. Mexico is mountainous between the two coasts (Mexico City International Airport is at 7,300 feet). Most recreational pilots stick to the coasts. Mexican FBOs at the airports near the larger towns might have aircraft available for rent to pilots with a validated license, but the best bet is to rent in the United States and fly south.

Make sure you have the additional aircraft liability insurance to cover the airplane in Mexico. The coverage has to be issued by a Mexican insurer, but is available through MacAfee and Edwards in Los Angeles (213 388 9674) and other United States agents. Necessary papers to fly a rental airplane across the border are a notarized affidavit from the owner authorizing the trip, and the usual aircraft registration, airworthiness certificate, weight and balance, and radio station license.

The West Coast. This is the traditional strip—a rather long strip—for those in quest of plush resorts in the sun: from Mexicali on the United States border to Acapulco, is approximately 1,400 nautical miles. There are good resorts every couple of hundred miles along the route, many of them with their own airstrips. Main fly-in destinations from Mexicali southbound are Guaymas, Mazatlan, San Blas, Puerto Vallarta, Manzanillo, Zihuatanejo, and Acapulco. Puerto Vallarta is the most logical point to branch off to Guadalajara and Mexico City. Check the tourist guidebooks for specific places that attract you.

Baja California. Pilots in the Southwest United States have been flying to this wild, windswept, peninsula for decades to get away from it all. Though somewhat tamed by development over the last 20 years, it is still an outstanding place of escape—700 nautical miles long—and parts of it are as remote as ever, especially beyond La Paz. Many of Baja's numerous dirt strips serve hideaway resorts. Fuel is available at controlled fields only. Tijuana and Mexicali airports are convenient border crossings. Destinations southbound are Bahia Los Angeles, Mulege, Loreto, La Paz, and the San Jose del Cabo area at the southern tip. A treat between January and March at Scammon Bay near Guerrero Negro Airport (about halfway down on the Pacific side) is the chance to watch the migration of vast numbers of huge California gray whales from the Bering Sea, 6,000 miles to the north, off the Alaska Coast.

The Yucatan. This peninsula in eastern Mexico on the Carribean has become the country's showcase tourist haven in the last 10 years. Major resorts of Cancun and Cozumel have large airports. Nearby is the 4,100-foot paved airfield of Chitchen Itza, site of Mexico's most famous Mayan ruins. The Yucatan is a relatively long trek for a light airplane following the coastline, even from Brownsville on the east coast of Texas more than 700 nautical miles to the north, with few attractions in between (and you have to get to out-of-the-way Brownsville first). An alternative is a long haul over water from points along the United States Gulf Coast and the tip of Florida. Perhaps something could be arranged locally at Cancun or Cozumel.

VFR QUESTIONS & ANSWERS

What are good sources for VFR regulations? Consult the Mexican AIP. The Texas Aeronautics Commission's *Mexican Flight Manual* also contains some useful information.

How can I get a weather briefing? You may pick up briefings in person at the major airports, or by telephone. American pilots have been known to call the closest United States FSS long distance. Another source of weather updates is commercial airline pilots who will relay information to flyers in out-of-the-way places.

What are VFR visibility and ceiling minimums? In controlled airspace, minimums are 3 miles and 1,000 feet; in uncontrolled airspace, one mile and clear of clouds.

Is night VFR permitted? No.

Must I file a flight plan? You must file a written flight plan for all flights in Mexico. If you fly from uncontrolled airfields, you must file retroactively upon arrival at a controlled field—odd, but true.

May I fly the airways VFR? Yes. Observe the standard ICAO hemispherical separation altitudes.

Must I maintain en route radio contact with ATC on or off the airways? No.

Is VFR on top permitted? Yes, if a VFR descent and landing is assured at the destination.

ADDITIONAL INFORMATION SOURCES

If you are going to do any serious flying in Mexico, you must get Arnold Senterfitt's *Airports of Baja California and Northwest Mexico*, and *Airports of Mexico and*

Central America, as well as Don and Julia Downie's *Your Mexican Flight Plan.* Other helpful publications are the Texas Aeronautics Commission's *Mexican Flight Manual* (free), and the Aeropuertos y Servicios Auxiliares *Welcome to the Friendly Skies of Mexico.*

29

Argentina

Country rating: **Moderate**

ONC Charts: **Q-26, Q-27, R-23, R-24, S-21, and T-18**

Rental cost range:
- 2 seat trainer   **$50-80**
- 4 seat fixed gear   **$100-140**
- 4 seat retractable   **$150-180**

QUALIFICATIONS AND LICENSE VALIDATION

Argentina requires local validation of your license, but if it is issued by an ICAO member state, the procedure is routine. On the strength of your license and supporting documents, the Civil Aviation Authority in Buenos Aires will issue a validation. No written or flight test is required, other than a checkout by the operator from whom you will rent.

Ease of flying in the country is rated Moderate for several reasons. Argentina is rich in bureaucratic traditions and validation might take more than a few days, potentially putting a time constraint on the short-term visitor. Once validation is in hand, you might find it difficult to rent aircraft to fly solo on short notice. Due to Argentina's harsh economic conditions and the high costs of flying, operators customarily under insure hull values, and are very picky about the pilots to whom they are willing to rent for solo flight. They will turn you loose solo only after they fully trust you, and that will most likely take more than one checkride.

After you are signed off to fly solo on a validated license, a minor inconvenience is a security measure restricting you to flying only in and out of controlled airports and having to file a flight plan for all flights, conditions that do not apply to holders of Argentine licenses. For short-term visitors, the smoothest option might be to fly with a safety pilot.

If you do go ahead with validation, it might be worth your while to rely on what makes all things possible in Argentina: the "Amigo Principle." Everything becomes much easier if a well-placed friend or a friend of a friend is there to help things along. The whole country thrives on it. Argentinians don't impress easily,

Iguasu Falls on the Argentine Brazilian border.

but once you become their "amigo," it is for life. Whatever is theirs, is yours, and they will spare no effort to unselfishly help you in any way they can. Rather than go straight to the Civil Aviation Authority, go out to an airport first. Take a flight or two with the flying school and hang out with the locals for a while. You'll enjoy it, and soon you will find not only good friends, but all the help you will need.

An instrument rating generally cannot be validated for noncommercial recreational flying in Argentina; you must have a commercial license to be issued an instrument rating, and foreign commercial licenses are not validated, as a rule.

Speaking at least elementary Spanish is most helpful everywhere, and is a must outside big cities, where ATC and airport officials are unlikely to speak a word of English.

Apply for validation in person, rather than through the mail.

DOCUMENTS YOU SHOULD TAKE

Pilot license
Current medical
Logbook
Radio operator license (if separate from pilot license)

Bring original documents and your passport, plus at least six passport quality photographs, to be on the safe side.

USEFUL FLYING ORGANIZATIONS

Direccion de Fomento y Habilitacion
Edificio Condor
Calle Comodoro Pedro Zanni 250
Oficina 437
Buenos Aires, Argentina

Government agency responsible for aircrew licensing and license validation. You may approach them on your own, but it is best to merely get information from them and subsequently apply for validation with the assistance of the establishment with whom you will fly.

Confederacion Argentina de Entidades Aerodeportivas (CADEA)
Anchorena 275
Buenos Aires, Argentina
Telephone   87 2320

Argentina's sport aviation organization representing all branches of sport aviation: a good source of information. Publishes *Aerodeportes*, Argentina's most informative magazine for recreational pilots.

WHERE TO FLY, WHAT TO FLY

Argentina is a vast country of great natural beauty with much to offer to the recreational pilot, from the rich central farm country, to the ranch land of the pampas, the Patagonian desert, the continent's wild and windy southern tip, and the formidable Andes to the west.

Since its earliest days, aviation has been important in bridging Argentina's great distances. The heritage of the 1930s mail pilots, immortalized by Antoine de Saint-Exupéry in *Night Flight*, lives on today. Yes, the country has serious economic problems, and has also had its political troubles, but the will to fly is not easily broken, and recreational flying continues to be widely available.

Commercial flying establishments are to be found near most large population centers, and the country is also covered by a network of aeroclubs, mostly subsidized by the Air Force. Buenos Aires, the country's capital, is ringed by several general aviation airports, and an aeroclub equipped with one or two Piper Cubs and Luscombes and perhaps a more modern four-seater is to be found at the local airport outside most of the bigger cities.

Argentina has its own aircraft industry, producing mostly military aircraft, among them the Pucara ground attack aircraft, which became known worldwide during the Falklands/Malvinas conflict.

A light airplane of local manufacture that you should try to fly is the Aero Boero 115, a ragwing taildragger reminiscent of the Super Cub.

Flying opportunities can be found around the destinations you are most likely to visit:

San Fernando, (744 8859, Aeroposta Argentina), is a half-hour drive north of Buenos Aires. Several operators offer flying in an assortment of classic taildraggers. There are limited opportunities to fly more modern equipment. The telephone number is that of a local flying school whose owner, Zenon Lopez Wallace, speaks English well. Popular flights out of San Fernando are over the picturesque Rio de La Plata estuary, the farm country to the west and the Atlantic coastline southeast of Buenos Aires.

Don Torcuato, (748 0763, Aero Kern), is Buenos Aires' main general aviation airport, in a northern suburb adjacent to San Fernando. It is an international point of entry, popular with pilots flying to nearby Uruguay and Brazil (mostly on business). It is also home to several big flying schools operating fleets of Tomahawks, Cessna 152s, and an assortment of four-seaters. Flying opportunities for the recreational pilot are the same as San Fernando.

San Justo and Matanza are two smaller grass strips around Buenos Aires best visited by airplane from San Fernando or Don Torcuato.

San Andres de Giles, approximately 50 miles west of Buenos Aires is home of the Club Albatros, the capital's main soaring center. The club offers a good selection of gliders, and dozens of private owners also base their sailplanes here.

Mendoza Airport is home to the Mendoza Aeroclub. Mendoza is Argentina's principal town in the Andes along the main highway to Chile. It is also famous for the vineyards around it. For pilots, it is an excellent staging point for some spectacular Andean flying. Respect the locals' cautious attitude to flying the mountains.

Batan serves Mar del Plata, one of Argentina's main beach resorts, about 220 nautical miles southeast of Buenos Aires. You can fly locally out of Batan, or make it a destination out of Buenos Aires.

Rio Gajegos is a principal coastal town on the southern edge of Patagonia. Flights over Patagonia can be arranged at the local aeroclub. About 150 nautical miles west in the Andes is the Moreno Glacier. Depending on weather and available equipment, a flying visit from Rio Gajegos might be possible.

Ushuaia, 180 nautical miles south of Rio Gajegos, is in the heart of Tierra del Fuego, at the southernmost tip of South America. The area is becoming increasingly popular with tourists and has a major airport. Though the status of the local aeroclub is uncertain, according to the Argentine flying community, there are always possibilities to arrange private flights over the spectacular network of channels and straits made famous by Magellan and Darwin.

VFR QUESTIONS & ANSWERS

What are good sources for VFR regulations? Consult the Argentine AIP, and local instructors.

How can I get a weather briefing? Most airports have weather offices or teletyped weather information.

What are VFR visibility and ceiling minimums? Argentina deviates in some respects from the ICAO minimums. Check the AIP.

Is night VFR permitted? Restricted night VFR is permitted.

Must I file a flight plan? Flight plans must be filed when flying from controlled airports. Visitors on validated licenses can only fly between controlled airports.

Is VFR on top permitted? No.

ADDITIONAL INFORMATION SOURCES

There are two good aviation magazines in Argentina. *Aerodeportes*, published by CADEA, the country's sport aviation organization, is the magazine to be read by active recreational pilots. It carries a good selection of articles on local flying clubs, flight tests, how-to topics, and accident reports. It also covers parachuting, soaring, and model airplanes. It has a good selection of commercial and classified ads. The other magazine, *Aeroespacio*, is aimed more at the aviation enthusiast who is not necessarily a pilot. It is sponsored by the Air Force and mostly covers military and commercial aerospace topics.

A good source of information on airplanes for sale is *Aerovente*, a local version of *Trade-A-Plane*. The Argentine yellow pages are surprisingly devoid of ads for flying schools and clubs, but a brief call to one of the more extensively covered charter operators would probably get you on the right track quickly.

30

Overcoming
language problems
on the ground

WHILE THE LANGUAGE OF THE AIR IS ENGLISH practically everywhere, the language of the ground is still as varied as the palaver at the proverbial Tower of Babel, and there are quite a few places where English is not widely spoken as a second language. Once you make it to the airport, someone in a position of authority will speak sufficient English, broken as it might be, to get you airborne with as little fuss as possible.

How do you make contact in the first place and get to the airport if, for instance say, Tagalog is the local tongue and you don't speak a word of it. The language barrier is one good reason to take a package tour. Because the average package tour does not extend to the local flying club for the pilot in the group, far too many pilots come home saying "What fun it would have been to track down that Skyhawk I saw over town, if only I spoke Tagalog." It is a mistake not to try, because with a little organization you will find that Skyhawk every time without speaking a word of the local language.

GETTING THROUGH ON THE PHONE

After you have identified the most likely telephone numbers, the first obstacle is getting through on the telephone to someone who can speak English. Where English is not in wide use, the secretary or receptionist handling the flying club telephone might not speak it. The key on your end is to get a local to make the initial call.

You will find the hotel concierge or receptionists as helpful in making this call as they are in making dinner reservations or arranging theater tickets. It is important to brief them accurately. Tell them to explain that you want to do recreational

One motion of the hand is worth a thousand words.

flying under whatever arrangement is possible, and would like to speak to someone in English about it.

If the English on the other end is too broken for a telephone conversation, get the concierge or receptionist to make the appointment for you. You will find it much easier to sort out the details face to face, once you get there.

Ensure that the organization called on your behalf does offer recreational flying, if not, ask your caller to inquire who does. It might take a call or two, but eventually you will reach the right place. And make explicitly clear that when you say "small airplane," you mean one engine, one propeller, and four seats. It is embarrassing to show up at the airport to discover that when you said "small Cessna" the concierge thought you meant the Citation I instead of the Gulfstream IV (true story).

Don't be put off if the initial response to the person calling on your behalf is that foreigners can't fly in the country. This is a common first response by receptionists or secretaries on the other end who think you just want to show up and rent an airplane like a car. Be politely insistent to the person making the call for you, that your wish, initially, is to accompany a local pilot. Explain the rest later, in person.

GETTING TO THE AIRPORT

The next step is getting to the airport. If you are lucky, you might be able to arrange a ride over the telephone with someone from the flying club. If not, you can take a taxi, rent a car, rent a car with a driver, or even take public transportation, depending upon where you are. Get advice from the people at the flying school and the hotel staff. If you go by taxi, be sure to find out beforehand if it should wait for you. In some places, especially the more out-of-the-way general aviation airports, taxis might not be readily available and it might be difficult to call one.

THE DRIVER-INTERPRETER

In many developing countries where self-drive car rental is not practical, a popular but somewhat expensive option is renting a car with a driver. Many of them speak English well enough to translate any basic information that is necessary to reach the English speakers at the airport. An added advantage is that you will not have to worry about transportation home when you are done. Cars with drivers often rent at half day or full day rates, so you might be able to combine time at the airport with other activities around town. Countries where the driver-interpreter option is a good choice are Kenya, India, Brazil, and the Philippines.

PERSONALIZED PHRASE CARDS

If you are not taken to the airport by someone speaking rudimentary English, and it is not widely spoken, a practically fail-safe way to communicate is with personalized phrase cards. Take an index card and write on one half of it, in English, each phrase that you are likely to need. Have the concierge or someone who speaks English write the same phrase on the card's other half in the local language in local script. It is much more effective to show the phrase card with a useful phrase rather than trying to say the phrase and massacring it beyond comprehension:

"Take me to . . . ."

"I have an appointment to see Mr. . . . ."

"Please write on this paper what time Mr. . . . will be here."

"Give my driver directions to . . . ."

"Wait here until I return." (Useful if the driver does not speak English.)

"Please get me a taxi."

"May I make a telephone call to . . . ?"

"Destination." Various destination cards are a must. Always carry one listing your hotel, complete with address, plus one or two other major hotels where English is always spoken, and consider carrying a card with the address of your country's embassy or consulate.

"In my country, this is not against the law!" Some folks claim that this card is the most important phrase card, to be carried with you at all times in any country.

31

Brazil

Country rating: **Moderate**
ONC Charts: **M-26, M-27, M-28, N-26, N-27, N-28, P-27, P-28, and Q-28**
Rental cost range:
  2 seat trainer   **$50-75**
  4 seat fixed gear   **$80-100**
  4 seat retractable   **$100-150**

QUALIFICATIONS AND LICENSE VALIDATION

The Departamento de Aviacio Civil will validate foreign licenses for private VFR flight, but the requirement to pass a written test on Brazilian air laws and regulations will deter most applicants on short term visits. Even if you do speak Portuguese, the time it would take to arrange the examination and process the paperwork may take longer than the time you will spend in Brazil. Apply in person.

DOCUMENTS YOU SHOULD TAKE

Pilot license
Current medical
Logbook
Radio operator license (if separate from pilot license)

If you go ahead with license validation, you will also need to present your passport. A notarized photocopy of your logbook is sufficient.

USEFUL FLYING ORGANIZATIONS

Departamento de Aviacio Civil
Divisao de Habilitacao
Aeroporto Santos Dumont
Rio de Janeiro

Uirapuru being readied for flight at Rio de Janeiro's Jacarepagua Airport.

This government office is responsible for license validations.

APPA-Brazil
Caixa Postal 19009
04599 Sao Paulo, Brazil
Telephone 55 11 881 0433
Facsimile 55 11 853 7152

APPA is the local AOPA organization. Though it is difficult to fly solo for foreigners who do not speak Portuguese, there is a lot of internal Brazilian general aviation, and APPA is its representative organization. APPA is a good source of contact if you want to get in touch with local business or recreational flyers. It is better to call than write.

EAA Chapter 854
c/o Mr. Sergio Machado
Av. Cristovao Colombo 508/1405
Porto Alegre, 9000 Brazil

This is an active EAA chapter founded in 1983 in this southern agro-industrial town. Members are very hospitable to visitors. The chapter organizes a Brazilian EAA convention every two years.

WHERE TO FLY, WHAT TO FLY

Brazil has one of the world's most sophisticated aviation industries. Its best known product abroad is the Bandeirante series of commuter airplanes, but a whole variety of other aircraft are produced, ranging from license manufactured Pipers to sophisticated military jets. There is a far flung domestic air carrier network, and Varig is among the best international airlines. Many private companies and wealthy individuals own their own aircraft, and some of the best bush flying anywhere is to be found in Brazil's vast rain forests.

It is unfortunate that the civil aviation authorities have not structured the regulations to make it easy for visitors from abroad who do not speak Portuguese to participate in all this flying. Nevertheless, flying in the company of a local safety pilot is easy to arrange and Brazil's many stunning aerial sights make it worth the effort. The aeroclubs offer temporary memberships on a case by case basis.

Noncommercial recreational flying is available in Brazil through a national network of nonprofit aeroclubs. There are no commercial flying schools, except for helicopter schools. The aeroclubs are well equipped with Uirapurus, a Brazilian basic trainer reminiscent of the French Rallye. Other aircraft in wide aeroclub use are Piper Warriors, Archers, and Arrows, produced locally under license.

A sampling of the aerial sights in store for you are Rio de Janeiro, the coast and many islands south of Rio, the immense city of Sao Paulo, and the magnificent Iguasu Falls.

Jacarepagua Airport, (325 9044), is the home of the Rio branch of the Aero Club do Brasil. The club is well equipped with a range of light aircraft, and the members are very friendly. Jacarepagua is a short drive south of Rio and is the place from which to stage flights past this outrageously beautiful city. The area over Rio south of Sugarloaf along the beaches is unrestricted to light aircraft at low altitudes. You can fly right down Ipanema and Copacabana up to Sugarloaf, and around the Corcovada, the famous statue of Christ overlooking the city. With some additional flight planning you can also also go into Santos Dumont Airport on the bay north of Sugarloaf, from where the Rio-Sao Paulo shuttle still flies immaculate Lockheed Electras. Jacarepagua is also ideally located for flights along the coast and islands south of Rio, where some of the most secluded resorts are to be found.

Marte, and the aeroclub there, serves Sao Paulo, Brazil's main business and industrial center. Sao Paulo is not particularly attractive, but its drab high-rises go on for miles and miles. To be down low over this immense sea of a city is downright intimidating. After a week in Sao Paulo it is great to fly out to somewhere green.

Iguasu is the town and airport at the famous waterfalls where the borders of Brazil, Argentina, and Paraguay come together on the banks of the Parana River. The falls rank right up there with Victoria Falls and Niagara Falls. Nearby is the immense Itaipu dam. At last count, there was a small local aeroclub at Iguasu. As with all big falls, the best way to fully appreciate Iguasu, is by seeing it from the air.

Other big Brazilian towns where you will find aeroclubs are **Recife**, and **Campinds**, **Porto Alegre**. Visit EAA Chapter 854 in Porto Alegre. Its 1990 Brazilian EAA convention attracted 160 airplanes and 25,000 visitors. Aircraft built by members include a Christen Eagle.

Soaring centers are at **Bauru** and **Tatui** in Sao Paulo state, and **Osorio** in Osorio R.G.S.

VFR QUESTIONS & ANSWERS

What are good sources for VFR regulations? Consult the Brazilian AIP, and the club instructors.

How can I get a weather briefing? The controlled airports have met offices or relayed weather information.

What are VFR visibility and ceiling minimums? Brazil has adopted the ICAO VFR minimums for controlled airspace. These minimums also apply in uncontrolled airspace.

Is night VFR permitted? No.

Must I file a flight plan? You must file a flight plan for all flights totally or partially within controlled airspace if the services of ATC are to be used.

May I fly the airways VFR? Yes. You must make periodic position reports and adhere to the standard ICAO VFR hemispherical cruising altitude rules.

Must I maintain en route radio contact with ATC off the airways? On flights in controlled airspace for which you filed a compulsory flight plan, you must make occasional position reports.

Is VFR on top permitted? No. Flight above clouds is not permitted if the cloud cover obstructs more than 50 percent of the ground.

32

Chile

Country rating: **Moderate**
ONC Charts: **R-26, Q-26, R-23, S-21, and T-18**
Rental cost range:
  2 seat trainer **$30-40**
  4 seat fixed gear **$45-55**
  4 seat retractable **$65-80**

QUALIFICATIONS AND LICENSE VALIDATION

Pilot licenses issued by ICAO member states are routinely validated by the Chilean civil aviation authorities for flying Chilean registered aircraft VFR. No written examinations or flight tests are required. Expect a comprehensive checkride from the operator who will rent the airplane. The country rating is Moderate because the validation paperwork might take a week or two, possibly presenting a time constraint for the short-term visitor. Apply in person.

Though, theoretically, English is the international language of aviation, a good basic knowledge of Spanish would be most useful for flying in Chile.

DOCUMENTS YOU SHOULD TAKE

Pilot license
Current medical
Logbook
Radio operator license (if separate from pilot license)

Bring your original documents for inspection, as well as half a dozen passport photos and photocopies of these documents and your passport to leave with the authorities.

Weaving among the Andes.

USEFUL FLYING ORGANIZATIONS

Ministry of Transportation
Department of Aviation
Subdireccion de Operations, Seccion Licencias
Eliondoro Yanez 2394
Santiago

This agency handles the validation of pilot licenses.

Club Aereo de Santiago
Tobolaba Airport
Santiago

The Club Aereo Santiago celebrated its 60th anniversary in 1988. It is Chile's premiere aeroclub, and is an excellent place to seek advice on license validation and flying opportunities throughout Chile.

WHERE TO FLY, WHAT TO FLY

Chile is more than 2,000 nautical miles long and barely between 100 and 200 nautical miles wide. It is a country of great natural beauty, primarily because to the east it lies for its entire length along one of the most impressive mountain ranges in the world, the Andes. What makes the Cordilleras los Andes so dramatic is that it is very narrow and rises almost vertically from sea level to between 10,000 and 20,000 feet for most of its length. This makes for spectacular recreational flying.

Chile is an air-minded nation. The airplane's utility in this rugged, mountainous land has been recognized since the earliest days; Aeropostale ran a scheduled air mail route in the 1930s from Santiago across the Andes to Europe via Buenos Aires. Today Chile has an aircraft industry, producing the Pillan, a tandem two-seat military trainer developed for the Chilean Air Force by Piper Aircraft Corporation.

A wide network of aeroclubs is found throughout Chile, with a number of commercial flying schools. Though many of the clubs are self-supporting, the Chilean Air Force provides significant direct and indirect support, making club flying delightfully inexpensive by world standards.

The Andes mountain range is a soaring pilot's paradise, and there are a number of well equipped soaring clubs. The crossing of the Andes by sailplane is one of the most rewarding soaring flights in the world, accomplished only by a handful of high performance sailplane pilots at the top of their sport.

Tobolaba Airport in an eastern suburb of Santiago is where most visitors are likely to make their initial contact with the Chilean recreational flying community. The airport is home to the Club Aereo de Santiago. The club is well worth a visit, because it is a club most of us would make up if we were asked to define the ideal aeroclub. First, consider the equipment: 10 Piper Tomahawks, 4 Cessna 152s, 2 Cherokee 140s, 4 Cherokee 180s, 4 Cessna 172s, 2 Piper Arrows, 2 Cessna 182 RGs, 2 Cherokee Six 260s, 2 Beech T-34s, a Pitts S-2A, a Decathlon, a Lake Amphibian, a Super Cub, and a Twin Comanche.

The restaurant is notable with every table covered by a white tablecloth, the china and glassware is first class, and the food rivals the outstanding eateries in town. Then there is the patio bar, the big, sparkling, kidney-shaped pool, and the well maintained tennis courts. In short, it is an aero-country club. And that is how it is used. There is no rushing in to bore holes in the sky and disappearing as soon as the airplane is tied down. Most members come for the day and socialize at least as much as they fly. Temporary memberships can be arranged, and members are always ready to go flying with a visitor.

Tobolaba also has a commercial flying school operating mostly Cessnas, for those who find such an arrangement more convenient and less demanding on their time than going the aeroclub route.

The area around Santiago, Chile's capital, is one of the more attractive regions to fly over. A short flight to the north is 23,000-foot-high Mt. Aconcagua, the Andes' highest peak. Also to the north, just before Aconcagua, is the main trans-Andean land and air route to Mendoza in Argentina. At the midpoint the flight passes over Portillo, Chile's world class ski resort. The minimum crossing altitude for this route is 14,000 feet, yet the flight from Tobalaba to Mendoza in an aircraft with the performance of a Piper Arrow is only an hour and a half. Two additional VFR routes through the Andes are farther to the south with MCAs of 12,000 and 10,000 feet, respectively.

The Chileans treat the Cordilleras los Andes with great respect and don't venture into the valleys except in the most ideal conditions. Even on the clearest days, wind generated turbulence can bend a light airplane's wings. Fortunately there is gentler flying over the narrow coastal area around Santiago, above the the country's best vineyards and the picturesque and historic port of Valparaiso. The big TCA around Cerrillos, Santiago's international airport, has to be carefully circumnavigated.

Aerodromo Municipal de las Condes, in the northeastern section of greater Santiago is home of the Club de Planeadores de Santiago, one of Chile's best soaring clubs. The club has a wide selection of equipment, ranging from trainers to high performance fiberglass sailplanes. There is also a restaurant, pool, and tennis courts.

Temuco and **Purranque** are airports in the southern lakes region of Chile; each airport has an aeroclub.

Chile's lakes region about 400 miles south of Santiago is rich in alpine charm. It is beautiful from the air and is a favored destination of pilots from far afield.

Farther south near the tip of the continent are the wild glacial regions and the thousands of islands around the Strait of Magellan. The weather can be atrocious. You are unlikely to fly down all the way here in a light airplane from Santiago or even from Temuco, but if you plan to be in the area, check out beforehand if any flying clubs are active at Puerto Natales and Puenta Arenas. Seek advice from the Club Aereo de Santiago.

VFR QUESTIONS & ANSWERS

What are good sources for VFR regulations? Consult the Chilean AIP and get a good briefing from an instructor. Chile is a security conscious nation; obtain an especially thorough briefing about prohibited airspace.

How can I get a weather briefing? Most bigger airports have met offices for a personal visit, or call for a briefing.

What are VFR visibility and ceiling minimums? Chile deviates from the ICAO standards in some respects. Check the AIP.

Is night VFR permitted? No.

Must I file a flight plan? You must file a flight plan for all cross country flights.

Must I maintain en route radio contact with ATC on or off the airways? You must make brief, periodic position reports.

Is VFR on top permitted? No.

ADDITIONAL INFORMATION SOURCES

The Club Aereo de Santiago publishes *Tobalabaereo*, a newsletter, and various periodic bulletins.

33

Weekend wings over Latin America

LEVEL AT 6,500 FEET, we were dwarfed by the Cordilleras Los Andes towering above us at three times our altitude. Barely 20 minutes flying time behind us was Santiago de Chile, home base for the weekend. Ahead to our right was 23,700 feet Mt. Aconcagua, the highest peak along the massive wall of sheer rock and snow that snakes for 2,000 miles down the length of South America's Pacific coast. The well used Cherokee 180 was humming along at 120 knots, yet I felt as if we were motionless, a soothing illusion in the dead calm air of early morning. It was a Saturday in November, and the sun already promised a fine southern summer day.

Since takeoff from Tobolaba Airfield in an eastern district of Santiago, we had been skirting rugged milk chocolate foothills and now we approached the valley near the town of Los Andes. To the east, the valley narrowed; it was the main route across the Cordilleras to Mendoza, barely an hour away in Argentina, and it had a minimum crossing altitude of 14,000 feet.

I thought of Henri Guillaumet while making a course adjustment to tentatively sample the first few miles of the pass on this weekend joyride. He left Santiago on Friday, June 13, 1930, in his robust Potez 25 biplane on the same route we had flown, and rounded the corner into this pass in a long, continuous climb for his 96th crossing of the Andes.

Guillaumet was the most experienced trans-Andean pilot of Aeropostale, the plucky French line whose fliers had been pioneering the air mail route from South America to Europe in their frail craft of sticks and fabric since 1928. Fellow pilots were Antoine de St. Exupéry, who modeled Pellerin in *Night Flight* after Guillaumet, and the legendary Mermoz.

Fewer than 15 minutes after he passed the point where I turned around and headed toward the coast, Guillaumet was blinded by snow showers. He saw a pass, he took a chance, and was hopelessly trapped. He was in a bowl over a frozen lake at 19,000 feet, ringed by a wall of peaks. His little Potez 25 flew on and

Panama City: Paitilla Airport in the foreground.

on barely above the field of ice, but wouldn't climb an inch. The aircraft ran out of fuel in two hours and glided to a landing with Guillaumet's guidance. For five harrowing days, he slogged through the snow during the day and burrowed into it at night, surviving to complete a total of 343 Andean crossings before Aeropostale went bankrupt a few years later.

Andean weather is as capricious as ever: flying in sunshine one minute, engulfed by billowing snow clouds the next, pummeled by raging winds that might make short work of you even when visibility is a hundred miles. Guillaumet's tale and dozens more since, with fewer happy endings, have convinced Santiago's weekend flyers to admire the Andes mostly on flights parallel to the mountain range, but to avoid all the mountain passes in favor of the beach. A handful of experienced mountain pilots do fly the Andes regularly, and the Aero Club de Tobolaba gives mountain flying instruction, but the chief instructor's personal permission is required for any mountain pass flying.

We set up a lazy circle in the valley to admire Aconcagua and the surrounding sawtooth peaks. Passengers were Joaquin from Spain, who had done his share of scooting around the Pyrenees in a Piper Tomahawk, and Hugo, who was working on his professional ratings at the aeroclub and hoped to soon fly jets for a paycheck. "Once a year, when conditions are perfect, the aeroclub organizes a mass crossing of the Andes to Mendoza," said Hugo. "Everyone is carefully briefed, and the experienced pilots lead the pack. But if the wind picks up when you are halfway across, or the thermals kick in . . . Dios mio! On my first crossing with the group in a Cessna 182, the turbulence really went crazy. Vario pegged up one minute, down the next, full control deflections with no effect. It didn't last long but I said every prayer I knew, and a few I made up."

"Let's go to the beach," said Joaquin. We turned west and flew past more barren foothills that anywhere else would have passed for a respectable mountain range. The weather had played a trick on us. Clear over the Andes, a thick blanket of fog hid the centuries-old coastal town of Valparaiso and its promised charm. Still, the fog, too, was pretty in its own way, and we meandered over it for some time before carefully circumnavigating the formidable Santiago TCA back to Tobolaba.

Some weeks later I was in Rio de Janeiro. I had come to know its striking natural beauty from decades' worth of airline posters long before my first visit. With some assistance on the phone by the hotel concierge I discovered that the place where I really wanted to be was the suburb of Jacarepagua, home of the Aero Club do Brasil. It was a postcard perfect day, and I relished the thought of seeing the world's most scenic city from the air. Unfortunately, so did the entire membership of the club, or so it seemed. They did have some interesting aircraft, but it had rained three weekends in a row and all were booked solid. Still, this was an excellent chance for some hangar flying.

The Aero Club was run more like a training camp; groups of students assigned to an instructor, learning not only by doing, but also by observing each other. It is the only game in town, free of commercial competition. The aero clubs receive a mix of support from industry and the government, and are the only places that provide initial fixed-wing training, after which the students' prospects are quite good. Aviation has an important role in the wild, inaccessible spaces of this vast developing land, as well as a rich heritage going back all the way to Santos Dumont, who many Brazilians believe to be the first man to fly a heavier-than-air machine.

Not all the airplanes on the Aero Club's ramp looked unfamiliar: a Warrior, an Arrow, or so I thought, until told that they were a Tupi and a Corsico. Brazil has gone to great length to develop its aircraft industry. Embraer's line of commuter aircraft and military trainers are exported worldwide and the country also produces several foreign designs on license, among them a line of Pipers that have all been given Brazilian names. Basic instruction is in a Uirapuru 150-hp side-by-side two-seater resembling a French Rallye design of the '60s.

I wanted to fly a Fokker T-21, a racy looking two-seat taildragger of '50s vintage. It had a big faded shark mouth, and promised quite a workout with its small rudder. Instead, because of the club's full schedule, I was offered an unexpected treat: my first flight ever in a light helicopter. A helicopter FBO that was located a few hangars from the club gave lessons during the week in a Bell 47. In the midst of scenic rides, he would fit me in for an introductory lesson just before lunch.

Flying the Bell was like chewing gum, patting your head, and rubbing your stomach at the same time—on a stool in a fish bowl. The instructor always snatched back the controls in the nick of time, but my dilettante ideas of real danger raced ahead of his professional perceptions, and once in awhile he sure fooled me: would have been nice if I spoke Portuguese, too. When he took over the controls, and the world around us stabilized, I had time to take note of the outrageously clear visibility. We darted and hovered at will and I was hooked on helicopters for good.

Sport aviation was everywhere as we whirled above the magnificent beaches. Ultralights droned in slow motion south of the airport, colorful hang gliders were staying aloft for hours along a massive ridge overlooking a particularly attractive strip of sand (dual flights are available; all the hotels have the brochures), and some fortunate soul was even earning some money towing banners up and down the beach front.

My next stop was Buenos Aires, Argentina's capital with an old-world flair. The country was in economic crisis, the annual inflation rate at 7,000 percent. What would my flying options be, if any at all? First, in an apartment in the old city, I found Ricardo Schillaci in the midst of a pile of Stearman parts, many of which he fabricated from scratch himself. We talked of the Argentine vintage airplane scene. His immaculate Stearman project was nearing completion. Someone at his local airport was restoring a Staggerwing, and in 1986 a local Robin restoration, which took 13 years, won the FAI's Phoenix trophy, the world's grand champion of grand champion awards. The only drawback in these hard economic times was that most restorations were leaving Argentina for dollars as soon as the last coat of dope was dry.

Then came a chain of telephone calls to friends of friends, and in the end, a difficult choice. On Sunday morning on the tarmac at San Fernando Airport, just north of Buenos Aires, I had to choose between a silver-and-blue Luscombe 8 or a fiery orange Piper Cub. The Luscombe was tempting. I had never flown one and had heard its landing gear could be quite demanding. I dearly love to fly Cubs, and would immediately feel comfortable in this one. In the end, my nonexistent Spanish and the broken English of Rodolfo, my local accomplice, decided the day. The chances for misunderstandings and errors would be reduced while flying an aircraft that I already knew. Handpropping the Cub proved easy as she purred to life on the first lethargic swing.

The scene we taxied past on the way to Runway 23 was local airport, USA, circa 1940s as Norman Rockwell would have painted it. Quonset hut hangars of corrugated metal, and on the grass out front, Cessna 120s, Luscombes, Piper Cubs, and even a stock Apache that looked like it had just rolled off the Lock Haven assembly line. "Argentina is the best place to fly classic airplanes today," explained Zenon Lopez Wallace, the proprietor of Aeroposta Argentina, which rented the Cub. "In the 70s when the economy was booming, everyone was running around in the latest airplanes and the old taildraggers were gathering dust in the back of the hangars. Now the fancy machines have all been sold abroad and we have rediscovered stick-and-rudder flying. The sad thing is that except for a few well-to-do business people, we now don't have the choice to fly anything else." When the choice returns, as it surely will, I hope they will continue to fly the ragwing fleet that saw them through.

Rodolfo and I took a right turn out of San Fernando and set course for the Rio de La Plata. Buenos Aires is only a few miles downstream from where the Rio Parana and the Rio Uruguay merge to form this formidable river—you cannot see the other side. We never flew higher than 800 feet and lost ourselves for a long time among the marshland and the countless tributaries and maze of creeks. We circled sailboats and cabin cruisers, rowboats and outrigger canoes, and watched weekend retreats, accessible only by water, slide past below. And when we were alone with the riot of bushes and trees, we eased on down as close as we dared, and felt the exhilaration of speed in the ponderous little Cub.

Then we were over the northern suburbs and Buenos Aires was off to our left, the downtown airport clearly visible. It is only for airliners now, but well worth a visit for the rare, if somewhat unkempt airplanes in its open-air museum. For awhile we flew west, passing Don Torcuato, the city's other general aviation airport, before we circled around back to San Fernando. It, too, is affected by the economic crisis, but the local flight schools mostly instruct in Tomahawks and 152s.

In some ways, the best part of the day came later, in the local cafe, where we "hangar flew" well beyond the time available. I heard of the aeroclubs in most small towns, a Cub, or a Luscombe, or two, subsidized by the air force, which are the best places to fly for less. But that far out, Spanish is a must. We talked of Zenon's cargo flights in 707s to North Africa and we delighted in discovering which obscure desert hamlets we both knew. And we were joined by Signor Cilveti, a marvelous old gentleman who flew Avro Lancastrians (Lancaster bombers converted to civilian use) across the Atlantic just after World War II and then traded up to DC-4s. Well into his 70s today, Cilveti still runs his air taxi service with a Cessna 310 and a Skymaster. In his 27,000 hours of flying, he had seen far more of the world from above than the rest of the pilots at the table had seen, combined.

Sunday night: heading for home. The 747 has just climbed out of Buenos Aires and is slowly rising to its initial cruising altitude of 29,000 feet. Only a door on the upper deck separates me from the cockpit's friendly reddish glow. It would be nice to sit in a jump seat and ask the pilots doing the driving if a Waco is waiting for one of them somewhere in a country barn. But the door remains locked, the cockpit off limits. The hijackers and terrorists have seen to that.

I think of San Fernando in the inky darkness behind us, Rio's beaches, and the Cordilleras. Scribbled in haste among my notes are telephone numbers for Anna, Julietta, and Gabriella. Only another pilot would believe that we had never met, that they were merely friends of friends asked to help because they spoke English well, a trail of cheerful voices on the telephone that ended at the fiery orange Piper Cub in an Argentine field.

34

Panama

Country rating: **Easy**

ONC Charts: **K-25, K-26, L-25, and L26**

Rental cost range:

  2 seat trainer **$60-80**

  4 seat fixed gear **$80-120**

  4 seat retractable **Generally not available**

QUALIFICATIONS AND LICENSE VALIDATION

Pilots holding a license issued by an ICAO member state need to obtain validation, but this is an easy administrative process. Apply at the Direccion de Aeronautica Civil at the address below, presenting your license, logbook, and current
medical. No written or flight test is required except for the usual checkride at the
flying school where you intend to rent an airplane.

Unless you are in Panama for some time and want to maintain solo flying
rights, you might consider flying with a safety pilot instead. Touring opportunities are limited, and to fully appreciate the canal from the air it is best to have a
guide.

DOCUMENTS YOU SHOULD TAKE

Pilot license
Current medical
Logbook

Have the original documents with you. A radio operator's license is not required,
according to the civil aviation authorities.

On final to Paitilla.

USEFUL FLYING ORGANIZATIONS

Direccion de Aeronautica Civil
Air Security Office, License Section
40 Street, Balboa Ave., De Diego Building
Panama City, Panama

Panama's civil aviation authority, responsible for license validation.

Aeroclub Enrique Malek
Paitilla Airport
Paitilla, Panama

Nonprofit aeroclub, very helpful to visitors. Operates single-engine Cessna equipment.

WHERE TO FLY, WHAT TO FLY

A flight over the Panama Canal is a must for every recreational pilot visiting Panama. But while it is the main attraction, other opportunities include flights to nearby islands and rough bush strips.

Paitilla Airport in suburban Panama City is the country's main general aviation airport. It is the base of the Aeroclub Enrique Malek, as well as at least one commercial flying school. Both fly Cessna 150s and 172s. A lot of commuter airlines that connect to domestic destinations fly Islanders, Twin Otters, and a collection of smaller twins. Because Paitilla is much closer to the city, it is preferred to the much larger international airport.

The flight over the canal can be flown comfortably in about an hour in a Cessna 150 or 172. You will leave Paitilla on a northerly heading. As the continent narrows, it also twists in a big S in an east-west direction and the Canal cuts across the continent along a north-south line (in fact, if you want to qualify as a trivia quiz entry, at one point of the narrows, you can fly east from the Atlantic and reach the Pacific).

One novelty of the canal flight is that in good visibility you can see the Atlantic and the Pacific soon after takeoff. You can get to within two miles of the canal, which positions you for a perfect view. It is best to fly low level in one direction to see the details and return at a higher altitude to see how narrow the isthmus really is. Be sure to read about the canal and study a map of it prior to your flight to better understand the canal's history and operations.

Other aerial excursions, which you can combine with a look at the canal, are to the San Blas Islands on the Atlantic side, and Contadora Island off the Pacific coast. The San Blas Islands are home to an Indian tribe that still lives as it has for centuries. An overnight stay in rustic conditions is possible. Contadora is a pleasant beach resort to enjoy for a day or an extended stay.

Exposure to bush flying technique can be arranged with a local flight instructor who has bush flying experience. Undeveloped strips are scattered throughout the jungle.

VFR QUESTIONS & ANSWERS

What are good sources for VFR regulations? Consult Panama's AIP.

How can I get a weather briefing? From an airport weather office.

What is the status of Panama's VFR regulations? Panama is currently revising its VFR regulations to bring them into conformity with ICAO standards. By publication this process might have been completed. Check upon arrival and obtain a thorough regulatory briefing from a local instructor.

35

Puddle jumping in Panama

"EIGHT FOUR SIX, CLEARED TO LAND," came the controller's voice through the speaker. It had been a memorable flight. We had just completed a nonstop out-and-return crossing of the American continent in a Cessna 150. It had taken approximately one and a half hours, sightseeing included. No, you did not miss anything in the news.

We had just flown the length of the Panama Canal from the Pacific Ocean to the Atlantic Ocean and back, a round-trip of approximately 70 miles. We were in the 150 of the Aero Club Enrique Malek of Panama City and I was doing what I always try to do on weekends during business trips, catch up on flying and the sights at the same time.

I found Aeroclub Enrique Malek's telephone number in the yellow pages and had someone (at the local office of the company that I work for) who spoke Spanish call early in the week because weekend schedules tend to fill up quickly everywhere. Yes, they could rent me a Cessna 150 or 172, and Jose Harris would be pleased to accompany me on an orientation flight.

The type of flying that I choose during foreign travels depends upon available time, equipment, and scenery—and whether the dollar fell out of bed or soared to new heights that morning. My first preference is to get checked out in and get as much experience as possible in any interesting airplane not easily available in the Boston area. A good look at the local scenery is a close second. I usually get a local sign-off in a common light airplane only if I am in-country for awhile or if I owe rides to friends. My stay in Panama was brief, the equipment familiar, and the Canal one of the greatest engineering feats of all time. This would definitely be a scenic flight.

The aeroclub was at Paitilla, Panama's main general aviation airport in a pleasant suburb. It was a short taxi ride from most hotels and even within walking distance from some. "May you have interesting approaches." I silently paraphrased the ancient Chinese curse while examining the runway jutting into the

Pacific. Bordering the runway, close in, was a massive row of high-rise apartment buildings that made the runway look more like another neighborhood street rather than a landing strip.

Air traffic was coming and going at a furious pace. Commuters were hustling fares to remote jungle communities and the islands off Panama's coast. Weekend pilots were out in force.

Jose was in his early 20s, and spoke English well. He flew Bandeirantes for a living with a local commuter line, and was a part-time instructor at the Aero Club on the weekends. He came with a big canvas bag. "Survival kit," he explained.

The entrance to the Panama Canal's Gatun Locks, in the right channel, from the Atlantic.

Among its contents was an enormous machete to hack our way out of the jungle if need be. I didn't ask how many times people like me have made him play canal guide, or what they thought of the machete.

The best scenic flights are low and slow, so I had chosen the 150. The ground formalities were minimal. Though both civilian and military controllers watch over the canal (there are several military airfields and thousands of soldiers nearby), it was enough to air file a flight plan for a VFR scenic tour. We taxied out behind two ungainly Trislanders and were cleared to go in sequence. We took off toward the Pacific and I made a left turnout while Jose air filed our flight plan.

We leveled off at a mere 1,000 feet and continued a wide left circle around Panama City to pick up the canal. We could clearly see the huge bridge that takes the Pan American Highway across the canal's entrance. We also picked up the three sets of locks on the Pacific side and moments later we were looking not only at the Pacific Ocean to the left, but also the Atlantic Ocean to the right through good visibility.

We eased to within two miles of the canal, as close as the regulations allow, and paralleled it toward Colon, its entrance on the Atlantic side. I had been reading *The Path Between the Seas*, but no book could do as much justice either to the enormity or the ingenuity of this turn of the century accomplishment, as my bird's-eye view.

The canal's structure is strikingly simple. In large measure it takes advantage of the natural lay of the land. Three locks on each side dam up the center of the isthmus, turning it into a big lake called Lake Gatun, 85 feet above sea level. The lake is fed by an inexhaustible tropical water supply that ensures navigable water levels at all times. Only on the Pacific side at the Galliard Gap, which was just below us, does the canal look like a real canal, where its builders had to excavate their way through a 10-mile-wide mountain range.

We watched the toy ships moving imperceptibly: eight hours to cross. Our one-way time was fewer than 30 minutes, even in the 150, to view the result of three decades of hard labor and the forgotten memory of 25,000 lives that the unforgiving jungle had extracted as a price.

"A few miles south of here a light twin went down three years ago," said Jose. "They were found last week." The jungle has changed little since 1914. We flew on at 1,000 feet MSL, just below a broken cloud cover, dodging isolated turbulence. Ignorant of the local weather's ways, I would have slept late that morning, but Jose had assured me that a thin broken layer meant no trouble until later in the afternoon.

Soon the canal widened into Lake Gatun and then we were circling over Colon on the Atlantic, and the Gatun locks. A passenger ship was just beginning its crossing. Off to the left, plainly visible and forming a V with the main waterway was a narrow channel leading nowhere. It is sad testimony to the first abortive attempt at digging across the isthmus by Ferdinand de Lesseps, the builder of the Suez Canal. Similar to the Suez, de Lesseps planned to dig across at sea level, but here the task was far more monumental. After a whole decade of clawing at the jungle with monster steam shovels that had produced only the modest ditch now below us, he had to admit defeat and declare bankruptcy. Then came

Teddy Roosevelt and his engineers, with the concept of damming up the center of the isthmus with the locks, which dramatically reduced the need to dig (ironically, first suggested by one of de Lesseps' men), and two more decades of fever plagued work that would also solve the mystery of yellow fever and malaria. No wonder some think of the canal as the moon shot of the turn of the century.

On the way back, Jose and I talked of flying in Panama, of the island resorts, the deserted beaches, and the rough bush strips that beckon the weekend pilot. Favorite flyouts are the San Blas Islands on the Atlantic side, where time has stood still and you can visit Indians living as they have for centuries, and the beach resort of Contadora, a mere 40 miles off the Pacific coast. Both are easy day trips.

We also talked of the tempestuous weather that must always be respected. But tropical storms clear up as quickly as they form, so the patient flyer is rarely delayed for long. We ambled along over the Pan American Highway and circled the spot where it ends, to restart miles farther to the south in Colombia because the jungle is too dense to make bridging the gap worthwhile. Then we headed back to Paitilla. The clouds were scattered by the time we slid down on final approach, past the high-rises.

36

Curacao and Aruba

Country rating: **Difficult**

ONC Charts: **K-27**

Rental cost range:

   2 seat trainer **$60-70**

   4 seat fixed gear **$75-90**

   4 seat retractable **$100-120**

QUALIFICATIONS AND LICENSE VALIDATION

Validation for short-term visitors and for long-term visitors with fewer than 1,200 hours is not possible in Curacao and Aruba, collectively known as the Netherlands Antilles; therefore, a Difficult country rating is assigned. The exception is a Dutch license, which is recognized by the Netherlands Antilles, based on their long-standing ties to Holland. Non-Dutch foreigners moving to these islands can obtain a validated license if they have at least 1,200 hours flying time. All others must get a local license by passing local written examinations and flight tests and obtaining a local medical. These popular tourist destinations are included in this guide because flights with a safety pilot are easy to arrange, and a morning or an afternoon of flying might be a welcome change to a pilot-vacationer into a second week on the beach.

There is a good chance that in the near future license validation for visitors might be introduced, given the islands' close ties to Holland, where ICAO licenses are automatically accepted without need for validation. There is also a big push on both islands to attract more tourists by trying to be as accommodating as possible to their every need.

United States license holders may fly N-registered aircraft solo. Though it is not their standard practice, an aeroclub might have one available for rent at the time of your visit, so it is worth checking out.

DOCUMENTS YOU SHOULD TAKE

Pilot license
Current medical
Logbook
Radio operator license (if separate from pilot license)

Bring original documents in case an N-registered aircraft is available and you are qualified to fly it. A chance to see the license and logbook will also be comforting to a safety pilot.

USEFUL FLYING ORGANIZATIONS

Aero Club of Curacao
Plesman Airport
Hato, Curacao

This active club has many members who work for the local airline ALM, which is affiliated with KLM Royal Dutch Airlines. It is a well equipped organization, flying Cessnas and a Piper Lance. The club stages an annual air show and open house.

Aero Club of Aruba
Queen Beatrix Airport
Aruba

A nice aero club with a good fleet of Beech and Cessna equipment.

Ministry of Communications
Department of Civil Aviation
Hato, Curacao

The civil aviation authority of the Netherlands Antilles. At the moment Aruba is also under its jurisdiction, although there is a movement toward greater autonomy for Aruba.

WHERE TO FLY, WHAT TO FLY

Besides Curacao, the main business center, and Aruba, the favored tourist destination, the Netherlands Antilles also includes the island of Bonaire. Curacao and Aruba have numerous daily international flights in and out of their large airports. You will be sharing the pattern with passenger-laden jumbo jets flown by airlines from Europe, the United States, and Latin America.

Don't be surprised if you are told to look out for the "Coke Machine" on downwind. That is what the local controllers call a certain South American airline based not too far away on the mainland. Some say the name comes from the swirling red-and-white color scheme on the aircraft.

Plesman Airport serves Curacao. **Queen Beatrix Airport** serves Aruba. Both airports have an aeroclub, mentioned in this chapter; at the moment, there are no commercial flying schools. Bonaire Island has an airport of the same name, unfortunately, aircraft are not available for rent, but the field is a popular destination for flights from the two other islands.

Flights around Curacao and Aruba, and flights among the three islands, are the most common form of recreational flying. From Curacao, Aruba or Bonaire are approximately half an hour away in a Skyhawk. Flight time between Aruba and Bonaire is approximately one hour. A good plan is to fly from one island to the other for the day. Aruba and Curacao are major resorts, and Bonaire is a less developed, quiet island where you can loaf in seclusion on the beach all day.

Flights farther afield are also possible. Caracas, Venezuela's capital, is approximately 150 nautical miles to the southeast, but many people consider dealing with the Venezuelan immigration and customs officials too much of a hassle to be worth the trip. Flights farther east to the Grenadines and beyond, island hopping northward along the French Antilles is also popular with the locals, but the distances are quite long. Grenada is approximately 400 nautical miles away, and the chain of islands north of Grenada is spread out along another 350 nautical miles.

VFR QUESTIONS & ANSWERS

What are good sources for VFR regulations? Consult the Netherlands Antilles AIP and the aeroclub instructors.

How can I get a weather briefing? Both Plesman and Queen Beatrix airports have met offices that supply comprehensive weather briefings. Up-to-date satellite photos are available. Watch out for thunderstorms and hurricanes in season.

What are VFR visibility and ceiling minimums? The Netherlands Antilles has adopted the ICAO VFR minimums.

Is night VFR permitted? No.

Must I file a flight plan? You must file a flight plan for all flights. For local flights, an abbreviated flight plan, filed over the radio, is sufficient. Cross-country flights require filing a written flight plan.

May I fly the airways VFR? Yes, you must fly the airways on cross-country flights. ATC will assign altitudes to fly, and will require position reports and time estimates between reporting points.

Must I maintain en route radio contact with ATC on or off the airways? Yes. Position reporting is mandatory.

Is VFR on top permitted? Yes, as long as a VFR descent and landing at the destination is assured.

ADDITIONAL INFORMATION SOURCES

The Aero Club of Curacao publishes a newsletter; back issues may be read at the club.

Asia

37

Hong Kong

Country rating: **Easy**

ONC Chart: **J-12**

Rental cost range:

  2 seat trainer **$75-90**

  4 seat fixed gear **$90-105**

  4 seat retractable **$100-130**

QUALIFICATIONS AND LICENSE VALIDATION

Recreational VFR flight in Hong Kong is possible for anyone with a license issued by an ICAO member state. The only requirement for solo flight is meeting the checkout requirements of the local aeroclub. Requirements are extensive because the sensitive border with the People's Republic of China is only a few minutes away by airplane, plus the airline traffic in and out of Hong Kong's Kai Tak Airport, where the club is based, is heavy. The aeroclub manager estimates a minimum of four flight hours for experienced pilots to fulfill the checkout requirements, and more time if a pilot flies primarily from a small, uncontrolled airport.

A local IFR license from the Civil Aviation Department is required for instrument flying in an aircraft that is registered in Hong Kong; acquiring the local license involves various testing procedures.

DOCUMENTS YOU SHOULD TAKE

Pilot license
Current medical
Radio operator license (if separate from pilot license)
Logbook

Take original documents.

USEFUL FLYING ORGANIZATIONS

The Director
Civil Aviation Department
Queensway, Government Offices 46th Floor
66 Queensway
Hong Kong

The people to bother if you want to do more than fly with the local aeroclub.

Hong Kong Aviation Club
Song Wong Toi Rd.
Kowloon
Hong Kong
Telephone   3713 5171

Local flying club at Kai Tak Airport, the only good show in town.

WHERE TO FLY, WHAT TO FLY

If you think that flying past Manhattan VFR below 1,100 feet is something, you haven't flown with the Hong Kong Aviation Club located just to the right of the threshold of Runway 13 at Hong Kong's **Kai Tak Airport**. The Hong Kong skyline is as spectacular in its own way as Manhattan, and an aeroclub at Kai Tak is like finding a little house surrounded by Cessnas for rent—right next to a main runway at Kennedy.

Checkerboard approach: Refueling of the Hong Kong Flying Club's Cessna 172 while an Airbus turns final.

The Hong Kong Aviation Club is the only game in town, and a delightful, friendly game it is. It also provides the unique experience of flying from one of the world's busiest airports. Because Kai Tak has only one runway, you will not be directed to some remote auxiliary strip in a far corner of the field, but will be told to hold for the 747-400 and taxi into position ahead of the DC-10. With a bit of careful preflight planning, you can even do it at night in a Cessna 152.

The drawback of flying out of Kai Tak is that after the spectacular Hong Kong skyline, and the tiny territory's outer islands, there is nowhere else to go. Flights to mainland China are possible but their arrangement is a complicated and lengthy business. Nor do the limited options and the thorough checkout required make it attractive for the short-time visitor to get signed off for solo. If you are not in town for the duration it is best to fly with a townie to experience the thrills of flying over Hong Kong and mixing it up with the heavies.

The aviation club has a fleet of two Cessna 152s, two C-172s, one C-182 and a brand-new Piper Cadet. The club has been in existence for 25 years and plans to be in Hong Kong indefinitely. The territory reverts back to China in 1997 and there are plans for a new airport on reclaimed land (turning Kai Tak over to the developers). Given preliminary indications, the club is optimistic that neither event will threaten its existence. Of 750 club members, 150 actively fly, the rest belong for social reasons. Temporary memberships are available for up to three months.

Hong Kong is also home base for several privately owned light aircraft, parked at the Aviation Club, among them a CAP-10 and a Saratoga. Their owners often take along visiting pilots who have befriended them.

One of the most memorable experiences for the pilot landing at Kai Tak is the infamous "checkerboard approach" to Runway 13 from the mountainous side of the airport. The approach requires that the pilot fly straight at the mountains at 600 feet MSL (a lot less agl) until two huge flashing red-and-white checkerboards on the mountainside come into sight.

An immediate descending right turn is required and the gear and flaps better be down because the threshold will be "right there" as the wings roll level. It is an awesome sight from the cockpit of a 747, whose pilots must hand fly the final stages of this approach. There is a lot more room for a Cessna 152 with a tighter base-to-final, well inside the checkerboard approach path, but you still get the idea.

VFR QUESTIONS & ANSWERS

What are good sources for VFR regulations? The AIP, and the aeroclub's instructors.

How can I get a weather briefing? From the met office by phone from the aeroclub.

What are VFR visibility and ceiling minimums? Hong Kong operates under the ICAO minimums.

Is night VFR permitted? Yes, but only patterns by prior arrangement.

Must I file a flight plan? Yes, in fact you have to file two, one each with civilian and military controllers. You file by telephone and the flight plan is less detailed than a regular flight plan. Hong Kong airspace is divided into sectors and you basically have to tell the controllers what sectors you propose to fly into and the approximate time.

Must I maintain en route radio contact with ATC? Yes, you have to give brief position reports when transiting from one sector to another.

38

Hong Kong hop

"INDIA GOLF, POSITION AND HOLD," said the controller as the China Airways flight swooped past the threshold, which was in front of us, descending toward the touchdown zone. With great relief, we lined up for takeoff. For half an hour after the initial call for taxi clearance, we had to watch a relentless procession of airliners streaming in for landing from all over the world. Now, stretching before us into Kowloon Bay toward the Lei Yue Mun Gap and the South China Sea beyond, was Kai Tak Airport's Runway 13.

Off to the right was the jagged outline of Hong Kong Island and Victoria Harbor separating it from Kowloon on the Chinese mainland. A normal departure route for the airlines is straight out through the gap, but we were about to head for Victoria Harbor in the Hong Kong Aviation Club's Cessna 172 for a scenic tour of Hong Kong.

Hong Kong's deeply rooted freewheeling capitalist traditions of equal opportunity permits an aeroclub to share one of the world's busiest single runways with commercial traffic. Kai Tak has always been the only civilian airport in the tiny, crowded territory, and was established in 1920 only because a group of sporting Englishmen was looking for a suitable spot for the aeroclub they were about to form.

It would take another 16 years before the first scheduled flight was to touch down at Kai Tak. In those days, a public road ran straight across the runway, and a set of railway crossing gates were lowered to stop the traffic whenever an airplane was taking off or landing.

The present aeroclub, a nonprofit organization supported by membership dues and income from its fully licensed restaurant, traces its origins to the less hectic days of the 1960s. Kai Tak's commercial traffic has grown since then by leaps and bounds and the pilots who fly the club's fleet of two Cessna 152s, two 172s, one 182, and a Piper Cadet have had to become increasingly more patient and flexible in their coexistence with the heavy iron.

Training new pilots is as important a task for the club as providing affordable flying for certificated pilots. Unfortunately, flight training has felt pressure from the steadily growing commercial traffic. The club had a longstanding arrange-

Hong Kong skyline: Bank of China is the tallest building.

ment with the only other airport in the territory, the little used military field at Sek Kong, closer to the Chinese border, to conduct training flights.

Gradually, Kai Tak became too busy for solo student departures and arrivals, requiring an instructor to accompany students to and from Sek Kong. The Sek Kong option disappeared all together when its runway proved to be the most suitable place in the crowded territory to house the tens of thousands of Vietnamese boat people seeking refuge in Hong Kong, and was closed to all aircraft except military helicopters.

Students had to go abroad for the cross-country portion of their training before the closure of Sek Kong. Now they go abroad, mostly to the United States, to complete the training as soon as they reach solo standards with club instructors at Kai Tak.

The Hong Kong Aviation Club is a favorite stop on the itinerary of visiting recreational pilots keen on the thrilling experience of flying along the Hong Kong waterfront at 500 feet, an experience equalled only perhaps by a low-level flight through the VFR corridor past the New York City skyline. As I was about to find out, it is not just a thrill but also a lot of work.

"Come as early as possible," club manager Ruth Golden had said when I called to make a booking. "Your chances of getting out without an ATC delay will be much better." The earliest possible slot was at 10:15 a.m., the agile locals having beaten me to the earlier times starting at 7 a.m. I was to fly with Peter Wells, the club's resident flying instructor. The club, located on Sung Wong Toi Road at the corner of Runway 13, opposite the commercial terminal, is difficult to miss on the way to the airport from Kowloon.

When I arrived, Wells, an affable Briton, handed me a topographic map of Hong Kong. Superimposed on it was what looked like a technical drawing of my television set's electrical circuitry. "We have quite a bit of airspace detail with which you should get familiar," said Wells. I counted 22 different sectors over an area less than half the size of Rhode Island. This compartmentalization is made necessary by the close proximity of the People's Republic of China, until recently a border as tense as the old Iron Curtain, and air traffic control considerations for commercial traffic in and out of Kai Tak.

Two telephoned flight plans were required: one for civilian ATC and one for military ATC. Both like to know where you are. Hong Kong's airspace is bisected roughly east to west. Sectors north of this line consist mostly of the mainland area known as the New Territories because that was the last area to be acquired by Britain. The northern sectors, which form an airspace boundary with the People's Republic of China, are managed by military ATC. Southern sectors are under civilian ATC.

Following the airspace review and filing the flight plans, we strapped on life jacket packs, settled into the Cessna 172, started it up, and had the attendant open the electric gates to the elaborate security fence enclosing the club fleet. We called ATC, only to be informed, through the headsets, to expect a 30-minute delay. "At least you are getting a realistic introduction to flying out of Kai Tak," said Wells as we shut down. "We have a very good relationship with the controllers, though, and they always get us out as soon as they can. Many of them fly with the club."

It is important for the visitor to realize the need for patience. Booking an hour and flying at the appointed time might not always be possible. Also, there is a restriction on local flying between 2 and 4 P.M.: depart or arrive, but not both.

During a quick tea in the club's pleasant (high-class by American airport standards) restaurant, I learned that for noncommercial recreational flying, a pilot certificate from any ICAO member state is accepted in Hong Kong at face value. Solo flight would only require a checkout by the club, but this would consist of at least four hours of flying, if not more, given the complexities of the airspace system and the dire consequences of border violations, not to mention the fur that would fly if an inexperienced pilot forced a 747 to perform a go-around at the end of its 13-hour flight from the United States.

According to Ruth Golden, a checkout is only worthwhile if a pilot lived in Hong Kong for an extended period. Flights to the People's Republic of China are possible, but a bear to organize because permission is required from Hong Kong and Beijing. The red tape is usually not worth the effort.

Given the Pacific Ocean's vast distances, flights farther afield require the range and comfort of the privately owned Saratoga parked at the aeroclub. Aerobatics is an ideal Hong Kong alternative to touring that requires minimal range; a privately owned CAP-10 is parked at the aeroclub.

Thirty minutes after postponement, the controller promptly cleared our Cessna 172 to taxi into position and hold; after a religiously observed two-minute pause for wake turbulence, we were off. (The office of the aeroclub has a series of photographs depicting visible wake turbulence created by a Cathay Pacific 747 landing through smoke from a burning building.)

All the magic of Hong Kong was at our feet upon executing a right turn after takeoff and leveling off at 500 feet: skyscrapers of Hong Kong Island lining the shore; Wanchai, made famous by Suzie Wong; the towering business district; and the futuristic new headquarters of that ancient pillar of trade and finance, the Hong Kong and Shanghai Bank.

A forest of residential high-rises climbed a hillside and above it all, Victoria Peak, the island's highest point. It was named after Queen Victoria, who ruled Britain during the height of its Imperial splendor in the last century and secured for her opium-dealing subjects the rights to this mysterious little land, under a lease from China set to expire in 1997. As if to herald in the new age about to make its debut when the lease runs out, the tallest building overlooking the Cessna was not some bastion of high capitalism, but the elegant glass headquarters tower of the People's Republic's foreign trade arm, the Bank of China. Only the tower is new, the bank has existed since the earliest days of Chairman Mao's rule, trading profitably to meet the hard currency needs of the socialist masses, and waiting. Such are the complexities of this place.

Kowloon was on the right side, strangely flat by comparison to the island skyline across the water because the buildings are limited to 12 stories by their proximity to the airport. Dazzling neon signs at night appear frozen in time, forbidden to blink, lest they confuse some weary airline crew on final approach. Across from the waterfront was another Hong Kong landmark, the Peninsula Hotel, commonly called the "Pen" by the locals, that opened in 1928 and remains one of the finest hotels in the world. Acres and acres of shopper's paradise behind the hotel draw tourists by the thousands.

Directly below was the harbor, littered with ships, boats, and junks of all vintage and size, crisscrossing the water every which way in an apparent state of anarchy. Most recognizable were the Star Ferry's oval-shaped cream-and-green tubs, which have linked Kowloon and Hong Kong since the turn of the century, and still give you one of the best views in the world for less than a quarter per crossing.

My only problem with flying along Victoria Harbor immediately after takeoff was that the excursion concluded too soon. There was so much to see and absorb that a bit of meandering was imperative.

The flight was also demanding: maintaining ATC's 500-foot maximum altitude restriction; constantly watching for helicopters, for whom the harbor is a favorite low-level haunt; and trying to absorb all there was to see. Rounding Hong Kong Island and climbing to the luxurious altitude of 1,500 feet for a look at its other side felt like a coffee break. Aberdeen was below us with its waterborne town of junks and floating restaurants. Beyond was Stanley, home of a famous open market (mostly clothing), which is just as popular as the stores of Kowloon for tourists and locals alike.

Minutes later we ran out of airspace again and turned east along the sector's outer limits, flying over a smattering of lesser islands toward Lantau, the biggest island in the territory. Lantau is relatively unpopulated and might be the scene of an airport built on landfill to replace Kai Tak by, perhaps, as early as 1997.

En route, I had time to reflect on what a student pilot had to gain from this cramped operating environment: 22 airspace sectors, 16 of which he can enter; lots of low-level precision flying with many climbs and descents; and radio skills that would make him comfortable flying in and out of Kennedy. Any student who can hack that will be a darn good pilot.

Reaching Lantau, we turned north again toward the mainland and descended to 500 feet to fly around the island's tip, under Kai Tak's Runway 13 ILS approach path. We skimmed over a jetfoil on its way to the tiny island of Macau, approximately 40 miles to the east, still a Portuguese colony and a favored gambling center for the Hong Kong citizenry since the sport was outlawed in their own territory.

The mainland is dozens of rugged parched green peaks, the farthest of them well inside the borders of the People's Republic of China and strictly off limits. We checked in with the military controllers, wandered the valleys, and circled the Vietnamese refugee camp on Sek Kong's runway. The absence of jetliners in this area permitted larger altitude allowances, even a heady 2,500 feet.

I looked across the border deep into China, now wide open to foreigners, and my feelings were strangely flat, not at all as titillating as during the most melodramatic Cold War days. I stole a moment to daydream about Imperial Airways' and Pan Am's giant flying boats alighting on Kowloon Bay in the 1930s, and Robert Scott beating up the waterfront in his shark nosed P-40 a decade later. Just as he flashed over the "Pen" in my thoughts, the Kai Tak controller's voice crackled in the headphones. He could take us now, or there would be a hold; what were our intentions? I considered the amount of colorfully engraved paper from the Hong Kong and Shanghai Bank that was in my pocket—the aeroclub does not take credit cards—and reluctantly started to follow ATC instructions.

The approach went over the mountain range that forms a bowl, which the airport rests in, and momentarily we were on left downwind for Runway 13, available only to VFR light aircraft. Heavies fly the famous "checkerboard" approach, which is considered to be among the world's most demanding approaches, from the other side.

The mountains are too high for a straight-in approach, so the ILS is offset and aims the airplane at a huge red-and-white checkerboard on the mountainside. When the pilot nears the checkerboard, at a few hundred feet above ground level, he or she disengages the autopilot (if operating) and hangs a hefty right turn, assisted by a curved *rabbit* (sequentially flashing strobe lights) on the ground to line up with the runway and touch down within seconds. The ride is very exciting on a rainy night down to minimums.

Cathay Pacific pilots, whose line was started at Kai Tak with one surplus C-47 in the aftermath of World War II, and who regularly shoehorn the airline's fleet of 747s and L-1011s into the airport, do it best. The hairiest moments are reserved for the unwary passenger who relaxes because he can almost touch the highrises below him during what appears to be the verge of an uneventful touchdown, only to find himself staring straight at someone's kitchen rushing toward him at great speed as the airplane enters an aggressive descending turn.

No such excitement for us on left downwind, but plenty of fun jumbo-watching on the acres of concrete below us. If our approach had been from the other side, we also could have flown sufficiently close to the checkerboard to get the idea, although the VFR light aircraft approach is much less dramatic than the ILS. We landed behind a Thai Airbus, then watched a United 747 take off and climb out through the Lei Yue Mun Gap as we taxied in.

39

Singapore

Country rating: **Easy**

ONC Chart: **L-10**

Rental cost range:

  2 seat trainer   **$80-110**

  4 seat fixed gear   **$105-175**

  4 seat retractable   **$185-215**

QUALIFICATIONS AND LICENSE VALIDATION

Singapore requires validation of a license for noncommercial VFR flying, but it is an easy process if you come prepared with the appropriate documents, and your license meets ICAO standards. Validation is issued by the Civil Aviation Authority of Singapore at Changi Airport, which you flew into upon arrival in the country. Validation takes two working days and is a routine procedure.

It is important to have documentation properly prepared as outlined in this chapter. Apply in person when you arrive. Visiting pilots most often fly with the Republic of Singapore Flying Club at Seletar Air Base on the other side of the island from Changi. Check with them in person, or at least give them a call, before approaching the CAA to get an update on validation details. A preliminary call to the CAA might also be helpful.

The validation will be effective for three months. If you stay in Singapore for more than three months, you will have to get a full Singapore license; get the validation first and arrange the full license while you fly under the validation. A full Singapore license normally requires a local medical certificate and passing a written test on aviation law and a flight test. The exact requirements vary with a pilot's experience, and will be specified in writing by the CAA. The flying club will be happy to provide guidance.

Validation of an instrument rating is not possible. You must take a local IFR flight test given by the CAA.

DOCUMENTS YOU SHOULD TAKE

Pilot license
Logbook
Current medical
Radio operator license

You have to present the original documents to the CAA. The total time in the logbook has to be authenticated. You might have the last page notarized, or have an instructor sign it off with a seal of a flying school or FBO stamped for authentication. Outside the United States, official or official looking rubber stamps are often required for authentication, and never hurt.

You must also present two passport photos and photocopies of your license, medical, radio operator license, and the last two pages of your logbook. They will keep these on file following the inspection and return your originals.

USEFUL FLYING ORGANIZATIONS

Civil Aviation Authority of Singapore
P.O. Box 1
Singapore Changi Airport
Singapore 9181
Attention: Flight Operations
Telephone   65 541 2482
Facsimile   65 545 6519

The government organization that issues validations and Singapore equivalents of foreign licenses.

Republic of Singapore Flying Club
Building 140B, East Camp
Seletar Air Base
Singapore 2879
Telephone   65 481 0200 or 0502

Postal address:
P.O. Box 33
Jalan Kayu Post Office
Singapore 9180

This is the only nonprofit flying club in Singapore to offer light aircraft flying, and also represents IAOPA. It offers a visiting membership for a reasonable fee.

WHERE TO FLY, WHAT TO FLY

Singapore is a tiny island city-state, smaller than Hong Kong, but it offers more flying opportunities than its size suggests at first glance. Singapore has been an important trading center for centuries, strategically placed along the region's central nautical thoroughfare and favorite pirate hangout, the Strait of Malacca.

Firmly entrepreneurial, the island remains one of Asia's most important commercial centers to this day.

Aviation touched Singapore as early as the 1920s and 1930s when commercial flights from Europe followed the pioneers into the region, and on to Australia. It was also a favorite way station for the periodic Europe-to-Australia air races that became popular during this time.

The **Republic of Singapore Flying Club,** (481 0200 or 0502), which is based at Seletar Air Base, dates back to those early days, founded in 1928. The club maintains the pleasant traditions of the typical old-fashioned flying/social club and is the ideal organization for recreational flying.

It is a well equipped club, operating (as of early 1990) a fleet of two Piper Tomahawks, a Cessna 150, two Cessna 172s, an Aerospatiale Tobago, and a Piper Lance. Beyond flying with an instructor, the club will check you out for local and regional flying, then turn you loose on their equipment upon license validation.

Commercial flying schools also exist and might be an option for a quick trip around the patch if availability and scheduling at the flying club do not suit your plans. The club will be glad to point you in the direction of the commercial schools in business at the time of your visit, if you wish to compare, which is always a good idea.

Local flying is restricted because of the island's small size, but an aerial view of the city, the Strait of Malacca, and a peek toward the Indonesian island of Sumatra to the south and the Malaysian Peninsula to the north is an interesting sortie.

Regional touring is a more interesting proposition. Flights to peninsular Malaysia's nearby west coast beach areas, such as Pulau Tioman, Malacca, and Penang, are easy to arrange. Depending on how you want to divide your time between flying and the beach, the closer destinations, such as the town of Malacca, are within comfortable day-trip distance. Flights to Thailand and Indonesia are also possible. If you don't have the time to checkout and validate your license, go touring in the company of a local pilot.

VFR QUESTIONS & ANSWERS

What are good sources of VFR regulations? Consult the Singapore AIP.

How can I get a weather briefing? Comprehensive briefings are available at Seletar Air Base.

What are VFR visibility and ceiling minimums? Singapore has adopted the ICAO VFR minimums.

Is night VFR permitted? No.

Must I file a flight plan? Flight plans must be filed for all VFR flights requiring ATC services.

May I fly the airways VFR? Yes. You must file a flight plan or notify ATC before joining an airway, and you must fly under ATC control.

Must I maintain radio contact with ATC en route, off the airways? You must make hourly position reports.

Is VFR on top permitted? No.

What are VFR cruising altitudes? Standard ICAO hemispherical VFR altitudes apply in controlled airspace. The British quadrant rules apply in uncontrolled airspace between 3,000 and 25,500 feet.

40

Malaysia

Country rating: **Moderate**

ONC Charts: **L-10 and L-11**

Rental cost range:

  2 seat trainer **$75-90**

  4 seat fixed gear **$90-110**

  4 seat retractable **$110-130**

QUALIFICATIONS AND LICENSE VALIDATION

Temporary validation of a foreign license is required, and is issued by Malaysia's Department of Civil Aviation (DCA), based in the capital, Kuala Lumpur. Validation of ICAO member state licenses for VFR recreational use is granted routinely. The procedure is administrative. No written or flight test is required. Validation is granted for three months and is extendable for additional three month periods.

Most visitors to Malaysia go to destinations far from Kuala Lumpur, mainly the beach resorts. From outside Kuala Lumpur, validation requests have to be mailed to the DCA and short-term visitors might face time constraints; hence, the country classification is moderate.

If Penang, the country's main beach resort area, is your destination, you might speed up validation by sending document photocopies to the Penang Flying Club before the trip and request that the club apply on your behalf, in advance.

The validation of an IFR rating requires a checkride administered by the DCA.

DOCUMENTS YOU SHOULD TAKE

Pilot license
Logbook
Current medical
Radio operator license
Passport

Original documents should be available for inspection by the aircraft rental facility. Photocopies will have to be submitted to the DCA for validation.

Visitors to Penang should contact the Penang Flying Club, which is willing to obtain advanced validation of a license if the club receives document photocopies at least 45 days prior to arrival; notarizing the photocopies is a good idea. Only the relevant demographic, checkride, and total time information (last page) of your logbook need be copied.

USEFUL AVIATION ORGANIZATIONS

Department of Civil Aviation
Third Floor, Wisma Yen San
Lot 13A, Jalan 225
46100 Petaling Jaya
Selangor
Malaysia

This government office, located in greater Kuala Lumpur, issues license validations.

Penang Flying Club
Clubhouse and Hangar
Penang International Airport
11900 Penang
Malaysia
Telephone   04 843367
Facsimile   04 847221

This flying club is in the country's best known beach resort area, headquarters of Malaysia's AOPA, and the area representative of IAOPA.

Beautiful beach weather can quickly turn sour.

WHERE TO FLY, WHAT TO FLY

Malaysia's western part is located on a peninsula extending below Thailand. The eastern part is on the island of Borneo, which it shares with Indonesia. The area below Thailand is commonly referred to as Peninsular Malaysia, and for most visitors, this is where the action is. Its excellent beaches, most notably those on the island of Penang, have become a popular tourist destination in recent years.

The Penang Flying Club (04 843367) at **Penang International Airport** is a non-profit flying and social club, in operation since 1935. A fleet of Cessna 150s and Skyhawks is used for member training and touring, and also for scenic and photographic flights on a charter basis. In addition to helping with license validation, the club also offers visiting memberships.

Other clubs and commercial flying schools can be found throughout Malaysia. Besides Penang, popular destinations offering recreational flying are **Alor Setar, Ipoh,** and **Malacca,** all on the west coast of the peninsula. Malacca also specializes in parachuting. Contact the local airports on arrival.

Touring up and down the peninsular coast is most attractive. A popular flight from Penang is north to **Alor Setar** on the coast, past the fishing grounds of Pulau Song Song and Kedah Peak. Continue from Alor Setar to **Langkawi Island** and enjoy the views of the surrounding coral cays before landing at its airport. Return straight to Penang over the water, or pick up the coast before turning south again. The round trip is approximately 180 nautical miles.

A southern round-trip from Penang to Ipoh is approximately the same distance. Flights farther south to Kuala Lumpur and Malacca are also possible.

Rally flying might be a possibility if your timing is right. Periodically, Malaysia's aeroclubs organize rallies to compete against each other in cross-country flying, requiring precision navigation and performance according to your flight plan. Participating crews consist of pilot and navigator. Rallies are as much a social occasion as an exercise to sharpen airmanship. Check the schedule for such events with the Penang Flying Club.

VFR QUESTIONS & ANSWERS

What are good sources of VFR regulations? Consult the Malaysian AIP.

How can I get a weather briefing? Comprehensive briefings are available at Penang, Kuantan, and Kuching airports. Teletyped weather information is available at most other airports.

What are VFR visibility and ceiling minimums? Malaysia has adopted the ICAO VFR minimums.

Is night VFR permitted? No.

Must I file a flight plan? You must file for all VFR flights.

May I fly the airways VFR? Yes, but only if you have an instrument rating because the flight will be handled as an IFR flight. In the Kuala Lumpur and Johor TMAs you can fly only under IFR rules, except for the Subang and Simpang VFR corridors.

Must I maintain radio contact with ATC en route off the airways? Yes, you must give hourly position reports.

What are VFR cruising altitudes? In controlled airspace, the standard ICAO hemispherical VFR altitudes apply. In uncontrolled airspace from 3,000 feet to 25,000 feet, you must observe the British Quadrant VFR cruising altitudes.

Is VFR on top permitted? No.

41

Philippines

Country rating: **Moderate**
ONC Charts: **J-12, K-11, and L-11**
Rental cost range:
  2 seat trainer   **$70-80**
  4 seat fixed gear   **$80-120**
  4 seat retractable   **$120-160**

QUALIFICATIONS AND LICENSE VALIDATION

The Philippine air transportation office will validate a foreign private license issued by an ICAO member state, but requires a checkride with a government checkpilot. There is no written test and the checkride format is similar to a flying school's prerental checkride.

Upon arrival you are immediately given a temporary prevalidation certificate that allows you to fly solo locally in preparation for the government checkride. You also need to get a letter from your embassy stating that you intend to fly for noncommercial, recreational purposes. The Philippine Air Force will run a security check. The whole process can take a week or two. The quickest way to get validation is to work through the aero club or a commercial school with the appropriate local contacts. Flying with a safety pilot is easy to arrange.

DOCUMENTS YOU SHOULD TAKE

Pilot license
Current medical
Logbook
Radio operator license (if separate from pilot license)
Letter from your embassy stating that you intend to do noncommercial flying only
Six passport photos

Take original documents, for review, with some photocopies that the authorities can keep.

USEFUL FLYING ORGANIZATIONS

Manila Aero Club
Andrews Avenue
Domestic Airport
Pasay City, Philippines (Pasay City is a suburb of Manila)
Telephone   831 7009

The club has been in business since 1965, is very helpful to foreign visitors, and will assist with license validation.

Air Transportation Office
Domestic Airport
Pasay City, Philippines

The civil aviation authority responsible for license validations. Make contact through the Aero Club or a commercial operator.

Air Ads, Incorporated
Andrews Avenue
Domestic Airport
Pasay City, Philippines
Telephone   833 3264

Corregidor from the Manila Aero Club's Sundowner.

Ask for Joey Roa, the owner. He is an outstanding pilot, and is extremely helpful to foreign visitors. He is one of the best known members of the Philippine general aviation community. His business is primarily a charter operation. He will not rent out his airplanes on self-fly hire without a safety pilot, but his advice is invaluable. He also owns a business making high quality static desktop model aircraft, which have become very popular in the United States.

WHERE TO FLY, WHAT TO FLY

The Philippines is a beautiful country with more than 7,000 islands and an airplane is the best way to get around. Once America's only colony, the country is becoming increasingly popular with tourists, especially Europeans and Australians, as one of the last great, unspoiled beach destinations in the Pacific. The Philippines has had its share of political upheaval, and there are insurgents, but they are active in areas hundreds of miles from where the average visitor is likely to go.

The center for private flying in the Philippines—and most likely your initial point of arrival—is Manila, the country's capital, on Luzon Island. Manila's main airport is descended from Nichols Field, a famous U.S. Army air base predating World War II. Separate terminal complexes handle international and domestic flights.

General aviation hangars are on the domestic side with row upon row of hangars, full of aircraft ranging from Cessna 150s to Beechcraft King Airs. The Philippines has only a handful of airports large enough to handle airliners; therefore, charter business is brisk among the many islands. Several charter companies also operate flying schools, mostly equipped with Cessna and Beech airplanes. Flying schools come and go over time; therefore, your best bet is to look in the yellow pages under the aircraft schools category when you arrive.

Manila Aeroclub, (831 7009), also on the domestic side of the airport and in business since the middle 1960s, is a nonprofit alternative to the commercial operators. It is as much a social organization as an aeroclub, and has a fully licensed clubhouse restaurant right at the airport. Many aircraft owners/operators are also members. It is an excellent place to make contacts in the flying community.

The club's equipment was somewhat sparse at our last visit in early 1990, consisting of one rather tired Beech Musketeer, and an Aeronca Champ under restoration. The addition of another Musketeer and one or two Sierras was imminent.

Though Manila is where most private flying originates, there are aeroclubs elsewhere in the Philippines. Among them are **Cubi Aeroclub** at Cubi, on the ocean side of the Bataan Peninsula, and **Bacolod Aeroclub** on Bacolod Island, in the central Philippines near some of the country's best beaches.

Two reasons to fly for fun in the Philippines are aerial tours of some of World War II's most famous battlefields and beach trips.

Historic battlefield flights

A popular flight of approximately two hours in a Musketeer is a tour of the Bataan Peninsula and Corregidor Island, scenes of the first big Pacific battles between the United States and Japan after Pearl Harbor. The best way to approach the peninsula is to first fly north past the Manila waterfront and the famous Manila Hotel to a small training airstrip inland; turn west to fly over fish farms and head straight to Bataan's 3,000- to 4,000-foot ridges. Fly along them at low level, southbound, to get a good look at the rough terrain.

Beyond the peninsula's tip, a stone's throw away is Corregidor, the Rock, shaped like a tadpole, made famous by General MacArthur's men who held out here for four months against enormous odds. It is only when you see how small the island is, and how close it is to the mainland that you fully appreciate their accomplishment.

You might land at Corregidor's recently reopened Kindley Field where four lonely P-40s faced half the Japanese Air Force. Continue south across the bay to pick up the mainland again and follow the shore back to Nichols Field, taking care to stay south of Cavite, now a navy base and once the site of the Japanese artillery batteries that bombarded Corregidor.

A longer variation of the battlefield tour is to first fly north-northwest for 78 miles to Linganyen where the Japanese made their initial beach landings. It is a picturesque coastline dotted with hundreds of islands. From here you can follow the Bataan Peninsula back on the ocean side past Subic Bay to Corregidor.

Beach flights

Beach landings are still the thing in the Philippines but for more pleasant reasons than in MacArthur's days. Flights to the beach are the most popular form of recreational flying. The best beach resorts are all within easy striking distance of Manila. The most popular destinations are listed below:

Borocay on Panay Island is the country's premier beach resort, only 187 air miles southwest of Manila. It is a favorite for weekend mass fly outs, an easy day trip or overnighter.

El Nido Beach Resort on Palawan Island, 220 miles southeast of Manila, is off the beaten path and fortunately accessible to light aircraft. The scuba diving is excellent.

Tambuli Beach Resort on Cebu Island is served by Mactan Airport. Cebu Island is approximately 350 miles southwest of Manila.

Bohol Beach Club on Bohol Island, approximately 30 miles from Cebu, is another favorite rustic hideaway among tall coconut palms near the local airport.

A good option if you have the time and money is to go resort-hopping for a week or two before heading back to Manila.

Weather is an important consideration on any flight in the Philippines, especially during the rainy season when the storms blowing in from the Pacific Ocean can be particularly violent. The weather pattern is typically tropical year round, with frequently clear morning skies followed by heavy vertical cumulus development during the day, and clearing again by sunset. Get all the weather wisdom you can from the local instructors.

VFR QUESTIONS & ANSWERS

What are good sources for VFR regulations? Consult the Philippine AIP.

How can I get a weather briefing? The bigger airports have full met offices. Most other airfields have teletyped weather information.

What are VFR visibility and ceiling minimums? The Philippines has adopted the ICAO VFR minimums.

Is night VFR permitted? No.

Must I file a flight plan? You must file a flight plan for all VFR flights requiring ATC services. Flight plans are strongly advised for all VFR cross-country flights, considering the rather wild terrain.

May I fly the airways VFR? Yes. A flight plan and position reporting at compulsory reporting points is required.

Must I maintain en route radio contact with ATC off the airways? No.

Is VFR on top permitted? No.

ADDITIONAL INFORMATION SOURCES

The Manila yellow pages section of the telephone book has a substantial number of possibilities in the aircraft section.

42

IAOPA:
What it does for you

IAOPA MAKES IT EASIER TO FLY WORLDWIDE, whether in your aircraft or a rental aircraft. The International Council of Aircraft Owners and Pilots Association is a federation of the world's 32 national AOPAs that attempts to achieve on an international level what the national AOPAs achieve within their own countries. IAOPA and the constituent organizations are nongovernment and nonprofit; IAOPA is a member of ICAO, the International Civil Aviation Organization, which is the international body charged, among other responsibilities, with standardizing aviation systems and regulations worldwide. IAOPA represents the interests of general aviation within ICAO.

At no time did aviation develop at such a rapid rate than during World War II. As the massive new four-engine bombers and transports flew their last missions in the war's closing days, it became clear that civil aviation was about to grow worldwide as never before. The nations of the world founded ICAO in 1945 to develop a standardized operating environment. ICAO did outstanding work for 15 years, but concentrated almost exclusively on the operation of air transport aircraft.

General aviation, defined by ICAO as "all civil aviation operations other than scheduled air services and nonscheduled air transport operations for remuneration or hire," was being neglected. IAOPA was founded in 1962 to bolster general aviation and was subsequently granted ICAO member status in 1964.

IAOPA's objectives emphasize the undertaking:

To facilitate the movement of general aviation aircraft internationally.

To coordinate with other organizations the requirements of general aviation.

To integrate the views and requirements of the national AOPA organizations.

To advance the interests of general aviation at the meetings of ICAO and other international organizations.

To encourage the implementation of planned systems, facilities, services and procedures, to promote the safety, efficiency and utility of general aviation aircraft.

To encourage the national AOPAs to meet with their own national authorities to promote the interests of general aviation.

To encourage the collection of statistical and other information among ICAO member states, pertinent to general aviation.

These formal objectives boil down to a vigorous program by IAOPA to eliminate red tape imposed on the international movement of aircraft by national authorities, prevent the loss of airspace for use by general aviation, and standardize licensing requirements and operating procedures.

Because IAOPA is essentially a lobbyist (as are the constituent national organizations), its recommendations cannot be legally binding, either internationally or on individual nations. Rather, IAOPA presents its position to lawmaking bodies and hopes that its case is sufficiently compelling to result in laws, regulations, and procedures that best serve the interests of general aviation pilots.

IAOPA is funded entirely from a fraction of the membership dues paid to its national organizations, and senior officers serve voluntarily, without pay.

Opinions can be divergent among the respective national AOPA organizations. IAOPA works on a consensus basis, hammering out differences, and establishing as common a stance as possible among its members through regional coordinators, working committees, and periodic international meetings of all members. That IAOPA finds it easy to speak with one voice, by and large, is primarily because the interests and aspirations of general aviation pilots tend to be the same worldwide.

IAOPA has represented general aviation since 1964 in more than 100 major international meetings and countless smaller committee meetings, panels, and working groups. It has become highly respected as general aviation's voice worldwide. Opinions and recommendations are routinely considered not only by the ICAO but also by the European Economic Commission, where it has a liaison office, and other international organizations.

If the present state of general aviation worldwide is an indication, IAOPA has been a remarkable success. Important contributions, directly affecting the users of this book, have been an initiative to facilitate the validation of foreign private licenses by ICAO member states (previously a pilot had to be reexamined and relicensed in every country), extensive work on standardizing VFR airspace definitions and regulations, and a successful bid to greatly curtail placement of a "permanent IFR airspace" designation on large portions of low-level airspace by numerous ICAO member states. It is primarily because of IAOPA's efforts that ICAO's *International Standards and Recommended Practices* has an extensive section entitled "International General Aviation."

Work continues in all these areas. An outstanding recent IAOPA accomplishment has been the passage by the European Parliament of the European Community Council's IAOPA-sponsored *Directive on the Mutual Acceptance of Personnel*

Licenses in Civil Aviation. This means that private pilot licenses (certificates) issued by any European Economic Community member state will be accepted automatically in any other member state. Ratification by the national parliaments is required, but under the EEC's rules, this is practically guaranteed.

As Europe's economic borders disappear, there is progress on devising and implementing rationally conceived, standardized Euroairspace, and IAOPA is in the thick of it.

Yes, more could always be done; more needs to be done, especially in further standardization of recreational VFR flying elsewhere in the world. Consider how much more forbidding the skies would be for general aviation pilots had it not been for the efforts of IAOPA since 1964.

IAOPA can help recreational flyers abroad in a more direct way, through the national AOPAs that constitute its membership. These member organizations, depending upon their size, are often an excellent source of information about recreational flying in their respective countries. Many publish a variety of books and pamphlets on local general aviation.

And from the impressive United States headquarters of AOPA near Washington, D.C., to one-man offices such as AOPA Malaysia in Penang, all stand ready to help visitors from abroad, especially AOPA members. Review the aviation organizations section of respective country chapters to find a national AOPA office.

43

Japan

Country rating: **Difficult**

ONC Charts: **F-10, G-11, and H-13**

Rental cost range:

   2 seat trainer **$200-250**

   4 seat fixed gear **$250-350**

   4 seat retractable **$450**

QUALIFICATIONS AND LICENSE VALIDATION

Japanese take full advantage of the noncommercial aviation that the rest of the world has to offer, but make it practically impossible for foreigners to fly in Japan without a safety pilot. In fairness to Japanese private pilots, they are not entirely happy with this state of affairs; they would much rather see recreational aviation in Japan open and affordable to everyone.

    The civil aviation authorities will issue you a Japanese license based upon the license you hold, if you are not a Japanese citizen and do not reside in Japan, but have a Japanese mailing address. It takes approximately two months to get the equivalent license. The catch, according to AOPA Japan, that makes it almost impossible to fly solo is the requirement to have a Japanese aeronautical class radio license that must be obtained by examination. A standard radio operator license is not recognized, and the examinations for the Japanese radio license are given only twice a year. Contact Japan's AOPA if you want to take on the challenge of obtaining a Japanese license.

DOCUMENTS YOU SHOULD TAKE

Pilot license

Current medical

Logbook

Radio operator license (if separate from pilot license)

It is pointless to take these documents if you are only a short-term visitor, but they might help confirm your experience to a prospective safety pilot and make him feel comfortable with allowing you to fly. Photocopies are sufficient.

USEFUL FLYING ORGANIZATIONS

Japanese Aircraft Owners and Pilots' Association (JAOPA)
6-30, Tsutsujigaoka
Hanayashili, Takarazuka-shi
Hyogo-ken 665, Japan
Telephone   81 6 251 5560

JAOPA is the logical contact for additional information about recreational flying in Japan. It has few employees; be patient while waiting for a mail response. It might be best to call, with a Japanese interpreter close at hand on your end.

WHERE TO FLY, WHAT TO FLY

Japan offers beautiful aerial views for the recreational pilot, and the country has quite an aviation heritage dating back to the equipment and exploits of Japanese military aviators during World War II. Unfortunately, in a land where free time has been minimal and conformism is still the rule, such hedonistic individual activities as flying small airplanes for sheer pleasure have not been a high priority.

Japanese interest in recreational flying is on the rise, but the cost of flying in Japan is astronomical so the locals flock overseas for certification. The total cost of a round-trip airline ticket, the license, and room and board leave plenty in the checkbook for designer flight jackets and pilot's shades, and the newly minted private pilot is still ahead financially in comparison to getting the certificate in Japan. Flying schools on the United States' west coast that are operated by Japanese, for Japanese, are especially popular.

So where does this leave the visitor wishing to fly in Japan? The sights can be stunning, and there are plenty of opportunities if you are willing to foot the bill. But it might cost more just to get to the local airport than an hour or two of flying would cost at home. Most big cities have general aviation airports nearby where you will find the usual American light aircraft fleet and most likely an all-metal low-wing Japanese four-seater, the Fuji 200, made by the same folks who build the Subaru automobile.

Language might be a problem, so it might be most productive to have a Japanese interpreter with you, especially during a first visit to a particular airport. Check around upon arrival for the closest airports; JAOPA has a couple of recommendations:

Chofu Airport is in the southwestern section of greater Tokyo. It is reasonably accessible from downtown and is a good staging point for scenic flights around the city and to nearby Mt. Fuji and the surrounding national parks.

Honda Airport at Okegawa in Saitama Prefecturate to the northeast of Tokyo is farther from the city center than Chofu and offers the same scenic touring opportunities. An added attraction of Honda is the availability of skydiving.

Yao Airport in Yao city is in the eastern section of greater Osaka. It is also within easy reach of the imperial city of Kyoto.

VFR QUESTIONS & ANSWERS

What are good sources for VFR regulations? The Japanese AIP is in Japanese and English.

How can I get a weather briefing? Most airports have met offices for comprehensive briefings.

What are VFR visibility and ceiling minimums? In controlled airspace, 3 miles visibility to 15,000 feet, and 1,000-foot ceiling. In uncontrolled airspace, 1 mile visibility, clear of clouds below 1,000 feet, with additional cloud separation distance above 1,000 feet. Consult the Japanese AIP for precise minimums.

Is night VFR permitted? No.

Must I file a flight plan? Flight plans must be filed for all VFR flights that depart farther than a radius of five miles from the airport.

May I fly the airways VFR? Yes, under ATC control.

Must I maintain en route radio contact with ATC off the airways? Periodic position reporting is mandatory in certain FIRs.

Is VFR on top permitted? Yes.

ADDITIONAL INFORMATION SOURCES

JAOPA recommends the Japanese aviation magazine, *Tsubasa*. If you don't read Japanese, find a translator. The translation might be worth the effort to obtain current information regarding general aviation.

44

India

Country rating: **Difficult**

ONC Charts: **G-7, H-8, H-9, J-8, J-9, and K-8**

Rental cost range:

  2 seat trainer   **$40-65**
  4 seat fixed gear   **$70-90**
  4 seat retractable   **Generally not available**

QUALIFICATIONS AND LICENSE VALIDATION

India is an intensely bureaucratic and a highly security conscious country; thus, at the moment, it is impossible for the short-term visitor to get a license validated for flying Indian-registered aircraft on private, VFR flights. A short-term visitor must obtain a security clearance prior to flying dual with one of the 26 aeroclubs nationwide that offer recreational flying opportunities. It is easier to fly a glider dual with one of several local glider clubs.

Foreigners who move to India for a long time can obtain license validation for noncommercial VFR flight. Validation procedures include a written test on air regulations and a flight test. The best way to obtain validation is join an aeroclub and work through it.

India is included in this guide because in spite of the onerous license validation regulations and limited cross-country opportunities, determined long-term visitors will be rewarded with flying over one of the world's most ancient lands, and will experience great camaraderie among the members of the local flying club. A number of foreign residents in India who did not fly before moving to the country have obtained a pilot certificate at an Indian aeroclub.

DOCUMENTS YOU SHOULD TAKE

Pilot license
Current medical
Logbook
Radio operator license (if separate from pilot license)

The Aero Club of India headquarters at Safdarjung Airport in suburban New Delhi.

It is most important for the long-term visitor who wishes to obtain license validation to take these documents, but they may also come in handy for the short-term visitor who tries to arrange some dual. Documents always impress the Indian bureaucracy. Be sure to have the last page of the logbook notarized.

USEFUL FLYING ORGANIZATIONS

Aero Club of India
Safdarjung Airport
Safdarjung, Delhi

The Aero Club of India is the governing body of the national aeroclub system. It will provide the visitor with information on the location and equipment of the individual aeroclubs, as well as with guidance on license validation.

Delhi Flying Club
Safdarjung Airport
Safdarjung, Delhi

This aeroclub serves India's capital. It is equipped with several aircraft of Indian manufacture and design, several Cessna 150s, 152s, and a Rallye. It is conveniently located in a southern district of New Delhi across from the ancient tomb of Safdar Jung, a short drive from most in-town locations.

WHERE TO FLY, WHAT TO FLY

India is an immense subcontinent of more than 750 million people and 5,000 years of civilization. It is a physically varied and attractive land of Himalayan peaks, balmy beaches, harsh desert, rich farmland, and dense forests where tigers and elephants still run wild. It is also a country rich in flying traditions, having been an important stopover on the main route between Europe and the Far East since aviation's earliest days.

India also has an extensive (mainly military) aircraft industry, in the form of the state owned Hindustani Aeronautics Ltd., which produces some of its own designs as well as foreign designs on license. Unfortunately, India has to carefully manage its limited resources to meet the basic needs of its vast population and recreational flying is not a high priority.

Recreational flying is available through a national system of 26 aeroclubs scattered throughout the country. Until recently, the mainstay of these aeroclubs has been the Pushpak aircraft, a local knockoff of the Aeronca Chief. Another light airplane of Indian make is the three-seat metal-and-fabric Revathi taildragger. The selection has improved recently with the importation of aircraft from Cessna and Aerospatiale.

Aeroclubs in some of the cities popular with visitors are the Flying Club of Delhi, the Flying Club of Jaipur (the famous Rajhastani pink city), and the Flying Club of Bangalore. Pay them a visit and see what you can arrange. On and off it has also been possible to fly in light aircraft over the Taj Mahal at Agra; lately, it has been more off than on. Glider clubs also operate at Delhi, Jaipur, and other locations. Most soaring is local.

VFR QUESTIONS & ANSWERS

What are good sources for VFR regulations? Consult the Indian AIP.

How can I get a weather briefing? Most airports have met offices.

What are VFR visibility and ceiling minimums? Below 3,000 feet in controlled airspace, the visibility minimum is 3 miles, otherwise minimums conform to the ICAO standard.

Is night VFR permitted? Yes.

Must I file a flight plan? Yes.

May I fly the airways VFR? Yes. Periodic position reports are mandatory. Below 15,000 feet, observe the quadrant rules for VFR altitude separation, inherited from the British. Above 15,000 feet, the hemispherical ICAO altitude separation rules apply.

Must I maintain en route radio contact with ATC off the airways? Yes. Periodic position reports are mandatory.

Is VFR on top permitted? No.

45

Over the land
of the Taj Mahal

AN INDIAN AIRLINES 737 TOUCHED DOWN at the numbers on the 4,500-foot runway and decelerated rapidly with an enormous roar of the thrust reversers. We had arrived in Jaipur, a medieval town of forts and palaces, the world of the legendary maharajas. But suddenly, off the left wing, I caught a fleeting glimpse of something just as intriguing— the unmistakable shape of an Aeronca.

An Aeronca?

In India?

It turned out to be a Pushpak, an aircraft of Indian manufacture, and the backbone of flight training and general aviation in the country, in spite of its dated design.

Aviation plays an important role in India, where distances are vast and industrial and administrative centers are scattered far and wide. Indian Airlines has 300 daily domestic flights and Air India flies to five continents. The late prime minister, Rajiv Gandhi (son of Indira Gandhi), was an airline pilot before turning to politics when his brother, Sanjay, a member of parliament, died doing aerobatics in a Pitts Special.

The Indian Air Force flies supersonic fighters produced locally on license, and a handful of corporations and wealthy individuals own airplanes. But India is also a land of the ox cart and subsistence farming, a developing nation of 850 million people, where scarce resources are almost entirely consumed by basic needs. What little is left for aviation has to go a long way; thus, while general aviation exists, it is quite different from the way most of us know it.

Indirectly controlled by the government and operating on a skimpy budget through a nationwide system of flying and gliding clubs, the nation's goal is to introduce as many would-be pilots as possible to the world of flight, creating a pool of talent from which the country's airlines and air force can pick and choose. The airlines are interested in the power pilots, the air force in the glider pilots who learn to soar while in high school.

There are 26 flying clubs and about as many gliding clubs, all under the supervision of the Aeroclub of India. They range from small regional operations—such as the Flying Club of Jaipur with 15 members, two Pushpaks and the world's oldest Cessna 140—to large operations—such as the Delhi Flying Club with a membership of 50 (and a big waiting list) training on a fleet of five Pushpaks and a Cessna 152. Delhi also has a Rallye GT 180, and a Revathi, a rather awkward and underpowered three-seat metal-and-fabric taildragger of Indian design that never caught on as a successor to the Pushpak.

All the clubs are subsidized by the government to varying degrees. The aircraft are government-owned and are on loan to each flying club on the basis of demonstrated need. The club at Jaipur also receives a federal subsidy for each hour flown, and is given an annual donation by Jaipur state. The Delhi Flying Club is the least subsidized, relying entirely on the annual dues and the hourly rental payments of its large membership to meet operating costs.

The members of all flying clubs pay modest dues and an hourly aircraft rental, which is standard throughout the country and amounts to approximately $40 per hour for the Pushpaks. If that is compared to typical Indian take-home pay, the cost is astronomical in United States terms, amounting to hundreds of dollars.

This explains why, although membership is open to anyone, the majority of club members are student pilots who qualify for a 75 percent federal subsidy per flying hour up to a certain number of hours within which they are expected to earn a license. It is also the reason why all but the wealthiest private pilots do little besides staying current in spite of such daunting possibilities as an aerial view of the Taj Mahal.

Flight training is quite extensive, a minimum of 60 hours for the private license and 250 for the commercial ticket. Given the Pushpak's modest VFR abilities, this means an awful lot of basic flying. Commercial students get 10 hours of instrument instruction in a Link trainer, but no instrument ticket. An interesting requirement for the commercial license is a 125-nautical-mile night cross-country flight. Though great emphasis is placed on pilotage, India has a highly developed system of VOR airways.

A Pushpak during taxi for takeoff.

And what about the Pushpak, this Aeronca look alike? It is nothing more than an outright and unabashed copy of the good old Aeronca Super Chief, a delightful high-wing, side-by-side, two-seat, taildragger of fabric-covered aluminum and welded steel-tube construction, first produced in Middletown, Ohio, way back in 1940.

The Indian version was "developed" in 1958 (a full decade after the final Super Chief rolled off the Middletown assembly line), when Hindustan Aircraft Ltd., the state aircraft production firm, was commissioned to meet the country's need for a basic trainer. The first ones even had the Super Chief's wooden spars, later changed to all metal. The biggest difference is the Pushpak's 90-hp Continental engine, license-produced by Rolls Royce, and 25 horsepower more powerful than the Super Chief's original powerplant.

The extra horses did not increase performance, according to the figures. Perhaps the engine's extra weight had a greater effect than the added power, or perhaps the Indian performance figures are more realistic than the original. A total of 150 Pushpaks were delivered by the time production ended in 1969 and approximately 90 are still flying today.

N. M. Patel, a retired Hawker Hunter fighter pilot, is the chief flying instructor of the Delhi Flying Club at Safdarjung Airport. A big sign on his desk proclaims "I myself am the greatest critic of my flying standards."

The airport is in a suburb of Delhi, across from the monumental marble and sandstone tomb of the 16th century Mogul commander, Safdar Jung. On downwind, the entire capital is spread out at your feet. The Delhi Flying Club shares the airport with a gliding club. The powered aircraft yield the runway to the winch-launched gliders around noon when the thermals start cooking.

Patel speaks fondly of the Pushpak. "It is an excellent trainer for one reason," he says. "It forces the student to learn the basics. He must look outside." He also thinks that beyond the solo stage, the Pushpak is way past its time. "We are finally going to see some changes, though," he says. "The Aeroclub of India has obtained a $4.5 million federal grant to be matched with $5.5 million from the state governments. The initial objective is to equip every aeroclub with at least one Cessna 152, and the first airplanes in an order of 28 have just arrived."

A Central Flying School to train commercial pilots is also being established with the most up-to-date equipment including turboprop twins. "All the buttons they will be wanting to punch," says Patel, tongue in cheek. The flying clubs will no longer offer commercial licenses, and the Central Flying School will accept only as many pilots as can be guaranteed jobs. Considering India's limited resources, that makes a lot of sense in Patel's opinion. "Maybe when we retire the Pushpaks, your antique enthusiasts will buy them for dollars, just as they did with all of our Tiger Moths a few years ago." he says with a grin.

Although the fancy new airplanes will go a long way toward modernizing India's aeroclubs, they will not be enough to retire the classic taildraggers and, in a way, that is just as well. Pushpaks will soldier on as they have for decades and many an Indian Airlines pilot will feel a pang of nostalgia for years to come when he taxis in a jet past a little yellow Pushpak.

Australia and New Zealand

46

Australia

Country rating: **Easy**

ONC Charts: **N-13, N-14, P-12 through P-15, Q-12 through Q-15, and R-11 through R-13**

Rental cost range:

  2 seat trainer **$60-80**

  4 seat fixed gear **$90-110**

  4 seat retractable **$100-140**

QUALIFICATIONS AND LICENSE VALIDATION

It became quite easy in 1989 for a visiting private pilot with a license from an ICAO member country to fly VFR in Australia. Largely due to the tireless efforts of the Aircraft Owners and Pilots Association of Australia, the Civil Aviation Authority has established a system of designated briefers solely for the purpose of briefing visitors who wish to fly.

From a regulatory standpoint, all you have to do if you are current and have a valid medical is to get a thorough briefing from a designated briefer covering general aviation flying procedures and the geographic areas that you plan to visit. Following the briefing, solo flight becomes a simple matter of a prerental checkride at one of Australia's many flying establishments.

The briefers are thoroughly trained in highlighting the differences between Australian flying rules, regulations and customs, and those back home. The CAA has approved 24 designated briefer positions to be based within the vicinity of major general aviation airfields throughout Australia's six states and two territories. Briefers are currently based at Sydney and Melbourne, and additional appointments are imminent.

If you are serious about flying solo in Australia, plan your trip carefully to reach a destination with a designated briefer early. You might not find one at the location where you ultimately intend to rent an airplane. For example, if you want to fly a rental from Alice Springs to Ayres Rock, get a briefing at Sydney, en

Sydney is stunning. The opera house is framed by the financial district and the Botanical Gardens.

route to Alice Springs. The aeroclub of Alice Springs is no place to find out that the nearest designated briefer is 1,000 miles away.

A list of designated briefers and locations is available from the CAA or AOPA-Australia; call upon arrival, or write in advance.

The designated briefer system is fairly new, so don't be surprised if the locals are not always entirely familiar with it. Be patient, but persistent, with a puzzled flying school and if you run into problems, have them call the designee who performed your briefing. If you encounter serious resistance or confusion, have them call AOPA-Australia. Offer to pay for any telephone calls.

Visual Flight Guide, which is available at most flying schools and clubs, is an excellent and inexpensive government publication that is a must for solo flight. The bright orange plastic binder contains approximately 100 pages of loose-leaf information on all aspects of VFR flying. Take it to the designated briefer session.

DOCUMENTS YOU SHOULD TAKE

Pilot license
Current medical
Radio operator license (if separate from pilot license)
Logbook

Bring the original documents.

USEFUL FLYING ORGANIZATIONS

AOPA-Australia
P.O. Box 1065
Fyshwick A.C.T. 2609
Telephone (6) 280 4221
Facsimile (6) 280 7341

Publishes a periodical for members, and will sell you a sample copy (useful for getting ideas for airports and flying schools through the ads). Also publishes an airport facilities guide. Due to budgetary pressures, the organization is not equipped to distribute aerial tourism information, but is very helpful if you encounter difficulties.

Sport Aircraft Club of Australia
c/o New South Wales Group
Wedderburn Airport
Wedderburn, NSW.
Telephone (046) 341 238

Australia's equivalent of EAA. Considering that the Aussies have been known to charter an entire 747 to fly sport aviation fans to Oshkosh, this is definitely the organization to contract if you are interested in experimental aircraft.

Civil Aviation Authority
607 Swanston St.
Carlton, Victoria 3053

Australia's FAA. The organization to contact for guidance on regulations covering flight beyond the noncommercial day-VFR flying outlined here. Among regional offices is New South Wales, 59 Goulburn St., Sydney, NSW 2000.

WHERE TO FLY, WHAT TO FLY

Australia is the natural habitat for the airplane if ever there was one. The general aviation airplane is often more a necessity than a luxury with 16 million people living in an area the size of the United States. The vast distances and the rugged, sparsely populated outback, which made the country's flying doctor service world famous, has also created an air-minded environment with plenty of scope for the private pilot.

Approximately 80 percent of Australia's population lives in the southeastern coastal region centered around Sydney and Melbourne, two likely places for your initial land fall. These are also good jumping off points for such faraway destinations of great natural beauty as the 2,000-mile long Great Barrier Reef, Ayres Rock in the middle of the outback, and the beaches of the Gold Coast in the vicinity of Brisbane. You will find rental possibilities in all of these areas, and if you are ambitious and appropriately qualified, you can cover hundreds of miles touring from area to area.

Sydney and environs

Bankstown, (02 708 1222), is the region's, and perhaps the country's, premier general aviation airport, southeast of Sydney. Bankstown has three parallel runways and scores of commercial flying schools, several of which also have aeroclub arrangements. Two designated briefers are also based here, at the Aero Club of New South Wales, and Navair. The usual fleet of Pipers, Cessnas, Aerospatiales, Trinidads, and Tobagos is also available. An aerobatic school offers high quality instruction in sporty French Robins, and for the history minded, at the time of our last visit, scenic flying with some dual was available in at least one Tiger Moth. A large met office is also on site, a good place to learn first hand about getting an Australian weather briefing.

Bankstown is a good base for local scenic flying over Sydney Harbor and up the north coast toward the Hawkesbury River, and the Hunter Valley wine country. Daytrips west over the Blue Mountains and a taste of the outback beyond are highly recommended. The airport is also a good staging ground for longer touring flights up the coast or inland.

Camden, (02 708 3888), is south of Sydney, somewhat farther than Bankstown. Beyond the standard possibilities for powered flight, Camden is also Sydney's most popular soaring center.

Wedderburn, (046 341 238), also south of Sydney, is the home of the New South Wales branch of the Sport Aviation Club of Australia, the country's homebuilders organization. Homebuilt airplanes abound here, and their owners are always happy to see fellow homebuilders from abroad.

Maitland, (049 328 888), near Newcastle, is approximately one and a half hours, driving, north of Sydney. Maitland is home to several Tiger Moths, some of which are available for rent. One of the flying schools is renown for hosting an annual two- to three-week organized tour by light aircraft, covering most of Australia. The safari, as they call it, usually takes place in August when weather conditions are most ideal.

Hoxton Park, (02 708 3888), and **Schoefields,** (626 8708), which is a Royal Navy base during the week, are two additional Sydney-area airports where noncommercial flying is available.

The rest of Australia

Below are other common destinations and the corresponding general aviation airfields where a good selection of rental light aircraft is available for the private pilot.

Melbourne-Moorabin, (03 587 3666), has a designated briefer on the field. Melbourne, on the southeast Australian coast, is the second largest city after Sydney. You will find attractive mountain scenery to the north, and pretty coastline west, toward Fort Campbell.

Canberra Airport, (062 435 911), serves Australia's capital city. It has several local operators and is also an Air Force base.

Adelaide-Parafield, (08 252 2500), is an ideal airport to initiate flights into the outback. This southern coastal town is historically important as a railhead and a main jumping off point for the outback.

Brisbane-Archer Field, (07 275 8222), is on the Gold Coast, Australia's Miami Beach. Take a leisurely aerial tour of the coastline to add some variety to lying on the sand.

Perth-Jandakot, (09 478 8770), is the general aviation field for this bustling, modern mining town in western Australia.

Alice Springs Airport, (089 507 211), is smack in the middle of the great Australian outback. Alice Springs is the nearest town for visitors to Ayres Rock. You may rent aircraft at the local aeroclub for the flight to Ayres Rock **(Yulara Airfield)** approximately one and a half to two hours away, depending on cruising speed. It is best to fly out, spend the night, enjoy the spectacular sunset and sunrise over the rock—if you are lucky—and return the next day. Make rental arrangements prior to departure for Alice Springs to avoid problems and disappointment.

Narromine, (068 891 322), is a world-famous soaring center on the edge of the outback beyond the coastal mountain ranges in a region known for some of the world's most fantastic soaring weather. Outstanding dual cross-country training and high performance single-seat sailplanes are available.

TOURING

Touring Australia by light aircraft is one of recreational flying's great adventures. Distances are vast, the countryside is wild, and radio navaids are sufficiently sparse to make navigation a bit of a challenge away from the coast. The Royal Aero Club of Newcastle in Maitland organizes an annual three-week air safari every August that takes approximately 20 airplanes around the entire continent. Reviewing a typical safari route is the best way to get an idea of touring possibilities:

From the Sydney area the route departs west over the 4,000-foot high coastal Blue Mountains, into the outback. The first stop is Broken Hill, a famous outback station, mining town, and flying doctor center, that is 500 nautical miles to the west. From here, the route turns south to the coastal town of Adelaide 230 nautical miles away and then follows the coastline to Kalgoolie and on toward Perth in the southeast corner of Australia, 1,200 nautical miles down the coast. From there, it turns north, still along the coast, to the pearling center of Broome, and on to Darwin. From here, it is time to start heading back toward Sydney, and there are two good options depending upon personal preference for more outback flying, or the beaches and the Great Barrier Reef.

The outback option is toward the south, through one of Australia's *Designated Remote Areas* to Alice Springs. In this particular DRA it is mandatory to follow specified roads, and to stay within five miles of them on either side. From Alice Springs, it is on to Broken Hill, and back to Sydney.

The coastal option from Darwin is east to the Gulf of Carpentaria and some of Australia's most deserted coastline. Then it is on to the Great Barrier Reef and the 2,000-mile journey south to Sydney through Cairns, the Whitsunday Passage, Brisbane, and the Gold Coast beaches.

These routes are the outer extreme of aerial touring. The hours are long, the flying intensive, and the total distance covered is approximately 6,200 nautical miles, or on average approximately 350 nautical miles per day, assuming three rest days along the way (in practice, there are longer legs and additional leisure days). The typical tourist would most likely opt for fewer doses, which still present formidable distances in comparison to what most pilots are accustomed to.

One popular option from Sydney, comfortably accomplished in two weeks, is to fly up to Alice Springs and Ayres Rock via Broken Hill, and then fly due east to the coast and the southern edge of the Barrier Reef, followed by a return to Sydney via the Gold Coast.

Two shorter variations are to fly out to Broken Hill, down to Adelaide and back to Sydney along the coast, or to fly straight up along the Pacific shore to the Gold Coast and back.

Weather

Australia is thought of as the land of sunshine, but as every VFR pilot knows, life is not as simple as that. The Sydney-Melbourne population belt along the southeast coast, where most touring flights originate, is bordered on the west by a coastal range, and that means trouble when a moisture laden wind blows inland from the Pacific: rain and low scud. Expect to be grounded longer than you prefer at any time throughout the year in this region.

The rest of the country is bone-dry except for the brief rainy season from December through March, or as the Australians call it, the **Wet**, so once you are past the Blue Mountains you should be all set. The Wet does take its toll throughout the land. Its steady torrential downpours can seriously upset any schedule everywhere, so it is best avoided.

Flight over remote areas

You have to give careful consideration to flying over Australia's sparsely populated outback, especially if you are not used to such terrain. Australian flight regulations go a long way to assure flight safety over remote areas and with a cautious, commonsense attitude, you should have few problems with an excellent chance of early rescue in the unlikely event of a forced landing. Three key issues arise when considering wilderness flying: not getting lost, being found quickly in case of a forced landing, and having sufficient emergency supplies.

Besides the usual accurate techniques of navigation, you can often plan a VFR flight over remote areas with a few things going for you. Chances are that you will have far fewer manmade features in a remote area than in a densely populated area; thus, it is quite easy to find and follow the road, the railroad, or the river leading to your destination. Fuel management becomes the only concern after the course is established.

The north-south VFR route through Central Australia's designated remote area requires that an aircraft remain within five miles left or right of the road or the railroad. The purpose of these regulations is not only to make navigation a no-brainer, but to make it easy to find you in case of a forced landing.

Outside designated remote areas, Australia's flight planning regulations also provide for measures to maximize the chances of your rescue, but it is up to you to use them. Australia has three categories of flight plans: *No Search and Rescue (SAR)*, *SAR Time*, and *Full SAR*.

No Search and Rescue applies to VFR flights below 5,000 feet; just jump in an airplane and go anywhere, cruising below 5,000 feet, in the entire country, outside designated remote areas, without saying a word to anyone.

Above 5,000 feet, a pilot must file a VFR flight plan, and designate SAR Time, which means that a search shall commence if you fail to show up at the flight plan's destination by a certain time.

A Full SAR requires en route VFR position reporting from the pilot. A pilot is foolish to venture over wilderness areas without filing Full SAR.

Concerned about survival after a forced landing? If you planned well, you will be found quickly. Know where you are at all times and broadcast your position on 121.5 MHz during the emergency descent, if not already in contact with ATC. There is a good chance that an airline will hear the Mayday and relay the message. If possible, on the ground, continue trying to contact an airplane on 121.5, but sparingly, to conserve the aircraft battery.

You can have all sorts of survival gear, but the most important item is at least a few days supply of water. A blanket or two would also be useful because the desert can get bitterly cold at night.

The designated briefer will provide thorough guidance if your plans include extensive wilderness flying.

VFR QUESTIONS & ANSWERS

What are good sources for VFR regulations? Consult the Australian AIP and the *Visual Flight Guide* published by the Civil Aviation Authority.

How can I get a weather briefing? You can get comprehensive weather briefings in person at the met office of a large airport, and elsewhere, by telephone. Telephone numbers are available at the airport where you fly.

What are VFR visibility and ceiling minimums? Controlled airspace minimums are 3 miles visibility below 5,000 feet MSL, 5 miles at or above 5,000 feet, and a 1,500-foot ceiling. Uncontrolled airspace minimums are 3 miles visibility and clear of clouds.

Is night VFR permitted? Yes.

Must I file a flight plan? You must fly a flight plan for all flights above 5,000 feet MSL. Check in the AIP or the VFG for the categories of search and rescue services available and required depending on your proposed flight.

Can I fly the airways VFR? Yes. You must have an airways clearance, which will be issued by ATC, based upon your flight plan.

Must I maintain en route radio contact with ATC on or off the airways? At or above 5,000 feet MSL you must provide periodic position reports in both cases.

Is VFR on top permitted? VFR on top is permitted only in uncontrolled airspace above 2,000 feet.

ADDITIONAL INFORMATION SOURCES

Two useful sources of information are the aforementioned *Visual Flight Guide* published by the Civil Aviation Authority, and the *Airfield Directory* compiled by AOPA Australia. The directory is especially useful if you plan to fly to numerous destinations on an extensive aerial tour of Australia. It is a listing of most Australian airports, the services available at them, and nearby accommodations. It does not contain airport diagrams.

Aviation magazines are also a good source of up-to-date information, and for a country with only 16 million people, Australia has a surprising number of aviation journals.

Australian Aviation is an attractive bi-monthly generalist flying magazine aimed as much at the aviation enthusiast as the licensed pilot. It contains a fair number of ads for flying schools, and is available on most newsstands.

Australian Flying is aimed at the private pilot. Most of its articles cover some aspect of piloting. Typical topics are training, cross-country, and flight test reports on aircraft of interest to the private pilot. Available at newsstands, but not widely distributed, so some searching is necessary.

Aircraft is a smaller circulation general interest magazine with some Australian content useful for the private pilot. Available on newsstands, but you have to search for it.

AOPA-Pilot is full of useful information and ads for the private pilot. Available by subscription only, but most aeroclubs have back issues lying around. AOPA will also sell you a sample issue.

Yellow pages in the large cities are also an excellent source of information on rentals and flying schools.

47

Flying down under

THE CHEROKEE WAS HUMMING ALONG above the vast Australian outback on a late evening flight from Thargomindah to Oodnadatta, when the engine failed. The pilot managed a quick position report to Alice Springs as the airplane began its depressingly silent glide toward the desolate salt flats of Lake Eyre. The three occupants' immediate fears were dispelled by a successful emergency landing, but they now had to contend with the thought of endless days in the arid bush and even the grim possibility of a slow death from exposure. The closest human settlement was more than 100 miles away. What happened next was extraordinary, even by the standards of pilots for whom flying in wilderness areas is all in a day's work.

Ansett Airlines Flight 42, a Boeing 727 with 122 passengers on board, was on its way from Alice Springs to Adelaide, cruising at 34,000 feet, 80 miles northwest of Lake Eyre, when its crew heard the Cherokee pilot's distress calls. They immediately altered course toward the lake, started to descend, and announced to the passengers that all on board were about to participate in a search for the stricken aircraft. "The passengers thought it was great," said Alan Potts, the 727 captain. "Not too many people get down low in that sort of country. It's a bit of an adventure."

The 727 descended to 1,000 feet agl, switched on its landing lights, and set up a search pattern. Radio contact was established with the Cherokee's pilot who soon saw the 727 and began providing directions. With only minutes remaining before total darkness, a sharp-eyed passenger on the 727 spotted the Cherokee. Its position was accurately established and relayed to Alice Springs Search and Rescue via another commercial flight.

Fixed-wing aircraft of the provincial police dropped blankets and provisions at the site during the night, and the following morning a helicopter rescued the three stranded flyers.

Everyone down under pitches in when a pilot gets in trouble.

Australia is two thirds the size of the United States, yet it is inhabited by only 16 million people. Many of them live on remote sheep and cattle stations and in

French-built Tobago being readied for flight in Australia.

obscure mining communities in the country's vast wilderness areas, commonly referred to as the *outback*.

Aviation plays an important role in their lives. Many ranchers have bush planes and the mining companies have big in-house flight departments. FBOs run a regular network of mail and cargo flights to individual homesteads. The Royal Flying Doctor Service is a local legend and it is not uncommon for even the priest to fly himself to his next sermon.

It doesn't take long to get on the aviation trail upon arrival in Australia. The Sydney telephone book is full of flying establishments; Chieftain Aviation, Professional Flyers, Kingsford Smith Aviation. My eye caught a set of old-fashioned wings around a flying kangaroo: Royal Aero Club of New South Wales. "Setting the standard since 1920," was beneath the wings. I found the club at Bankstown Airport, Sydney's primary general aviation field, approximately 40 minutes, driving, southwest of the city center.

The aeroclub is the Piper FBO. In spite of its name, it is a commercial training school. On the line is a spick-and-span fleet of 23 airplanes: Archers, Warriors, Senecas, 140s, Tobagos, Trinidads, and seven Tomahawks. The school has always painted its aircraft in its own distinctive color scheme, and the design had recently been revised. Most of the planes were in the new livery; all-white wings and fuselage, and a bright red tail with a white kangaroo, not unlike the color scheme of Qantas, Australia's international airline.

(During the 1960s, the aeroclub was Qantas' primary flight training school on contract. After a two-decade absence, the airline had just accepted new bids for a flight training program, and the aeroclub was hopeful. The color scheme wouldn't hurt, if they won.)

The office was formula FBO, except for the neat uniforms worn by the staff of full-time instructors. I met John Zarlenga at the flight desk, who, but for his accent, could have been a young instructor from Anytown, USA. We were to take an Archer for a look at Sydney and its environs, but first we sat down to talk about local customs.

Private pilot training is slightly more structured than in the United States. The first step is a restricted pilot license for a minimum of 33 hours of basic flight training; it is common practice to log more time, 25 hours of dual and 15 hours of solo for a total of 40 hours. The license restricts the holder to the pattern and practice area of his or her home base.

Next comes 27 hours of navigation training and a navigation flight test that removes the restriction, giving the holder the equivalent of a United States private license without night flying privileges.

The night endorsement requires 10 hours of night flying and 5 hours on instruments.

Writtens are also more structured, segregated by topic (aeronautics, navigation, meteorology, and the like).

The commercial license and instrument rating requirements are similar to the United States. A curiosity of the IFR rating is that it is possible and quite common to get one endorsed for only VOR and NDB approaches because the number of ILS facilities in the country can be counted on two hands. Single-engine IFR to carry passengers for hire is not permitted. An individual aircraft type endorsement is required for all twins, in addition to the twin rating.

Given the country's vast open spaces, pilotage is taken very seriously. The aeroclub maintains an extensive set of predetermined cross-country routes, and makes it a point to give students experience "outback," away from Sydney's relatively urban environment. (There is a note next to Crookwell on the cross-country list: "Call Mrs. Cummins to check that the airstrip is clear of sheep.")

The same flight that takes the student to Crookwell also includes a landing at Charles Kingsford Smith, Sydney's international airport, named after Australia's most famous aviation pioneer, who was first to cross the Pacific by air. His name is a mouthful though, and Smith alone just doesn't sound like Kennedy or La Guardia, so flying people (and cabbies) call the airport by its old name, Mascot. The names I liked most on the cross-country list were Wollongong and Boorowa and Katoomba.

Two types of VFR flight plans are Full Search and Rescue and Search and Rescue Time, which were also discussed in chapter 46. The former requires continuous position reports to ATC, resulting in an instant search and rescue effort if contact is lost. The latter is like a United States VFR flight plan, calling out search and rescue only if the expected time of arrival at the filed destination is exceeded. Filing is optional for VFR flights below 5,000 feet; position reporting to ATC is required above 5,000 feet.

Curiously enough, with all the wilderness around the place, ELTs are mandatory only in designated wilderness areas (which must be really wild), and only if the aircraft is not equipped with an HF radio.

Walking out to the Archer, we passed two airplanes rarely, if ever, seen in the United States. One was a Victa Airtourer, an Australian all-metal fully aerobatic

The Royal Aero Club of New South Wales, in business for five decades.

side-by-side two-seat trainer/tourer. Its clean lines are reminiscent of the Grumman AA-1 and belie the design's age. In 1953, it was the winner out of 104 entries of the Royal Aero Club of Great Britain's light aircraft design competition.

Subsequently, 170 were built by Victa Ltd. of Australia before the project was moved to Aero Engine Services of New Zealand where production continued into the 1970s. A novel design feature of the Airtourer that could be of great interest to homebuilders is its simple control stick. One column comes up between the side-by-side seats and a hollow square is attached to it. Each pilot holds a side of the square, which, in effect, amounts to a side stick.

The other intriguing plane on the ramp was a Scottish Aviation Twin Pioneer, a prehistoric looking taildragger with two big radial engines, huge windows, and three enormous vertical stabilizers. The Pioneer was a very effective STOL utility aircraft of the 1950s, capable of carrying more than a dozen passengers in and out of the shortest and roughest strips. Today, immaculately restored and equipped with genuine leather seats, this one loiters at 60 knots over Sydney with sightseers.

My flight with John was a pleasant CAVU excursion up to the Murray River, just north of Sydney, and back down along the coast to Sydney Harbor. Harbor Bridge, the unique opera house, and the city skyline is one of the most spectacular aerial sights anywhere. But there was no wandering around. We strictly held our reported altitude, and outside the TCA we gave old-fashioned estimates to checkpoints (to be accurate plus-minus two minutes), even though the controller had us on his scope (and a 1200 transponder code would have made things a lot simpler). We were given a code to circle over the harbor inside the TCA where the controller was operating on the theory that whenever two aircraft are in the air at the same time a collision might be imminent.

He sternly told us to stay north of the water until a solitary helicopter cleared the area; none of this "Helicopter at 10 o'clock, keep him in sight" business.

On the way back to Bankstown, I asked John about any exotic airplanes in the neighborhood. "Chap at the field flies people around in his Tiger Moth," he said. I thought of viewing the harbor from the open cockpit biplane and resolved to find the chap as soon as we got back.

David Voight must have the only Tiger Moth in the world painted like the Red Baron's Triplane. I knew Australians liked to play jokes on the British, but this seemed a bit much. "Belonged to a chap who played the bad guy in a World War I movie." explained Voight, "It was in great condition, so I announced that the Red Baron was here to give scenic flights and business has been booming ever since." The Moth has become a familiar sight over Sydney, and Voight looks like he should be somewhere in the past with the Great Waldo Pepper in his weathered sheepskin flying jacket, leather helmet, and flying goggles.

Though quite a few Tiger Moths flew out to Australia all the way from England during the late 1930s, Voight's plane was built locally in 1940 right at Bankstown by de Havilland Australia. It served with the 7th Air Training Squadron in Tasmania during World War II, and then embarked on a long second career as a crop duster. This was a common fate for Tiger Moths, just as it was for their United States counterpart, the Stearman.

The flight over Sydney in the Tiger was a real taste of the past, just like the old photos of all those biplanes over the Harbor Bridge. The modern buildings did not intrude on the illusion, and this time we had the airspace to ourselves: no helicopters. On the way home, we were cleared straight over the international airport, a view rich in historical perspective from the open cockpit. It is right on Botany Bay, discovered in 1770 by Captain Cook and site of the first colonial settlement a few years later. It was the ultimate destination of the Fokker Trimotor, "The Southern Cross," in 1928, piloted by Charles Kingsford Smith and his crew on the first flight across the Pacific (they landed in Brisbane, where the aircraft is now on display). It was also the last stop for many of the Tiger Moths on their long journey from Britain. Below us were the jumbo jets about to depart on their daily flights to San Francisco or London or Amsterdam.

Voight does not give instruction, or rent out the Tiger Moth to a solo pilot, but he can refer people to an accommodating Tiger Moth owner in nearby Newcastle.

I plan to look him up on my next trip down under.

Then I'll head outback.

Below 5,000 feet.

48

New Zealand

Country rating: **Moderate**

ONC Charts: **R-15 and S-13**

Rental cost range:

  2 seat trainer **$70-90**

  4 seat fixed gear **$100-120**

  4 seat retractable **$130-160**

QUALIFICATIONS AND LICENSE VALIDATION

Visitors who intend to fly solo VFR in New Zealand registered aircraft must get temporary license validation. A written test on New Zealand air regulations is required to receive validation, but this is less ominous than it sounds. The test is administered by one of any number of regular flying instructors who are designated by the government and will issue a validation on the spot as soon as you pass the test. The instructors will also prep you for the test, if necessary.

No flight test is required, and validation remains in effect for three months, or the expiry of your license, whichever comes first. AOPA-New Zealand has the list of designated instructors, as does the New Zealand Air Transport Division. Expect a thorough checkride from the operator renting an airplane.

DOCUMENTS YOU SHOULD TAKE

Pilot license
Current medical
Logbook
Radio operator license (if separate from pilot license)

Take original documents. The instructor validating your license will need to see the license and logbook, and the operator renting an airplane will want to see them all.

USEFUL FLYING ORGANIZATIONS

Examination Section
Air Transport Division
P.O. Box 31441
Lower Hutt

This branch of government oversees license validations.

AOPA-New Zealand
Claremont
RD 4
Timaru

The local AOPA is very helpful to visiting pilots. Contact them upon arrival for the current list of designated instructors who can issue validations, and for a few words of advice on recreational flying in New Zealand.

WHERE TO FLY, WHAT TO FLY

The Maoris (Polynesian people native to New Zealand) call New Zealand *Aotearoa*, the Land of the Long White Cloud. New Zealand is approximately 1,000 nautical miles long, yet no spot is farther than 70 nautical miles from the ocean. There are two main islands, the rather rotund North Island and the longer, more gracefully shaped South Island. The Southern Alps tower more than 12,000 feet and run almost the length of South Island. Under the right wind conditions, the mountains throw off a massive series of lenticulars that blend together and seem to run for hundreds of miles. Hence the name, Aotearoa. Soaring pilots take note.

The closest big land mass to New Zealand is Australia, 1,200 nautical miles to the west across the Tasman Sea. This distance has made New Zealanders great fans of airplanes ever since the earliest days, when only dreamers dared to think that the flying machine would cut their isolation from the rest of the world from days and weeks to mere hours. New Zealanders are an enterprising lot, and have provided a steady supply of pilots to the British Empire until its demise, and to any operator in need worldwide, ever since. The aviation bug is also alive and well back home in New Zealand, and opportunities for light aircraft touring, soaring, and vintage aircraft flying abound.

All of New Zealand is attractive from the air, but it is especially difficult to find superlatives to describe the wild, primeval beauty of the Southern Alps. Here, scenic tours by light aircraft are big business, and for the pilot with mountain experience, self-flying is the way to go. For the pilot without mountain experience it is one of the best places to learn.

Every big city has airports where light aircraft rentals are available. You will find the usual American fleet, as well as some fine antique and classic aircraft, mostly English. Be also on the lookout for the chance to fly an Airtourer, a spiffy low-wing, side-by-side, two-seat, all-metal tourer/trainer of Australian design also produced in quantity in New Zealand during the 1960s and early 70s.

Selected airports and touring opportunities should be considered because their surroundings are popular destinations for visitors.

North Island

Ardmore serves Auckland, New Zealand's commercial center and largest city, and is a common entry point for visitors. Flying schools and aeroclubs at Ardmore are complemented by warbirds and vintage aircraft.

Paraparaumu is the general aviation airport serving Wellington, the country's capital. New Zealand's governmental aviation departments are located in Wellington. It is only 20 miles from Wellington to the northernmost tip of South Island. A popular touring route is across the Cook Strait to Nelson, over the Tasman Bay and Marlborough Sounds, to Palmerston North, and back to Wellington.

Masterton is a short distance northeast of Wellington. It is well known for its vintage aircraft.

South Island

Harewood in Christchurch on the east coast of South Island is the ideal staging point for flights to New Zealand's highest mountain, 12,349-foot Mt. Cook and the 17 peaks more than 10,000 feet high that surround it. The route takes you west over rich farm land before it slips through a 7,500-foot pass and continues along the 18-mile-long Tasman Glacier to descend into Mt. Cook Airport at 2,500 feet.

Frankton, outside Queenstown on the alpine shores of Lake Wakatipu, is an excellent jumping off point for nearby Milford and Te Anau airstrips that serve the 3-million acre Fiordland National Park, Milford Sound, and Lake Te Anau. Plan to spend hours roaming over this splendid, glacier-sculpted terrain of barren granite, virgin forest, and bottomless fjord.

Taieri serves Dunedin, a Scottish settlement and onetime gold rush site on the southeast coast of South Island. Taieri is another good gateway for aerial tours of the Te Anau, Milford Sound, and Fiordland regions.

Nelson Airport serves the comfortable and balmy beach resort of Nelson, at the northern tip of South Island. Fly around Tasman Bay and Cook Strait, and fly over to Wellington or Masterton.

VFR QUESTIONS & ANSWERS

What are good sources for VFR regulations? Consult the New Zealand AIP.

How can I get a weather briefing? The met offices at the bigger airports give good briefings. Visit in person, or call.

What are VFR visibility and ceiling minimums? New Zealand has adopted the ICAO VFR minimums.

Is night VFR permitted? No.

Must I file a flight plan? Yes, for all flights requiring ATC services.

May I fly the airways VFR? Yes. You must give periodic position reports.

Must I maintain en route radio contact with ATC off the airways? If you are on a flight plan, you must give hourly position reports.

Is VFR on top permitted? No.

ADDITIONAL INFORMATION SOURCES

Wings is the local flying magazine.

Africa

49

Kenya

Country rating: **Moderate**

ONC Charts: **L-5 and M-5**

Rental cost range:

  2 seat trainer **$70-85**

  4 seat fixed gear **$90-110**

  4 seat retractable **$120-160**

QUALIFICATIONS AND LICENSE VALIDATION

Kenyan civil aviation authorities will validate private pilot licenses issued by other ICAO member states, but require a written test on Kenyan air laws and regulations. The test is not particularly difficult, but can be taken only at certain times, so it requires some careful logistics to arrange taking it, especially on a short-term visit. The best way to go about this is to work through CMC Aviation at Nairobi's Wilson Field (address and telephone number are elsewhere in this chapter). Write to them, or give them a call.

Glider pilots may soar solo on their foreign licenses without validation.

DOCUMENTS YOU SHOULD TAKE

Pilot license

Current medical

Logbook

Radio operator license (if separate from pilot license)

Bring original documents, as well as some notarized photocopies that the authorities might want to keep.

USEFUL FLYING ORGANIZATIONS

Nairobi's Wilson Field has three operators with light aircraft available for rent:

Aeroclub of East Africa
P.O. Box 40813
Nairobi, Kenya
Telephone   501772

This nonprofit club has been around in some form or fashion since the days when Beryl Markham and Denys Finch-Hatton flew Pussmoths out of Wilson Field in the 1930s to resupply hunting parties and spot game. The club has a nice fleet of trainers and touring aircraft of various makes. An important function of the club is flight training. Ask about temporary memberships.

CMC Aviation
P.O. Box 44580
Nairobi, Kenya
Telephone   501221

CMC Aviation is a commercial flying school and charter operator of long standing, experienced in charter services and flight instruction. CMC is an excellent choice for the short-term visitor wishing to fly with a local safety pilot instead of hassling with license validation; CMC can assist with license validation. The fleet includes Piper Tomahawks, Warriors, and Archers.

Rent A Plane Ltd.
P.O. Box 42730
Nairobi, Kenya
Telephone   501431

Rent A Plane is a relative newcomer at Wilson Field, providing aircraft rentals.

WHERE TO FLY, WHAT TO FLY

Aviation has long been a part of Kenya's often romantic, at times harsh, but always colorful, history. The countryside is wild and not easily traveled overland. It is an ideal environment for general aviation, and the bush is dotted with landing strips. Journeys to the country's famous game parks and wilderness areas that might take half a day or more from Nairobi in a jeep or a minivan are reduced to an hour or two in an Piper Archer or Cessna 182. Kenya's flying doctor service is rightly as famous as the one in Australia.

Kenya's terrain is attractive and varied. To the south of Nairobi is big game country. Here in the low-lying grassland you will encounter lions and elephants, buffalo and giraffes, hippos, rhinoceros, antelope, and countless other game in greater numbers than anywhere in the world. And rising from the savanna is 19,000-foot Mount Kilimanjaro, Africa's highest peak.

A short flight north of Nairobi is the highlands, the Aberdares, and 17,000-foot Mount Kenya. Farther north is the moonscape desert surrounding Lake Turkana.

The Great Rift Valley, man's ancestral home, conspicuously visible from the air, is west of Nairobi and beyond it stretch the vast waters of Lake Victoria.

The Kenyan coast is east of Nairobi with balmy, sparkling beaches of Mombasa, Malindi, and Fort Lamu. Too many options in Kenya make choosing a destination difficult.

A flight from Kilimanjaro to Nairobi in an Archer takes slightly more than an hour.

Nairobi's Wilson Field is the place to fly in Kenya, as detailed elsewhere in this chapter.

Nairobi's central location gives you a nice choice of flight planning options. If you wish to taste bush flying on a short local hop, head for the Ngong hills and the Great Rift Valley beyond. You can motor around the valley and be back in about an hour.

More attractive, but longer, excursions are flights toward Kilimanjaro to the south and the Amboseli game reserve at its base, or the Mount Kenya region to the north. You can fly these routes round-trip in approximately two and a half hours, including a generous aerial sightseeing allowance. An especially pleasant experience is to include a lunch stop at the Amboseli Buffalo game lodge or one of the northern country clubs. There are two main landing strips at Amboseli; Amboseli Buffalo is the one to the east. A cardinal rule on the ground at the game park bush strips is never stray farther or walk more than than a few wing-spans from the airplane and always be alert for game that could be dangerous.

The premier big game destination is the Masai Mara game reserve, Kenya's section of the Serengeti, sharing the border with Tanzania. The Mara is slightly more than two hours southwest of Nairobi and a number of its lodges and tented camps such is Keekorok, Kichwa Tembo, Governor's Camp, and Cotter's Camp have their own bush strips. You can easily fly the Mara route round-trip from Nairobi in a day, but it would be a shame not to stop for at least a day or two of serious game viewing. Find out beforehand the requirements for landing at the various bush strips (some might require prior permission) and make accommodation arrangements in advance.

The ultimate aerial safari experience is to fly from game park to game park. If you manage to get a validated license, such a trip is subject only to a thorough checkout. If your pilotage and wilderness skills are a bit rusty or nonexistent, a day or so of instruction should get you squared away. Another alternative is to plan a longer tour in the company of a hired safety pilot. This option might be less expensive than you think, and hired safety pilots are content to make themselves scarce during nonflying hours.

A nice tour of approximately 10 days is to fly down to the Mara for a few days, followed by a hop east to Amboseli, then on to Tsavo, and an Indian Ocean beach resort, before returning to Nairobi, or spending a few days up north. Build in some flexibility for possible weather delays. Book accommodations in advance.

The weather is not generally a problem during the dry season; for days, there will not be a cloud in the sky. But in the vicinity of mountainous terrain you might have to deal with occasional cumulus buildups or local fog and low stratus, especially north of Nairobi. Kenya has two rainy seasons, the short rains during November, and the long rains during April and May. Avoid big flying plans during the rainy seasons, especially the long rains. You might also have to contend with increasingly unsettled weather during the seasonal transition periods.

Much of Kenya is wilderness, though some areas are densely populated, and if you are forced down in an area where predators are on the loose, you would be foolish to venture far on foot. It is important, even on shorter flights, to have a supply of water and emergency equipment on board.

Perhaps the best option for a Kenyan visit is to prearrange a traditional safari, with room for a few days of flying at the end. Obtain any validations and reserve an airplane before you depart on the safari.

Exotic flying options are soaring at Meru airstrip in the Mount Kenya region and dawn ballooning in the Masai Mara. Ballooning has been a longtime and expensive favorite of many Mara visitors, most of whom are not flyers.

VFR QUESTIONS & ANSWERS

What are good sources for VFR regulations? Consult the Kenyan AIP, available at the flying schools and aeroclubs.

How can I get a weather briefing? Wilson Field and Moi Airport have weather offices where full briefings are available. Teletyped weather information is available at other controlled fields.

What are VFR visibility and ceiling minimums? Minimums are 5 miles visibility with a 1,500-foot ceiling in controlled airspace and uncontrolled airspace above 1,000 feet agl; 1 mile and clear of clouds in uncontrolled airspace at or below 1,000 feet agl.

Is night VFR permitted? No, except in the airport pattern by special arrangement with ATC.

Must I file a flight plan? Flight plans are required if you depart from a controlled airport, and strongly recommended for all cross-country flights, given Kenya's wilderness areas.

May I fly the airways VFR? Yes. You must file a flight plan and fly under ATC's positive control. Air filing is permitted if you decide after departure to fly on an airway.

Must I maintain en route radio contact with ATC off the airways? If flying under a flight plan, you must give brief, hourly position reports.

Is VFR on top permitted? Yes, above 1,000 feet agl. A VFR descent and landing at the destination must be assured. According to the AIP, visual contact with the surface is required only below 1,000 feet agl.

ADDITIONAL INFORMATION SOURCES

Kenya has no aviation publications of note. However, two books are a must to get a flavor of light aircraft flying, past and present, over this colorful and challenging land. Beryl Markham's *West with the Night* has become a classic portrayal of bush flying in Kenya during the 1930s. It is also an entertaining memoir of a lifestyle gone forever. It is available in bookstores worldwide.

Derek Wood's *Go An Extra Mile* is a contemporary account of the life and flying times of Kenya's original flying doctor. It is available in Nairobi's larger bookstores.

50

Fly to a game park

RUNWAY FREE AND CLEAR OF ELEPHANTS: Most pilots will never see this item on a prelanding checklist; but it's a must if you fly into Amboseli Buffalo, a game lodge in Kenya's Amboseli Wildlife Reserve at the foot of 19,000-foot-high Mt. Kilimanjaro, the highest peak in Africa. Amboseli Buffalo's laterite airstrip is approximately one hour flying time from Nairobi, the capital, and is one of several remote bush strips in the heart of Kenya's big game region.

On a recent visit to Nairobi, a friend and I flew down to Amboseli one morning in an Archer I rented from CMC Aviation, the local Piper dealer. I had made the flight several times before, but, like flying to the beach back home, I am always ready to do it again. We left Wilson Field, Nairobi's general aviation airport, on a southerly heading to pick up a dry riverbed. We followed it out to a vast, arid plain and intercepted another river that led us to the lodge. Ahead, disappearing into its self-generated shroud of clouds, was Kilimanjaro.

We landed in a stiff breeze and shut down next to a Cessna 414 that was unloading a group of Swedish tourists, and a Cherokee Six on a private safari. It was only a short walk from the airstrip to the lodge, but we went by minivan because in the game reserve there is always the chance of crossing paths with lions, elephants, or buffalo. Attacks are rare, but they do happen, usually to people who mock the recommended precautions.

The lodge is a comfortable oasis of thatch-roofed bungalows, a big pool, an excellent restaurant, and a complete bar. It is a great base for the game drives that are conducted in specially constructed minivans with roofs that lift up onto folding bars, and provide an unobstructed view and an excellent photo platform all around. The vans never hold more than six and parties of three or four are not uncommon.

It was the dry season at Amboseli, the best time to view large concentrations of game as they congregate around the river and the few wet water holes. On our first game drive, right after lunch, we quickly found ourselves amidst vast herds of zebra and gazelles, and one of the most populous and odd looking inhabitants of the East African grasslands, the wildebeest. They look like a small, skinny, and agile cousin of the American buffalo. They are forever on the move in a

A common inhabitant of Masai Mara.

migratory pattern, constantly grazing on the run, moving to give the grass a chance to regrow.

We stopped often, and shut off the engine to watch the peacefully feeding herds in silence. Driving past a dense thicket of thornbushes, we came upon a pride of lions. Sprawled in every direction, snoozing in the afternoon heat, they didn't even bat an eyelash while we watched. As we approached the river, we startled some giraffes. They sailed off across the plain, their long necks swaying elegantly to and fro. We also saw warthogs, hyenas, and an occasional jackal.

In the late afternoon, we heard the sound of crunching and crumpling coming from a clump of shuddering acacia trees, as if some giant was ripping them out of the ground. The trees were being ravaged by a herd of grazing elephants. We watched for a long time, fascinated by the elephants' casual strength.

Suddenly, just as the big beasts began to lumber past us, the clouds in the background parted to reveal the snowcapped peak of Mt. Kilimanjaro. It was an image straight out of Hemingway's books and the days of Baron von Blixen, the great professional hunter and naturalist of the 1930s.

I half expected to catch a glimpse at any moment of Beryl Markham's fragile biplane approaching from the north. A legendary East African bush pilot, she often flew in supplies from Nairobi for Blixen's safaris and spotted game for him. Her book, *West with the Night,* is a must for anyone with an interest in East Africa and flying in the early days.

Back at the lodge, we sat around an open fire late into the night, sipping gin and tonics, another great legacy of Africa; tonic water contains quinine and was once recommended to ward off malaria; the gin was added to make it go down more easily. Pleasant as it might taste, take the pills to prevent the chills and fever.

The next morning, we awoke before dawn to steaming pots of tea for the early morning game drive. It is the best time to see the predators in action before they settle into idleness to pass the heat of day. We were lucky enough to encounter a relatively elusive sight, a *kill.* A pride of lions was feeding on a water buffalo that was downed during the night. The males had already had their fill, and were lounging nearby. It was the females' turn, and already they were being accosted by the more aggressive cubs. Surrounding them at a respectable distance were the scavengers waiting patiently in their characteristically ominous pose: vultures, jackals, and a hyena.

We also saw a cheetah with her two cubs that morning, and watched as a baby wildebeest was born. The natural cycle of life and death on the vast plains of East Africa has remained unchanged for thousands of years.

We returned to the lodge for an enormous English breakfast and spent the rest of the morning exploring the more remote corners of the game reserve. We stumbled on a solitary rhino, one of only five known to be in the reserve at the time, and were treated to the spectacle of a mock charge by a large bull elephant, whom we had managed to annoy somehow. He did a lot of ear flapping, stomping, and trumpeting, but broke off his run at our van well before we would have had reason for real concern.

On the flight back to Nairobi that afternoon, we did a little aerial game view-ing. The minimum altitude above the reserves is 500 feet, not too good for pho-tography, but excellent for watching the huge herds.

Amboseli is by no means the only reserve accessible by air. Your itinerary should also include Masai Mara to the west, adjoining Tanzania's world-famous Serengeti game reserve and offering the best big game viewing in Kenya, and Tsavo to the East, famous for its thousands of elephants. Distances are short, less than two and a half hours flying time to any destination.

I have also had the chance to fly into Masai Mara's Keekorok airstrip, where the wisdom of not wandering around on foot was made obvious minutes after arrival. As we drove onto the access road from the runway's edge, we rolled by three lions lunching lazily on the remains of a wildebeest at the end of the run-way.

There are several lodges at Masai Mara, but I chose to rough it and stayed in a tent at Cotter's Camp. It was comfortably rustic, and what an atmosphere. The camp was run by an enterprising young Englishwoman who got tired of manag-ing a disco in Nairobi. A special treat at Cotter's is an opportunity to watch for that most elusive and nocturnal of cats, the leopard. Cotter's has a wood-and-grass lookout constructed next to a salt lick in a wooded area miles from the camp. You are driven there by a guide at approximately 10:30 in the evening and brought back the next morning. The sight of two leopards frolicking silently by the light of the moon is in itself worth the trip.

Also at Masai Mara, I saw more than 30 lions in a forenoon on a day when we didn't come across even the slightest hint of other humans until returning to camp; we were also charged by an angry rhino when we foolishly cut her off from her calf. Masai Mara also offers early morning balloon safaris, a most unu-sual way to view game. There is a champagne breakfast on touchdown in keep-ing with the best traditions of ballooning.

Don't miss a chance to do some flying if business or pleasure takes you to Kenya. Navigation is not too difficult in spite of a lack of navaids, especially VORs. Prominent landmarks abound and except for some bad spells in the northern mountains, the weather is mostly VFR, especially during the dry sea-son from October to March. You should get the aeronautical charts covering Kenya, but all the locals use a high quality road map.

Be it only a quick flight to Amboseli for lunch, or an extended aerial tour of several wildlife reserves, arrange for wings at Wilson Field, load up on film, and head for lion country.

51

Nigeria

Country rating: **Difficult**

ONC Charts: **K-2, K-3, L-2, and L-3**

Rental cost range:

  2 seat trainer **$100-120**

  6 seat fixed gear **$180-200**

  4 seat retractable **Generally not available**

QUALIFICATIONS AND LICENSE VALIDATION

Nigerian civil aviation authorities require that you obtain a Nigerian private pilot license to fly solo in a Nigerian registered aircraft. No government administered flight test is required, but you must pass a written test on Nigerian Air Law, and get a Nigerian medical. At the present time, because of national security concerns, you must also have a Nigerian residence permit to be eligible for a local license. This makes solo flying by short-term visitors impossible, but flights with a safety pilot are easily arranged at the Lagos Flying Club.

If work takes you to Nigeria for a long stay and a residence permit is obtained, contact the Lagos Flying Club for assistance to acquire a Nigerian license. Personal contacts are important in getting things accomplished in Nigeria, and the club will shepherd you through all the steps faster than on your own. Nigeria is rated Difficult because of the onerous license validation procedures and the limited availability of rental aircraft.

DOCUMENTS YOU SHOULD TAKE

Pilot license
Current medical
Logbook
Radio operator license (if separate from pilot license)

Take original documents. A Nigerian medical is necessary to obtain a local license.

USEFUL FLYING ORGANIZATIONS

The Lagos Flying Club
PMB 21587
Ikeja, Lagos
Telephone   935 273

The Lagos Flying Club is the only game in town, and, for all practical purposes, in the whole country. The club is based at a private airfield at Magbon, on the coast, 38 kilometers west of Lagos on the Badagry Expressway (there is a sign approximately one mile west of the toll booths on the expressway). The fleet consists of a Cessna 152 and a Cessna 206. Among the club members are a number of Nigerians and expatriates who work in various segments of the local aviation industry and benefit the club with their expertise.

Lutz Paap's Chipmunk at Magbon Airfield, home of the Lagos Flying Club.

It might be difficult at times to get through on the telephone. If you have a problem making contact, just show up at Magbon airfield on a Saturday morning. In weekend traffic, it takes approximately one hour to drive from the residential areas of Lagos. Also, ask around in the local business community. Someone will most likely know someone who knows someone . . . who is a club member. Be persistent because people who have not heard of the club might flatly tell you that there is no such thing.

WHERE TO FLY, WHAT TO FLY

Nigeria is included in this guide because visitors who are familiar with the country expect it to be the last place on earth where recreational flying would be possible, yet the Lagos Flying Club is an outstanding example of how, if there is a will, there is always a way. Nigeria is Africa's most populous state. Three out of four Africans are Nigerian.

Since the 1970s, the country's vast oil resources have played havoc with the economy, first overtaxing the infrastructure because of an explosive increase in wealth, then, as oil prices collapsed, causing great economic hardships at all levels of society and giving the country a reputation for being a very difficult place in which to get anything done without a big hassle. The government's security concerns caused by a three-year civil war at the beginning of the 1970s, and a history of military coups, have been major obstacles faced by private aviation, but through it all, the Lagos Flying Club has endured. The bottom line is that despite what outsiders familiar with Nigeria might expect, it is possible even for the short-term visitor to do at least some flying in a light airplane.

The Lagos Flying Club has been at it continuously since 1958. Through the mid 1970s the club flourished with as many as six club aircraft on the line including several good touring airplanes. Flight training supported full-time instructors and weekend flights to neighboring countries along the coast were common. Then oil prices collapsed and the cost of fuel, maintenance, and spare parts skyrocketed, almost putting the club out of business. A dedicated core membership saw the club through and now activity is on the increase again with the recent acquisition of a Cessna 206, in addition to a Cessna 152.

Most flying is in the local area around Magbon, along the coast, toward the border with Benin. The beach is beautiful and goes on forever, and an intricate maze of inlets and creeks conjures up images of the coast's rich, centuries-old history of trading and conflict.

Cross-country flying inland is also possible along various routes, but first you have to fly over to Murtalla Muhammad Airport, the international airport of Lagos, to pick up a flight plan in person. Getting all the approvals can sometimes take hours, requiring vast reserves of patience. Subsequent flight plans at other airports are more easily obtained. Nearby Ibadan Airport is a popular training destination.

Previously, flying clubs were in most big cities; today, the only club besides Lagos is at Zaria (approximately 400 miles north of Lagos), where the government operates its central flying school for professional pilots. The club is run by the flying school, but membership is open to outsiders.

A colorful figure and a main driving force of the Lagos Flying Club is Lutz Paap, an ex-Luftwaffe pilot turned architect who has been living and flying in Nigeria for nearly three decades. Paap has managed to spend more than 2,000 hours aloft strictly for his own amusement in this part of the world where flying for fun is supposedly so difficult to do. Among other adventures, he has flown a motorglider to Nigeria all the way from Germany. Paap is also a colonel in the Confederate Air Force, a member of the EAA, and a regular at Oshkosh. Since 1976, he has been flying Yellow Fever, a bright yellow Chipmunk he bought from the Nigerian Air Force. The Chipmunk has become a fixture over the beaches on the weekends, and always stands ready to whisk the visitor off the ground not only for a tour of the neighborhood but also for a good dose of aerobatics.

VFR QUESTIONS & ANSWERS

What are good sources for VFR regulations? The Nigerian AIP. The Lagos Flying Club has a copy.

How can I get a weather briefing? According to Lutz Paap, "Look outside," otherwise, at the met office at the international airport. Aside from the usual summer rainy season, a particular weather problem you might face during January and February is the *harmatan*, a fog-like dust storm that blows down from the Sahara.

What are VFR visibility and ceiling minimums? Nigeria has adopted the ICAO VFR minimums.

Is night VFR permitted? No.

Must I file a flight plan? A flight plan must be filed for all cross-country flights. Filing must be done in person at the airport of departure. For flights out of Magbon this means first hopping over to Murtalla Muhammad Airport to file a flight plan, and this can be time-consuming.

May I fly the airways VFR? Yes.

Must I maintain en route radio contact with ATC on or off the airways? Position reporting is required on cross-country flights, and on airways you might have to comply with instructions from ATC.

Is VFR on top permitted? No.

52

Zimbabwe

Country rating: **Easy**

ONC Charts: **P-4 and P-5**

Rental cost range:

  2 seat trainer **$50-65**

  4 seat fixed gear **$70-100**

  4 seat retractable **$120-160**

QUALIFICATIONS AND LICENSE VALIDATION

Zimbabwe requires foreign license validation. Licenses issued by ICAO member states are routinely validated for recreational flying without a written test or flight test. Validation takes, at the most, a day or two. Apply for validation in person at the Department of Civil Aviation's offices on Causeway in downtown Harare. Depending on workload, there is a good chance that you will be given the validation while you wait.

Validation will usually be issued for the duration of your stay, up to a maximum of three months.

DOCUMENTS YOU SHOULD TAKE

Pilot license
Logbook
Current medical
Radio operator license (if separate from pilot license)

Take original documents. For validation, only the license and logbook must be presented.

USEFUL FLYING ORGANIZATIONS

Department of Civil Aviation
Private Bag 7716
Causeway
Harare, Zimbabwe

Government agency that handles the validation of foreign licenses.

Mashonaland Flying Club
Charles Prince Aerodrome
(postal address: P.O. Box 343)
Harare, Zimbabwe
Telephone   32 922 or 32 916

Nonprofit flying club with numerous aircraft in the fleet. The best bet for visiting recreational pilots.

WHERE TO FLY, WHAT TO FLY

Say "Zimbabwe," and most people will think of Victoria Falls. But the falls are only one of many exotic destinations within easy reach by light aircraft from the main population centers. Zimbabwe is excellent farm country, and is also rich in minerals. Farming, mining, and a relatively sparse ground transportation network have given the airplane a workhorse role for decades.

Workhorses also like to play, and in Zimbabwe, the usually excellent weather gives the VFR recreational pilot strong odds of reaching a destination unhindered. The emphasis is on the great outdoors. Game parks, lakeside campsites, and centuries-old ruins are, at the most, a few hours flying time away.

Charles Prince Aerodrome outside Harare, Zimbabwe's capital, is the country's center for recreational flying. Here you will find the nonprofit Mashonaland Flying Club and its large fleet, as well as the more expensive rental aircraft of the commercial flying schools.

Try the Mashonaland Flying Club first. Its training fleet includes Piper J-3 Cubs and Cessna 150s and 172s. Touring aircraft include an Archer and several Cessna 182s. An aging, but delightful, DHC Chipmunk has previously been available for aerobatic training, and with any luck it is still there.

The club welcomes visitors as temporary members. It is as much a social club as a flying club, a good place to meet all sorts of flying types.

The commercial operators might be a good alternative if the club is unable to accommodate your needs.

Touring

One of the best reasons to check out in a light airplane in Zimbabwe is to take advantage of the outstanding cross-country touring opportunities the country has to offer.

Victoria Falls.

Victoria Falls and Hwange National Park, approximately 300 miles west of Harare, are the best known tourist destinations in Zimbabwe. The flight can be challenging to navigators spoiled by radio navaids and idiot-proof landmarks. It requires some careful dead reckoning, but a good initial VOR heading can be drawn from Harare, and the main highway and railroad to the south and the Zambezi River to the north all converge on Victoria Falls.

The airport is approximately 15 minutes from town by car. It is best to arrange a pick up in advance when making a hotel reservation. Rental cars are also available and strongly recommended if you plan to visit the nearby game parks.

Victoria Falls is truly one of the great natural wonders of the world, formed by the Zambezi River, which widens to approximately one mile and tumbles into a deep, narrow gorge; it has to be viewed from the air to be fully appreciated. Under humid conditions, a wide veil of mist rises as high as 300 feet from the gorge, giving the falls its local name, *Musi Oa Tunya*, "The Smoke That Thunders." Within walking distance is the turn of the century Victoria Falls Hotel, maintained and run in the grand old style.

Hwange National Park is less than an hour's drive from the falls and is one of the best game parks in Southern Africa, especially rich in elephants. Another option is a visit to Chobe National Park across the border in Botswana, along the Chobe River. It is best to arrange at least overnight stays in the game parks. Go on dawn and dusk game drives when the wildlife is most active. These game parks are usually closed during the rainy season from mid-December to early March when roads become impassable and the game scatters far and wide due to the abundance of water.

The Zimbabwe Ruins and Lake Kyle are a straight 140-mile run south of Harare, served by the airport at Maswingo (Fort Victoria). Rental cars are available at the airport. Reserve one in advance when you make hotel reservations in Harare. The Great Zimbabwe ruins are a magnificent mystery. Built approximately 600 years ago from stone in a complex, free-flowing style unlike any other form of architecture, the city was abandoned in a few decades by its inhabitants, who seemingly disappeared without a trace. Archaeologists are only now beginning to unravel the puzzle.

Nearby is Lake Kyle's national park, where you can go game viewing on horseback, and the chances of seeing rhinos is good.

Lake Kariba is a fisherman's and water sportsman's paradise, approximately 120 miles northwest of Harare. The enormous lake is man-made, formed by damming up the Zambezi, but it looks completely natural. Kariba Airport is near the lake's eastern edge and is convenient to an assortment of game lodges and resorts. Opportunities to view wildlife drinking at the lake are excellent. Elephants occasionally cross Kariba on marathon swims.

VFR QUESTIONS & ANSWERS

What are good sources for VFR regulations? Zimbabwe's AIPs. Also, a few good review sessions with a local instructor.

How can I get a weather briefing? From the airport met office at the bigger airports. Weather information is not exceptionally detailed.

What are VFR visibility and ceiling minimums? Controlled airspace: 5 miles visibility and a 1,500-foot ceiling; uncontrolled airspace: 5 miles visibility above 1,000 feet, 1 mile visibility and clear of clouds below 1,000 feet.

Is night VFR permitted? No.

Must I file a flight plan? Flight plans must be filed for all cross-country flights. From uncontrolled fields, VFR flight plans can be air filed after takeoff.

May I fly the airways VFR? Yes.

Must I maintain en route radio contact with ATC on or off the airways? Minor reporting requirements must be met, such as FIR boundary crossings, hourly position reports, and destination in sight. Zimbabwe has a notable arrangement with the telephone company for closing flight plans if you land at an uncontrolled field and are beyond radio range to close the flight plan before landing; simply say "air movement" to the operator, and the telephone call is free.

Is VFR on top permitted? Yes.

ADDITIONAL INFORMATION SOURCES

Printed information on aviation is scarce in Zimbabwe. An excellent VFR aviation map is available from the government mapping agency. Obtain a copy and arrange an extensive briefing for each route you intend to fly.

Flying is a social activity in Zimbabwe, so the best sources of information are the hangar flying sessions at the end of the day. If you intend to go touring by private aircraft, collect the wealth of tourist information available on popular destinations from travel agencies and bookstores.

53

In rented Cubs and Chipmunks over Africa

ROD BATER'S CLIPPED BRITISH ACCENT came through the intercom: "Right, then! The road is your reference line . . . let's begin the dive . . . watch the rpms . . . back on the stick now . . . full power, smoothly, more back pressure . . . head tilted back, look for the horizon . . . and smoothly to idle now, ease off a bit on the stick . . . over we go . . . not bad for an initial try."

I had just been talked through my first loop in a de Havilland Chipmunk. But we were not over England in the 1950s and Rod was not the RAF instructor that he sounded like. We were flying in the 1980s in the Chipmunk of the Mashona-land Flying Club and the road I had used for my reference line led to Harare, Zimbabwe.

A week before I was wondering just what I would be doing besides work in this southern African country where I would work for a month and a half. Now I wasn't so sure that I would find the time to do my work.

When I arrived in Harare, I started calling the local charter operators with a skeptical mind. I did not expect more than the occasional four-seater. A charter company I found in the yellow pages suggested the Mashonaland Flying Club. The name sounded promising. Joe Verronau, the club manager, answered the phone and said I would be welcome to fly with them. He didn't think my license validation would take more than a week. I'll believe that when I see it, I thought, as I politely inquired about the fleet. "Well, we instruct in Piper Cubs," said Joe. I was out the door and on my way to Charles Prince airport before he had a chance to hang up.

Restat Iter Caelo, "The Sky Always Remains," proclaimed the inscription under a winged springbok on the club's crest hanging over the entrance. The springbok, one of Africa's most graceful antelopes, seems to be the national beast down there and needs no wings to literally soar through the sky at a full run. Verronau's office was behind the club's swimming pool. Airplane models and pictures of airplanes were everywhere. Out on the patio overlooking the

Piper Cub, still instructing in Zimbabwe.

runways, Joe and I talked flying over tea served in silver and china by uniformed waiters with winged springboks on their ties.

The club had 24 airplanes ranging from two J-3 Cubs to a fully instrumented Mooney with an assortment of Cessnas and Pipers in between. A computer tracks the club's 700 members, approximately 150 are active. Two full-time instructors are complemented by many members with an instructor certificate, like Rod Bater, donating their time. A crop dusting operation that shares the airfield with the club performs maintenance on contract. A full kitchen staff and several waiters make things pleasant on the ground.

When I returned from a walk around the flightline, I commented enviously to Verronau about a Chipmunk I saw hidden in the back of a hangar. "Oh! Forgot to mention that," he replied. "One of ours, too. Ever flown one before?" The Mashonaland Flying Club was not at all something the uninitiated would have expected to find in what is commonly, but somewhat misguidedly, referred to as the middle of the African bush.

Things were looking up, but I still had misgivings about getting my license validated in time to fly solo. As it turned out, I was worrying needlessly. Verronau sent me to the Directorate of Civil Aviation in Harare where they examined my license and medical and issued me a Certificate of Validation on the spot. It was good for three months and allowed me to exercise all the privileges of my United States license.

Back at the airport that afternoon, the first order of business was the Mashonaland Flying Club's number one lesson in operating its Cubs: how to hand prop them. Pilots always have to get an assistant to swing the prop while they remain in the cockpit. The club strictly adheres to the "Switches off! Throttle set! Brakes on! Stick back! Contact!" exchange initiated by the prop man and acknowledged by the pilot before the prop is swung.

We were airborne in short order with Ron Saunders, volunteer instructor and a confessed Cub addict who used to fly B-25s in World War II. As soon as we were level at 3,000 feet agl, Ron announced "I want a spin, three turns to the left." I did better. I gave him three and a half. "Now to the right and keep it to three." The man meant business. He seemed satisfied and pointed out Delta Four, Charles Prince's enormous practice area to the north, measuring approximately 30 miles on each side. Delta Four is a convenient arrangement because it takes a solid 40 minutes simply to motor around it, and you need only a tower clearance, whereas for any cross-country flight, VFR included, you must file a flight plan.

On the way back, Ron cut the engine and didn't increase power until we had a patch of grassland made. At Charles Prince, I gave several demonstrations of my ability to land without grievous bodily harm to man or machine and as the sun set over the Umvukwe Range, I realized a lifelong ambition of soloing a Piper Cub. Could not have been in a more unlikely place for a naturalized Bostonian. Nor could it have been more satisfying with both windows down and the sky casting a reddish glow on the entire scene; the native African villages and the bush below, Harare's modern skyline in the background. As I was turning final, I was already thinking Chipmunk.

Bater had lent me the Chipmunk manual and gave me a thorough oral exam before telling me about this airplane. Victor Papa Whiskey Echo Victor was a most authentic Chipmunk. Produced in 1952, it saw service in the RAF and then spent several years with an aeroclub outside Paris prior to its arrival in what was then still Rhodesia. It had flown all its life without modifications. The engine was the original 145-hp Gypsy Major, which had to be hand propped; it drank a quart of oil per hour in straight-and-level flight and threw out an additional quart for every hour of aerobatics.

Rod showed me which nuts and bolts were the most likely to come loose in an aerobatic session, and how to check for stress wrinkles on the fuselage and wing skins. He explained the technique of moving mixture and throttle forward with a single motion of the left hand on takeoff until the engine sounded "just right." The mixture never went all the way forward at Charles Prince's 4,850-foot altitude, nor could it be preset before takeoff because full-power runups are not recommended.

I was also cautioned about the airplane's susceptibility to carburetor icing and the need to use carb heat at all times under 2,000 rpm. Many European operators permanently wired the carb heat in the open position. According to Rod, the two hardest things about flying the Chipmunk were learning how to start it and how to taxi it.

Engine start consisted of opening the left cowling, pumping furiously on a little priming handle next to the fuel pump until an overflow valve started to leak, buttoning up the cowling, turning the prop six times to work the fuel through the cylinders, racing around into the cockpit, strapping in and getting the throttle and mixture set just right (this was the hardest part) so that the engine caught when the prop was swung. If it didn't fire on the second swing the prime was usually gone and it meant repeating the whole vaudeville show.

Of course, it helped to know the airplane well and experience could come in the most embarrassing ways. I once struggled for a solid hour without any success, Medicine, the mechanic, swinging the prop like a madman. He kept asking if the switches were on. I said yes.

Finally, as he was about to faint, he staggered to the rear cockpit and reeducated me about the second set of magneto switches to be found there in some tandem two-seaters. The engine roared to life on the next attempt.

Taxiing was like chewing gum, patting your head, and rubbing your stomach all at the same time. The brakes were operated by a hand lever on the left. If you pulled it with the rudders in the neutral position, both wheel brakes would activate. If you pulled it while applying left or right rudder, only the left or right brake would work. This gave the Chipmunk outstanding maneuverability on the ground but on occasion you felt a frantic need for a third hand to manipulate the throttle. Chipmunks have a clever brake rudder interlocking device that frees up one hand, but on this "Chippie" it didn't work.

Bater was right. After all the hocus pocus on the ground the Chipmunk was a sheer pleasure to fly. It had the most balanced and harmonious controls among the airplanes I have flown. From the first instant, the act of flying seemed automatic. Whatever control movement felt the most comfortable for a maneuver somehow always worked out to be just the right amount required. Rod had me go through all the basics of a checkout and couldn't resist a barrel roll on the way home for some touch and goes.

On landing, the Chipmunk would float if you didn't get the speed right, which proved to be its only characteristic where the handling wasn't "automatic." We floated a little on the third landing and Rod told me to turn off.

"Want a few full-stop patterns?"

The Mashonaland Flying Club's unmodified Chipmunk.

"No," he replied. "I am going to get out and you will see how lovely it is to fly her alone."

"Oh, great!" I lied, as my legs turned to jelly. All of a sudden being entrusted with Zimbabwe's only Chipmunk seemed like an awesome responsibility.

As soon as I was airborne, under that World War II fighter-style canopy, with the military panel in front of me, I was immediately overcome by a "Snoopy-esque" glee. "And here is the famous fighter ace high over the English Channel prowling in search of the foe in the sun."

I actually managed to accomplish a good many schoolboy patterns that earned me the right to fly the Chipmunk whenever I felt the urge as long as I promised not to be a fool (the interpretation of "fool" being left up to me).

I kept my word and resisted aerobatics in the Chipmunk until Rod's demonstrations. The true connoisseurs of the art would most likely consider her to be an underpowered pig with the 145-hp Gypsy Major. A fellow named Ludgater who flew nothing but the Chipmunk was always muttering to himself that someone should put a 200-hp Lycoming in her with a constant-speed prop. For this novice, though, the pig was very much in sunshine as I watched the Zimbabwean horizon tumble, twirl and disappear every which way.

I did only the basics: loops, stall turns, slow rolls, barrel rolls, and Cuban eights, all gentle inside maneuvers. As long as I picked up enough speed, she never let me down and that delightful harmony of her controls was ever present. She also made me muse about the days when you could still have a decent dogfight without feeling like you were playing a video arcade game.

Aviation is either feast or famine. A week before I was resigned to missing a month and a half of good summer flying in New England and all of a sudden in the middle of Africa I could tie away a J-3 Cub and a Chipmunk whenever I felt like it without having to own either of them. The dilemma was which one of the two to fly. I decided to recognize a good thing when I saw one and fly both as often as I could even if the ensuing weight reduction in my wallet would upset British Airways' weight and balance calculations on the way home.

Summer settled down into a pleasant pattern indeed. I would go on a low-level dawn flight in the Cub, following the railway line, circling the *kraals* of the traditional African villages (several huts encircled by a thornbrush fence) or fly over the bush looking for springbok and impala.

I would then go to work and come back at sunset to unwind in the Chipmunk. There was nothing like cruising home in the "Chippie" with the canopy cracked open after a good workout. If I felt particularly energetic in the morning I would cavort around in the Chipmunk first and return to the Cub later. On the weekends, one day would be Chipmunk day, the other, Cub day.

In the evenings, we would always collect around a bar for some serious hangar flying. I learned that the soft-spoken Ron Saunders was sent to RAF disciplinary squadron for scattering hundreds of toilet paper rolls all over the English countryside returning from a mission over Europe in his B-25. Several unconfirmed stories floated around about the airport manager once flying a Spitfire under Tower Bridge ("It was drawn in the open position," he claims).

I also found out that the Mashonaland Flying Club got its name from the

Land of the Shona, the native tribe in this part of Zimbabwe. One night I met a distinguished old gentleman with an enormous handlebar moustache who told me he lived on a farm about 200 miles away where he spends most of his retirement flying an immaculately restored Tiger Moth. There would always be dinner as the night wore on, and on Sundays there were barbecues, *braais* as they are called in that part of the world.

Zimbabwe ranks among the most captivatingly beautiful countries in Africa. The weather is perfect most of the time and the outdoors is a favorite pastime. Most recreational and historic areas are accessible by air. A foremost objective of the Mashonaland Flying Club is to enable its members to tour the country by airplane, and there are arrangements for discounts with several resorts.

Victoria Falls, one of the seven wonders of the world, is only three hours west of Harare by light aircraft. The spectacular aerial view alone is worth the flight. The falls are three times the width and one and a half times the height of Niagara.

Up river, the Zambezi teems with hippo and crocodile. Other game often drink from the shore and can all be observed from daily river cruises. There is a crocodile farm and the Wankie Game Park's elephants, lions, giraffes, and lesser wildlife are only a short drive away, even shorter by air.

Staying at the Victoria Falls Hotel, overlooking the waterfall, is like going back in time to the lazy elegance of the late 1800s. The decor has been superbly maintained and the huge dining room is still kept cool by 40 ceiling fans. The Shona and Ndebele tribal dances around the open fire at night are dazzling and authentic, and the native embroidery on sale would greatly please your mother-in-law.

Lake Kariba, a 130-mile long man-made lake is also well within reach, an hour and a half flying time north of Harare. The fishing and sailing are excellent and the area is also famous for its picturesque lodges with their nicely maintained golf courses and tennis courts. Some lodges also have stables. Two elephants attracted international attention in 1982 when they crossed the lake in an 18-hour marathon swim at one of its wider points.

I did do some in-country touring in a Piper Archer, but my main priority was to fly the Cub and the Chipmunk. On my last afternoon in Zimbabwe I took the Chipmunk for a final flight, tucked her away in the hangar, locked up her canopy, and looked at her for a long time before I turned to go. That night, on British Airways, high over the Sudan, it suddenly occurred to me that the Chipmunk's keys were still in my pocket.

54

Botswana

Country rating: **Moderate**

ONC Charts: **P-4, Q-4, and Q-5**

Rental cost range:

2 seat trainer **$60-85**

4 seat fixed gear **Generally not available**

4 seat retractable **Generally not available**

QUALIFICATIONS AND LICENSE VALIDATION

License validation is required for recreational flying, but for a pilot holding a license from an ICAO member state, it is a simple, administrative process. You should apply in person at the Department of Civil Aviation in Gaborone, the capital. You will have to present your license and logbook; no written or flight tests are required other than the usual flying school checkride prior to solo rental. Even an instrument rating will be routinely validated, as long as your logbook shows an instrument proficiency check within the past 13 months. In spite of the easy validation procedures, the country is rated Moderate because of the limited opportunity for flying rental aircraft.

DOCUMENTS YOU SHOULD TAKE

Pilot license

Current medical

Logbook

Radio operator license (if separate from pilot license)

Take logbook and license for validation, other documents for the flying school.

USEFUL FLYING ORGANIZATIONS

Ministry of Transportation
Department of Civil Aviation
Flight Safety Division
Gaborone, Botswana

Government authority responsible for license validation.

WHERE TO FLY, WHAT TO FLY

Solo flying opportunities are restricted in Botswana for the visitor by the limited availability of rental aircraft. The last visit found two rentable Cessna 150s at Gaborone Airport, available from a charter operator whose main business was flying for the mines.

Tooling around in a 150 on the outskirts of Gaborone can be fun but Botswana is mentioned here because of the interesting bush flying experience available in its unique Okavango Delta, an off-the-beaten-path destination in the middle of the Kalahari Desert, growing more and more popular with wildlife enthusiasts.

Botswana is an arid land the size of Texas, inhabited by little more than 1 million people. It is the country portrayed in the hit film, *The Gods Must Be Crazy*. A large section of the country is covered by the Kalahari Desert. Approximately 500 miles north of Gaborone, the Okavango River spills into the Kalahari from the grasslands of Angola and is promptly swallowed up by the desert, never reaching the ocean.

The marshland it forms is unique and rich in every kind of African wild game. And the only reliable way to travel throughout this marsh, other than by dugout canoe, is by light aircraft from Maun at the marsh's southeastern edge. Maun is home base to several bush operators, among them Northern Air, one of the most enduring of the charter companies. From here, they ply their trade flying visitors and supplies into the tiny grass strips serving the tented wildlife camps scattered on the delta's many islands. Cessna 206s dominate the fleet.

Private charters for less than a full planeload of passengers are available, but expensive. Depending on the size of a party, you might get a private charter by default, but even in a group, it is easy to arrange for the right seat if you are a pilot. If you are reasonably experienced and talk to the charter company in advance, you might be able to arrange informal dual instruction in bush flying while you fly the various legs of the itinerary; it will be an unforgettable experience.

Pilots highly experienced in wilderness flying who insist on flying the Okavango solo might consider the expensive and somewhat time consuming option of obtaining a South African license validation and renting a South African registered aircraft. For less experienced flyers willing to part with their life savings, the ultimate flying adventure is to do the Okavango from South Africa with a South African safety pilot. In either case, the South African option requires detailed advanced planning initiated prior to arrival in Africa and carefully assessing the possibilities in view of your experience. Write to AOPA South Africa for the names and addresses of specific operators willing to consider such a venture.

VFR QUESTIONS & ANSWERS

What are good sources for VFR regulations? Consult the Botswana AIP.

How can I get a weather briefing? Gaborone, Maun, and Francistown have met offices where full briefings are available.

What are VFR visibility and ceiling minimums? Three miles visibility and 1,000-foot ceiling in controlled airspace; one mile and clear of clouds in uncontrolled airspace.

Is night VFR permitted? No.

Must I file a flight plan? Flight plans must be filed for all cross-country flights.

May I fly the airways VFR? Yes. In fact, private pilots with fewer than 500 hours total time and 50 in type may only fly the airways and follow designated railroad lines on cross country flights.

Must I maintain en route radio contact with ATC on or off the airways? Yes. You must provide hourly position reports and report crossing FIR boundaries.

Is VFR on top permitted? No.

55

Bush flying over
the Okavango Delta

EVERY WINDOW FLAP WAS ROLLED UP on the tent to catch what little breeze might come along. The towering thunderclouds of Botswana's rainy season darkened the sky. It was a perfect afternoon for a nap. A distant buzz snuck into my comatose mind, and then a blistering full-throttle roar, and I was wide awake and sure that this time he really clipped the trees. But, of course, he hadn't, and the engine noise subsided as he pulled the Cessna 206 up sharply to come around and land on the strip hacked out of the tall, wild grass.

He taxied to our line of six tents, the only habitation on Shinde Island deep in the Okavango Delta, Botswana's unique marshland on the edge of the Kalahari Desert. His name was Trevor McGuire, and he just made it to the tents before it started pouring. Tomorrow he would show me the pleasures of flying in the Southern African bush.

The delta is formed by the Okavango River that flows into the Kalahari, one of the most arid deserts on earth, and is swallowed up by its sands a thousand miles from the nearest ocean. It is a vast water hole about the size of Massachusetts.

Packed with an immense variety of African wildlife, it is a favored destination for ecologist, hunter, and adventure traveler. And like most true wilderness areas, it is bush plane country. The most efficient way to move people and the supplies they need is by air.

Trevor had flown in from Maun, the home base for the region's bush pilots, and the only real town and trading center on the edge of the Okavango. The 206 was one of five operated by Northern Air, the oldest and most enduring among the handful of bush operators in the delta. Other planes in Northern Air's fleet were two Beech Barons and two Britten Norman Islanders.

Around the evening campfire we talked of elephants and lions and buffalo, zebras and wildebeest, giraffes and antelopes, and how they all migrated, following the water's movement through the season. We talked of encounters with hippos and crocodiles, and the dozens of bird species that live among the papyrus reeds. We listened to the hyenas' nocturnal whooping, and noises too strange to identify.

And we got Trevor to talk about how he came to the Okavango from his native Australia three years before, with barely 500 hours in single-engine aircraft in his logbook. Now, still in his 20s, with nearly 3,000 hours under his belt, a fair share of it in Barons, he was about to go home. Tomorrow would be his last day with Northern Air.

There weren't many things for which he would trade his three seasons, but it was time to see what else there was to flying. Some pilots lasted only one season, he said. Some were there forever. Most were like him: a few good years, a great adventure, and then on to other cockpits.

During high season the pace could be brutal; going flat out from sunup to sundown, flying up to twenty sectors among the dozen strips that serve the 30-odd campsites scattered throughout the delta. It was more fun as the rainy season approached and fewer people came to Maun on Air Botswana's daily flights from the southern cities. Then there was time to see the wildlife, and stay overnight at the camps and tell tall tales around the fire at night.

Occasionally a watercraft is better than an aircraft, especially for a closer look at the Okavango Delta.

At dawn we took to the water for one last time in a *makoro*, a native dugout canoe as old as the river bushmen's history, and hoped not to startle a hippo. Crocodiles live-and-let-live (as long as you don't wash your socks at the river's edge where you can be easily mistaken for a drinking goat and snatched into the water for dinner). Hippos can be ill-tempered and might throw spectacular tantrums if you float into their domain. But no beady little hippo eyes disturbed the morning's tranquility, and eventually I made the makoro glide toward the grass strip and the Cessna 206's promise of aerial game viewing.

We loaded our bags in the cargo pod under the 206's fuselage and got underway with a soft field takeoff, which most pilots face only on flight tests, but this time was for real. The yoke was way aft on the roll across the grass, still soggy in spots from the previous day's rain. The 206 staggered into the air a hair above stall speed and leveled off briefly to accelerate.

We came around for the obligatory high-speed pass to say good-bye and turned east, pulling up to 300 feet, on course for Machaba, a bush camp on the edge of the Okavango. There we would drop off a companion and then fly to Maun for a connecting commercial flight to Zimbabwe. The two legs were typical sectors for the Okavango, each a little less than an hour's flying time.

We called in on the unicom frequency, which is monitored by all bush flights and the camps, and is usable in case a problem arose. The ground before us was a flat patchwork of papyrus-laden water pools, grassland, and acacia thicket, all in various shades of faded green. To the novice it is featureless terrain, a challenge where navigation is by pilotage.

"The real problem is that the water level keeps changing with the season and the terrain changes with it," said Trevor. "An island you picked as a sure-fire landmark one day may have disappeared by the time you try to find it a week later." The area under water increases from 6,000 square miles in the dry season to 9,000 square miles during the rains. But like all other terrain that at first seems devoid of landmarks, the Okavango offers plenty of guidance to the trained eye.

Some of the deeper channels and larger islands do not change and are easily recognized after a few flights. There are also seasonal *tracks* (roads). Even some of the islands, like Shinde, can be reached overland during the driest months. "There is actually a navigational advantage to having very few tracks around," said Trevor. "If you find one, you can be quite sure it is the one you are looking for." I suggested that a VOR at Maun would greatly simplify things. "It would also make things pretty boring," he replied.

The ultimate fallback for a disoriented pilot is the marked terrain change at the delta's edges. The Okavango can be thought of as a baseball diamond with Maun at home plate—all the way around the bases, the transition from marsh to desert scrub land is sudden and clearly recognizable from the air. This line can be intercepted at any point and followed home.

In some areas just outside the delta, cattle control fences that run for hundreds of miles (the Tswanas' lives revolve around cattle), can also be useful for navigation. Orientation is rarely a problem, though finding your way around can get quite difficult during the late dry season's extreme haze.

"Tsessebe!" shouted Trevor. We rolled into a dive toward the small specks in the grass field: stocky, short-necked antelope. They bolted as we roared past on the deck. We stayed only a few feet off the ground, dodging solitary trees, hopping over lines of scrub, looking for more game. Fat, "well done sausages," submerged in the deeper pools of water, became recognizable as thousand-pound hippos when we flashed by.

Giraffes disappeared aft in slow motion, their long necks swaying almost level with us. The deer-like herd of lechwe scattered, and Africa's most dangerous and unpredictable big game, the buffalo, simply glanced at us. So we raced from field to field and over acres of shallow water, always heading in the general direction of our destination. In case of trouble, it would have been easy to pull up and find a suitable clearing.

Twenty minutes out, we eased up to 300 feet again. Trevor recognized a clump of trees and behind them was an unattended grass strip, a drop-off point for hunting parties. The hunters were flown in and picked up later at an appointed time. On long expeditions, the strip was also used to bring in fresh supplies. Strong wildlife conservation policies carefully control hunting, yet those policies make the adventure available for those so inclined.

We dove again and roared past the lonely wind sock. "Wind check," said Trevor. Back on course, we talked of flying so low over wildlife. Airplanes are still few and far between, and the wild game is so rich that any restrictions to operations in the area are still far away.

A channel appeared off the right wingtip; next to the channel was a track leading to Machaba. The airfield turned out to be a luxuriously long laterite strip. No buildings, just a four-wheel-drive jeep waiting for our companion, and some tied down Piper Cherokees. "Game spotters," said Trevor.

We flew to Maun at 3,000 feet agl. At that height, the land seemed even more featureless and flat. I looked at the instrument panel, bare to the bones, except for the ancient HF radio. "A legal requirement, that radio," said Trevor. "Never works. Now that you mention it, there is something I've wanted to find out for the last three years." He got busy with a screwdriver trying to remove the radio's face to see if there was anything behind it. He was thwarted by some hidden bolt, and remembering that it was his last day and I would be going on to Zimbabwe within the hour, he turned to me gravely and said "Now we'll never know."

We flew on and reached the edge of the Okavango. A fence showed up, and then a light smudge on the horizon turned into Maun. It could have been LaGuardia, compared to those obscure clearings in the bush.

We rolled past rows of hangars and light aircraft after landing, even passing one of Air Botswana's brand-new blue-and-white ATR-42s.

I remember hoping that it would be a long time before they installed a VOR.

56

South Africa

Country rating: **Moderate**

ONC Charts: **P-4, P-5, Q-4, Q-5, and R-4**

Rental cost range:

  2 seat trainer **$70-90**

  4 seat fixed gear **$100-120**

  4 seat retractable **$130-150**

QUALIFICATIONS AND LICENSE VALIDATION

Recreational flying in South Africa requires license validation, which is expeditiously handled, dependent upon the help of a local flying school, theoretical (oral) and flight tests, and contact with the Department of Transportation's Division of Civil Aviation (DCA) in Pretoria, the nation's capital. From Johannesburg, Pretoria is only a short drive, but from other areas of the country where tourists are most likely to go, it is too far to visit in person.

The short-term visitor who is not well organized or cannot devote the time to some paperwork and preparation for an oral and flight test might find the option of flying with a local safety pilot more attractive; thus, the country rating is Moderate. But with a little planning and determination, license validation with the least amount of fuss should take only a few days. Considering the available flying adventures, the extra effort is worthwhile.

The key to validation is to work through an efficient flying school. Immediately upon arrival, express mail the following information to the DCA, referencing the flying school assisting you: copies of your valid license and medical; full name; address in South Africa; type of license held; license number; aircraft type ratings, if any; other ratings; medical expiration date; country issuing the license; passport number; passport's country of issue; passport's expiration date; full reasons for validation request; date of arrival and date of expected departure from South Africa.

The school can quickly familiarize you with South African flying regulations and procedures, check out your flying abilities, and administer the tests. You will have to take an oral test on South African air navigation regulations, and a flight test on cross-country flying, which are not particularly onerous requirements if you are comfortably current. The school should telex the test results to the DCA, who will grant validation by telex within three days.

Place a telephone call to the DCA upon arrival to confirm validation procedures and to obtain the name of a specific inspector to receive the validation. The validation of IFR ratings for noncommercial flying is also possible, but time consuming. It requires a written examination, a flight test by a DCA check pilot, and the validation of your radio operator license, via the mail.

DOCUMENTS YOU SHOULD TAKE

Pilot license
Current medical
Logbook
Radio operator license (if separate from pilot license)

A notarized photocopy of the pilot license is sufficient; other documents should be original.

USEFUL FLYING ORGANIZATIONS

AOPA South Africa
P.O. Box 1789
Pretoria 0001
SOUTH AFRICA
Local telephone   021 663 1296
International telephone   27 12 322 8716
Local facsimile   021 322 8722
International facsimile   27 12 322 8722

AOPA South Africa is a good source of advice for the private pilot, and will assist you if you encounter difficulties with license validation.

The Director General
Department of Transportation
Division of Civil Aviation (DCA)
Private Bag X193
Pretoria, 0001
SOUTH AFRICA

South Africa's government entity regulating and administering civil aviation, including the validation of foreign licenses.

WHERE TO FLY, WHAT TO FLY

South Africa is a natural habitat for the touring light aircraft. It is a mostly semi-arid, sparsely populated land of vast distances and wide open spaces, three times the size of Texas. It is rich in minerals, wildlife, natural beauty, and political controversy. It is experiencing an exciting time of fundamental political change and in spite of the tensions and difficulties, the future for its willing and dynamic people of all races is promising.

Being at the southern tip of the African continent, South Africa was a challenging destination for early aviation explorers and adventurers. The London-to-Capetown run was a favorite route during the 1930s golden age of long-distance-record flying. Far-flung commercial air links were established with the rest of the world early on, and recreational flying also spread rapidly.

Quite a few Puss Moths and Tiger Moths arrived from Europe on their own wings and some still share the sky with a large, modern fleet of light aircraft winging over the *veld*, South Africa's wide open grassland, for pleasure or business.

Recreational flying is available around most population centers from a variety

Sights such as this are common at any South African national park.

of commercial schools and flying clubs. Below is a selection of airports serving the areas you are most likely to visit.

Rand Airport is one of two general aviation fields serving Johannesburg, the country's business center in the Transvaal. It is in the eastern suburb of Germiston. A good variety of single-engine Cessnas and Pipers are available for rent from a number of flying schools, among them the Rand Flying Club.

Lanseria in the northwestern Kruegsdorp suburb is Johannesburg's other big general aviation airfield, especially popular with individual owners. Besides the rental fleets, expect to see a lot of personal Mooneys and Bonanzas on the ramp.

Wonderboom serves Pretoria, the capital. It is also easily accessible from nearby Johannesburg. Its location on the wide open veld, away from heavy commercial traffic, makes it a popular spot for specialty events, such as experimental aircraft fly-ins, and aerobatic gatherings.

D. F. Malan Airport is just outside Capetown. Many visitors consider the Cape Province, with its splendid beaches, picturesque vineyards, and rugged mountains, the most attractive destination in the country, and flying over such terrain is well worth the effort.

Other general aviation airports near big cities are **Virginia** outside Durban, **Ben Schoeman** near East London, and **H. F. Wervoerdt** serving Port Elizabeth.

Touring

Outstanding touring opportunities are available from the main population centers. They range from half-day or day-long scenic flights to overnight trips of several days.

Popular options from the Johannesburg-Pretoria area are flights to Kruger National Park, Kimberley, and Sun City. Kruger is the country's premier game park. It is on the Mozambique border covering an area about the size of Massachusetts. Facilities for visitors are excellent. Two airports serve **Kruger**, **Skukuza** (special permission required), and **Phalaborwa**. Coordinate land travel arrangements through a travel agent.

Kimberley, 200 miles southwest of Johannesburg, is South Africa's diamond center, served by **B. J. Vorster Airport**. The original open-pit mine, the Big Hole, discovered in 1868, and the restored mining town next to it, which is now a museum, are popular tourist sites.

Sun City is a Las Vegas-like entertainment and golf resort miles northwest of Johannesburg, served by **Pilansberg Airport**.

Capetown's Table Mountain is an outstanding site and an easy local hop. From Capetown, picturesque flights are possible up and down the coast as far as you care to go. The Garden Route east of the Cape toward Mossel Bay, George, and Plettenberg Bay is especially nice. Another option, and an easy half-day or day flight is touring the wine country around Stellenbosch and Paarl.

For the exceptionally adventurous pilot with a king-sized wallet full of excess cash, flights to Botswana's Okavango Delta, and Zimbabwe's Victoria Falls are possible. Such trips are the ultimate in African air touring, but you must be experienced in long-range wilderness flying.

Parts of South Africa are among the best soaring sites in the world. Many European glider pilots head for the veld's mighty summer thermals when winter sets in up north. Soaring sites are at Oudtshoorn, Vryheid, Vrede, Ermelo, Welkom, and Krugersdorp.

South Africa's usually excellent weather is an attractive feature of VFR flying. But as every VFR pilot knows, there is no such thing as perpetual good weather anywhere, and the degree to which weather deteriorates at the most inopportune moment is one notch below what the pilot can handle. To avoid frustration, it is best to plan your flying for the dry season, April to September up north, and October to March in the south. Even in the rainy season, the weather is never bad for very long, but delays of a day or two should be expected, and cross-country flights over terrain where airports are few and far between must be carefully planned.

VFR QUESTIONS & ANSWERS

What are good sources for VFR regulations? Consult the South African AIP.

How can I get a weather briefing? Detailed briefings are available at the bigger airports and over the phone. Get the numbers at the local airport.

What are VFR visibility and ceiling minimums? South Africa conforms to the ICAO minimums except for a 3-mile visibility minimum in controlled airspace, and 1 mile and clear of clouds in uncontrolled airspace below 1,000 feet.

Is night VFR permitted? No.

Must I file a flight plan? Fight plans must be filed for VFR flights in controlled and advisory airspace.

May I fly the airways VFR? Yes. Observe standard hemispherical ICAO VFR cruising altitudes.

Must I maintain en route radio contact with ATC on or off the airways? Yes, hourly position reports are required when a flight plan has been filed.

Is VFR on top permitted? No.

ADDITIONAL INFORMATION SOURCES

World Air News is a local flying magazine.

57

Cameroon

Country rating: **Moderate**

ONC Charts: **K-3 and L-3**

Rental cost range:
- 2 seat trainer **$80-100**
- 4 seat fixed gear **$100-140**
- 4 seat retractable **$140**

QUALIFICATIONS AND LICENSE VALIDATION

Validation of foreign licenses for recreational flying is required by the Cameroonian authorities and is granted without difficulty to the holder of a license issued by ICAO member states. Application must be made to the Civil Aviation Authorities in Yaounde, the nation's capital. Given the slow flow of paperwork in Cameroon, it might take a week or two to obtain validation. The process might take longer if an application is filed in Douala, the country's main commercial city, or other locations outside the capital; hence, for the short-term visitor, the best option is to fly with a safety pilot. For long-term visitors, the availability of an interesting mix of regular weekend flying and bush flying makes validation worthwhile.

Validation will cover whatever ratings you hold. It is issued for 90 days and is renewable.

It would be wise to seek validation assistance from the aircraft rental entity, a club or FBO, for instance. Application to the authorities must be made in person, but may be made by your designated representative.

DOCUMENTS YOU SHOULD TAKE

Pilot license
Current medical
Logbook
Radio operator license (if different from pilot license)

Kribi bush stop for a Cessna 310.

A few passport photos would be wise. Take original documents. Notarized photocopies might suffice if applying from outside Yaounde.

USEFUL FLYING ORGANIZATIONS

Ministry of Transport
Directorate of Civil Aviation
Yaounde, Cameroon

WHERE TO FLY, WHAT TO FLY

Cameroon is perhaps the most varied and picturesque country on the west coast of Africa. Up north, the country straddles an impressive volcanic mountain range that extends far into the Atlantic, forming a chain of islands. Few people realize that right on the shores of the Atlantic Ocean is 13,000-foot-high Mt. Cameroon. Classic African jungle lies to the south and southwest. Semiarid grassland to the east and northeast is rich with the big game of Africa.

Most of Cameroon was French territory once, and the French influence is still strong. Cameroon is a member of ASECNA, an aviation organization formed by France and former French territories to cooperate on technical and regulatory requirements.

Recreational flying is available in Douala, the country's commercial center on the Wouri River, a few miles upstream from the Atlantic, and only 25 miles south of Mt. Cameroon. **Douala International Airport** is home to the Douala Aeroclub and an assortment of charter operators, one of which, Avia Service, has been offering aircraft for noncommercial rental for years.

The Aeroclub flies a small fleet that offers great variety: a four-seat Aerospatiale Tobago for economical sightseeing; a Piper Saratoga for serious touring, and a slick, low-wing, Fournier RF-7 two-seat aerobatic trainer for some serious fun.

Avia Service has rented single-engine light aircraft to private pilots for a long time. The fleet always changes because the company also buys and sells aircraft. Bear in mind that charter operators tend to come and go for a variety of reasons, but someone always seems to take up the slack. Chances are good that any successor facility will have something for rent.

A number of destinations are within easy reach of Douala. A popular weekend fly out is to the beach village of Kribi, approximately 80 miles to the south. It is common practice to load up several aircraft with friends and head for Kribi's grass strip. Kribi has one of the best beaches in the country, and because it is a four-hour drive from Douala, the beach tends to be uncrowded. Get the rental facility to make arrangements for ground transportation at Kribi, because the airport is unattended. Usually, you will be told to buzz a particular house to announce your arrival. Do not be misled by the fancy sign at the airport listing the phone numbers of Kribi taxi cab companies. The airport has no phone.

Another popular flight is to the capital city of Yaounde, 100 miles west of Douala. Until recently, the road was so bad that the drive took nearly 10 hours; the local airline's shuttle service was frequently overbooked, giving the businessman-pilot a great excuse to fly himself. It still beats driving and is a fun way to take a few hours and see something of the countryside.

A pleasant local flight is poking around 13,000-foot Mt. Cameroon, 25 miles north, combined with a low-level run along the coastline. Several grass strips around Douala are available for soft-field practice.

More ambitious flights to the northern towns of Garoua and Maroua (approximately 400 miles from Douala) are also possible, depending on available equipment and your confidence in your navigational skills; VORs are far apart. Garoua and Maroua are the jumping-off point for the Waza game reserve where elephants, buffalo, and occasionally lion can be seen.

The weather can be a big headache for VFR pilots in West Africa. During the rainy season, usually between July and September in Cameroon, it can rain for days and thunderstorms are rampant. During the dry season, haze often restricts visibility considerably. A lack of comprehensive meteorological services compounds the problem. Great caution and good, current, basic instrument skills are a must for the pilot who ventures far afield on his own.

VFR QUESTIONS & ANSWERS

What are good sources for VFR regulations? The Cameroonian AIP. A good briefing by a local instructor is a good substitute.

How can I get a weather briefing? In person at Douala Airport. However, forecast capabilities are not very extensive.

What are VFR visibility and ceiling minimums? Cameroon has adopted the ICAO minimums.

Is night VFR permitted? No.

Must I file a flight plan? Yes, for all cross-country flights.

May I fly the airways VFR? Yes, according to the ICAO standard VFR altitude separation rules.

Must I maintain en route radio contact with ATC on or off the airways? Yes. Position reporting on cross-country flights is mandatory, including accurate estimates to the next reporting point.

Is VFR on top permitted? Yes.

ADDITIONAL INFORMATION SOURCES

Good sources for regulatory information and VFR airport diagrams are various periodic ASECNA publications, sporadically available at the flight service station at Douala International Airport.

Cameroon has no locally published aviation magazines. French aviation magazines are readily available in the larger bookstores.

58

Bush flying in turboprops

THE PEUGEOT PICKUP TRUCK came racing down Bela's 3,000-foot dirt strip as we kept the Cheyenne's engines idling for one minute before shutdown. The pickup had stopped alongside the airplane by the time we opened the cabin door and we were met by the driver, an anxious Frenchman of middle age who ran the logging camp where we had just landed.

He was waiting for a large envelope, which we gave him, then we watched him rush back to the truck, tearing the package open on the way. He laid out its contents on the hood and read hungrily for the next half hour, ignoring us as we unloaded the rest of the cargo. He reminded me of a man who had not eaten for a long time; he was reading his mail. We had flown 450 miles into the West African rain forest (dead reckoning the last 300 miles) and the airplane represented his only contact with the outside world, other than a thousand-mile journey by boat on the river bordering his logging camp.

We had also flown in logging machinery parts, saw blades, electrical equipment, iceboxes full of meat, fresh vegetables, bread, and bottled drinking water. This scene, so typical of general aviation's wide role in West Africa, would repeat itself at two more jungle strips that day before we headed for home by compass and clock. Home was Douala, the main port and commercial center of Cameroon, on the west coast of Africa where it starts to curve south toward Zaire and Angola.

Cameroon, like most of the other countries of West Africa, is a natural environment for general aviation. The transportation infrastructure is very poorly developed. The few roads that exist are mostly unpaved and often impassable in the long rainy season. Cameroon, which is approximately the size of Spain, has only 1,700 miles of hard-surface road; Spain has approximately 90,000 miles. The trains of the government-operated railway system run at erratic intervals and take a long time to get anywhere at 15 mph.

Scheduled airlines are also run by the government and serve only the few major population centers, most often only once or twice a week. They are frequently overbooked and delays or cancellations are not uncommon. The great rivers are available if you have a lot of time and own a boat, a rather unlikely proposition. Political instability and highway banditry in several areas can turn overland travel from a merely frustrating experience into a risky adventure.

Landing strips, on the other hand, are relatively easy to hack out of the jungle. Cameroon has approximately 60 of them. Gabon, a neighboring country of solid rain forest the size of Colorado has approximately 300 airfields, compared to only 280 miles of paved road. Combine the environmental factors with the entrepreneurial spirit of the privately-run charter operators and it is obvious why most businesses requiring mobility and punctuality make wide use of general aviation.

Cheyenne on final to Kika in the rain forest along the Cameroon-Congo border. An unimproved runway is an unfamiliar sight to most Cheyenne pilots.

The airplanes range from heavy singles to twin turbo props. The utility of singles is somewhat curtailed because single-engine IFR is not permitted, though special VFR is granted liberally once the authorities are familiar with the pilot. Most companies prefer rental to ownership because the number of trips they require per week does not justify the purchase of an aircraft. Some agricultural and mining concerns do have their own equipment.

Flying in West Africa is, well, different, especially if you are used to weather forecasts, radar coverage, and a VOR in every backyard. Do not expect FBOs everywhere with stocked spare parts rooms. Serious shortcomings exist in the airway system and maintenance facilities, compared to western standards. The weather is ranked, though somewhat undeservedly, among the meanest in the world. Navigation, maintenance, and weather factors combine to keep a pilot's flying skills sharp and push an aircraft to its limits.

The most striking difference in the airway system is a total lack of radar coverage for all of West Africa. Indeed, as you fly off the last European radar screen heading south, you would not be in radar contact again until reaching South Africa, approximately 4,000 miles away. Virtually the entire African continent, an area three times the size of the United States, is without radar service. Pilots must work extensively with estimates, which requires a great degree of accuracy to ensure the safety of the system.

VORs are also in short supply, by United States standards. Cameroon has five. The distance between VORs is often more than 200 miles, requiring alternate forms of navigation, especially if one of them is out of service (a fairly common occurrence in some countries). NDBs, which are inexpensive and more powerful than in the United States, are the primary radio navigation aid.

The few major airports, showcases of development, are well equipped with DME and ILS. Because most flights either originate or terminate at such centers, a trip to the bush can be quite a schizophrenic experience:

Take off following a 747 on a 10,000-foot runway lighted up like a Christmas tree. Track the appropriate VOR radial and watch the DME miles click off until beyond reception range and there is nothing to see but a solid undercast, or, if you are lucky, the wall-to-wall rain forest. Finally, arrival is hours later, by compass and clock, at an unmarked laterite strip next to one of many rivers in the jungle.

Perhaps the flashy twin should be a biplane, you should be wearing a fur-lined leather jacket, and your name should be Mermoz.

West Africa's weather has a rather bad reputation in aviation circles, primarily because the region is in a chronic low pressure zone and hardly a day passes without some form of instrument meteorological conditions. The rainy season is exceptionally long (July to September) and heat and humidity create a large amount of cloud cover. The rainy season gives way to the *harmattan*, a light but persistent wind that blows south from the Sahara, and blots out the sun with its dense clouds of fine desert sand. The best time of the year is late spring or early summer when the morning cloud cover burns off and the afternoons are sunny.

Thunderstorms—local pilots call them "Charlie Bravos"—are the most highly respected weather hazard, but the cells are usually quite isolated. Thunderstorms aside, IFR is fairly benign with a lot of cloudiness that looks worse than it is. Icing is not a problem. The prevailing winds are usually light even at altitude and the most extensive cloud cover is heavily layered with some breaks every 100 miles or so. The worst part of flying the weather is the total absence of weather forecasting. Careful fuel management and alternate destination planning are essential.

Terrain is also a consideration. Most people have little idea of just how mountainous parts of Africa are. A volcanic range running northeast to southwest into the Atlantic dominates the Cameroon-Nigeria border. When I was preparing to go to Cameroon, I was quite shocked to find a minimum en route altitude of 15,500 feet just north of Douala, which is at sea level; Mt. Cameroon, with a summit at 13,435 feet, is the highest point of West Africa and is a mere 30 miles north of the city's airport.

Operators who can afford it, make up for the shortcomings of the system by equipping their aircraft as extensively as possible. Weather radar, radar altimeters, and dual ADFs are the most useful. HF radios are required because air traffic control centers are too far apart for VHF communication. Most of Cameroon's en route traffic comes under Brazzaville Control, hundreds of miles to the south.

The maintenance of the fleets also demands a greater degree of self-sufficiency from the operators than would be expected in the United States. There are no maintenance facilities to speak of besides what each charter firm establishes

Unloading supplies at Bela.

for itself. Avia Service has its own avionics shop and engine overhaul facilities and maintains a large inventory of spares. Still, if a black box becomes so cantankerous that it has to be sent back to the factory, Avia can't just put it on next-day air and get a replacement in return the following day.

Problems away from home base can be frustrating for lack of maintenance capabilities. A small, concealed termite hill, hard as cement, collapsed a Navajo's right main gear upon landing at a small bush strip; the ensuing slide caused some spar damage and a bent propeller. Although this kind of damage is serious, it is certainly repairable, and anywhere else the Navajo would have been back in the air in due course. Not so in Cameroon. There was no economical method to get the airplane out or get a new wing in; therefore, the Navajo was cannibalized and the airframe will sit where it came to a halt until swallowed by the timeless rain forest.

Business took me to West Africa for a long-term stay, and often my best option to get around efficiently was to rent one of Avia Service's airplanes. I primarily flew either the Piper Seneca or Cessna 310, but I also managed a fair amount of time in the complex Cheyenne II and the T-1040, under close supervision from pilots who flew them every day. I also flew Avia's Archer, Turbo Saratoga, and Tomahawk, mainly to go to the beach.

These logbook entries are the record of some of my fondest flying memories:

12/15, PA-34-201T, Seneca III, Douala-Yaounde, 0.7 hours.

Yaounde is the capital of Cameroon and I go there often. It is only 120 nautical miles east of Douala, the commercial center, and main port. That is a short distance, but it is a six to seven hour drive on lousy roads. A commercial flight is another option. This route is one exception where service is frequent. The local airline runs anywhere from three to six flights a day depending on how many they decide to cancel for mysterious reasons at the last minute. It is also a bit tedious to show up at the airport every time only to watch them discover, yet again, that you cannot fit 200 people into a 150-seat airplane. It is quite different with Avia. I drive out to the airport, fire up the Seneca, activate my flight plan filed the night before, and 45 minutes later I am in Yaounde. Same thing on the way back. Everything should be as simple in Africa.

5/6, Cheyenne II, Douala-Sao Tome, 1.3 hours.

Sao Tome is an island country 285 nautical miles southwest of Douala. It was one of the last African colonies to gain independence. The Portuguese left in 1974. The island exports cocoa, coffee, and fish and imports everything else. I am going there to facilitate this trade. During the 18th and 19th centuries, the island was infamous for another type of trade: it was the foremost slaving center of Africa. I am flying with Bernard Grand, a Frenchman who logged more than 2,000 hours in sailplanes in the Alps before becoming serious about flying—he is only 28. Arrivals can be tricky; look up Sao Tome in the Jepps; the airport diagram reads: "NO PUBLISHED PROCEDURE."

We ascend into the soup at 600 feet, go through multiple layers, and are on top at 18,000 feet, climb to 21,000 feet, and dodge thunderstorm cells all the way.

Clearance is direct Sao Tome. Douala VOR is lost 80 miles out. Grand tunes the Sao Tome commercial radio station into the ADF and it is dead-on with a very powerful signal. No official navaids are received until picking up the Sao Tome VOR 40 miles from the island. Grand contacts Brazzaville on HF while I dodge more cells. We are lucky. The airport is clear.

1/11, PA-34-200 Seneca II, Douala-Libreville, 1.5 hours.

Libreville is the capital of Gabon, with commercial air service from Douala twice a week, departing in the evening and returning the following morning. Nighttime is not a good time to conduct business; therefore, I take the Seneca. It is almost like the real world. Both airports are equipped with full ILS-DME. I am out of VOR range for only 20 minutes at a cruising altitude of 9,000 feet. Halfway to Libreville, I am on the gauges and watch the radar. The subsequent ILS approach is uneventful. The Seneca, like most of Avia's aircraft, has an HSI.

1/1, Tomahawk, Douala-Edea-Douala, 0.5 hours.

The first flight of a new year. My plan is to introduce a friend to flying light aircraft by taking him 30 miles south of Douala to the Sanaga River, follow it west for 30 miles to the Atlantic Ocean, and return to Douala via the beach. The ceiling is 600 feet, broken; the Tomahawk has dual VOR/LOC; the controller verifies my ratings and issues a Special VFR Clearance. We go through a hole to get on top of a 1,500-foot cloud layer. Near the river, solid instrument meteorological conditions. I advise the controller, who subsequently issues a clearance for a localizer approach back to Douala. Imagine, this is January, the dry season; you sure wouldn't get much flying done around here without an instrument rating.

2/19, Archer II, Douala-Kribi-Douala, 1.8 hours.

For once, a beautiful sunny weekend in late February. A real beach day and that is the destination with three friends. Kribi is one of the most beautiful beaches in West Africa. We could drive, but it is the same old story: four hours on dirt roads. Better to fly to the long, unattended laterite strip a few miles inland and buzz a certain house on arrival to get a ride. The airport has a huge sign with a phone number for taxis but there is no phone.

The flight down is beautiful, low, over miles and miles of deserted beach. We see a shipwreck, one of many that came to grief over the centuries in the capricious weather and currents of the West African coast. On arrival we see that we are not alone. The Saratoga and the Tobago of the Douala Aeroclub are also there for the day. We circle an oil drilling rig on the way home and take advantage of the good visibility to fly past downtown Douala.

2/29, Cheyenne II, Douala-Bela-Kika-Moloundou-Douala 4.2 hours.

A typical forest resupply flight to the logging camps carrying food, drink, mail, payroll, and machinery parts. The Cheyenne is at 21,000 feet on top of a solid overcast with isolated thunderstorms dotting the area. The first stop is Bela, 450 miles east-southeast of Douala on the Sangha River where the borders of Cameroon, Congo, and the Central African Republic meet.

Eventually the Cheyenne is overflying the capital, Yaounde, and the last good radio fix, YDE VOR. Then it is compass and clock. There is a trick to forest

There is one slight problem at this unattended field: No telephone!

flying; most logging camps are along rivers; fly to the river, decide which way to turn, and if the the turn is correct . . . home free. ONC charts are the best maps; African editions have huge white spaces with "Maximum Elevation Believed Not To Exceed XXXX Feet." But the maps' terrain and waterway features are uncannily accurate, and should be, considering the satellite mapping technology utilized to produce them.

I am flying with Bernard Grand again and he is reporting our position to Brazzaville. Brazza comes back sounding like Donald Duck throwing a temper tantrum in French; HF does funny things to voice transmissions. Grand claims to understand the transmission, I don't.

Destinations Bela and Kika are not even on the map, having been recently hacked out of the jungle by the loggers. We have plotted them carefully. Moloundou is shown as "Position Approximate." The map also shows an NDB at Ouesso in the Congo (approximately 60 miles south of Bela), which never works.

Descent is initiated at the appointed hour and the Cheyenne breaks out at 1,500 feet. The winds were kind and the compass accurate—the Sangha River and Bela are straight ahead. A pilot is in big trouble in this area if a compass is not pointing to where it says it is . . . .

A few years ago, a pilot loaded a heavy generator, a mass of metal, into the nose of a Cherokee Six and didn't notice what it did to the compass. He completely missed his destination and had to crash land hundreds of miles from nowhere in a Congolese swamp after the Cherokee ran out of fuel. Fortunately, he was found by Pygmies, a nearly extinct forest people. It took them two weeks to get him back to civilization and his wife and three children.

We make several low passes over the logging camp to announce arrival and squeeze into the 3,000-foot laterite strip, grateful for beta power during rollout.

The next two stops are Kika and Moloundou approximately 50 and 60 miles, respectively, to the southwest along the Ngoko River. This leg is flown at 1,500 feet agl over a scattered to broken layer of low-level stratus that always forms quickly after a heavy downpour.

I marvel at the vast expanse of dense rain forest, which creates a feeling of isolation as powerful as that experienced flying over a frigid ocean. The forest looks like an endless sea of densely packed broccoli. The Cheyenne descends below the stratus and clips the forest at 200 feet agl. Kika is spotted one mile to the east, about to go past in flash.

On the ground, Avia's T-1040 is being refueled out of a drum, a chamois filters the fuel. It is interesting to compare the two aircraft. The T-1040 has a larger load-carrying capacity at 1.5 tons than the Cheyenne II but also burns much more fuel at its unpressurized operating altitudes. The Cheyenne will return to Douala without refueling.

I tread cautiously on the ground at these forest stops because I have a pathological fear of snakes and the loggers are full of horror stories about them. Snakes have also been found on the premises of Avia Service. Avia does crop spraying and one day a mechanic got into a Pawnee just in from the banana plantations. He found himself staring straight at a dreaded green mamba, one of Africa's most poisonous "two-step snakes" (that's how many steps you take before you drop dead after it bites you). Death is certain in a few minutes.

Despite the absence of an ejection seat, the mechanic broke the zero-zero ejection speed record on his way out of the Pawnee. The snake was subsequently dispatched and a great debate ensued on how to tell the Pawnee's pilot about the lethal stowaway he had flown home without a parachute the day before.

The payroll is deposited at Moloundou and the founder of the logging business climbs aboard for a ride back to Douala. The loggers are a hardy lot. They come out of the rain forest only once or twice a year and some choose not to come out for years. It is a lonely existence. A lot of scotch and wine is flown into the forest.

The flight back to Douala turns into a race with an enormous storm. All the scattered cells of the day seem to have consolidated and at 26,000 feet it is dark as the fringes of the system tower above.

We report Edea beacon inbound for the ILS. Douala tower is communicating with an Avia Service Seneca doing touch and goes. It is being test flown after a major overhaul by Luc Peres, the chief pilot. There are bugs. Peres has feathered a prop and is unable to restart the engine. He explains his predicament and is given a priority landing clearance. The feathered prop is obvious when the Seneca turns and Peres reports short final. Tower: "Will this be a touch and go or a full stop?"

Aviation progresses in Africa, too. Every year there are more VORs and new jetports, and radar is expanding its sweep. But the task of development is as enormous as this last truly exciting place on earth, and I am grateful for the years of adventure that still remain.

Index